The Home Front 1939–1945
in 100
OBJECTS

The Home Front 1939–1945
in 100
OBJECTS

Austin J. Ruddy

FRONTLINE
BOOKS

First published in 2019 by

Frontline Books
An imprint of Pen & Sword Books Ltd,
47 Church Street, Barnsley, S. Yorkshire, S70 2AS

The right of Austin J. Ruddy to be identified as the author this work has been asserted by him in accordance with the Copyright, Designs and Patent Act 1988.

HB ISBN: 9 781 52674 086 1
PB ISBN: 9 781 52676 733 2

CIP data records for this title are available from the British Library.

Printed and bound by Replika Press Pvt. Ltd.
Typeset by Mac Style

Pen & Sword Books Limited incorporates the imprints of Atlas, Archaeology, Aviation, Discovery, Family History, Fiction, History, Maritime, Military, Military Classics, Politics, Select, Transport, True Crime, Air World, Frontline Publishing, Leo Cooper, Remember When, Seaforth Publishing, The Praetorian Press, Wharncliffe Local History, Wharncliffe Transport, Wharncliffe True Crime and White Owl.

For more information on our books, please email: info@frontline-books.com , write to us at the above address, or visit: www.frontline-books.com

This book is dedicated to the memory of my mother, Cheryl Tagg Ruddy (1944–1980), and the Allied wartime generation. Just two words: thank you.

Cover image: Actually, it should be 101 Objects of the British Home Front! This rather imposing red object, middle left, is a small child's respirator for infants aged around two to four years old. It was manufactured with a bright red rubber face piece and blue filter to be less intimidating to young children. Mysteriously, it was known as a 'Mickey Mouse gas mask', even though it bore no resemblance to the Disney character. For more about respirators, see Object 6.

Contents

Acknowledgements

It is appropriate here to pay tribute to my family's wartime generation: my mother, Cheryl Tagg Ruddy, a war baby born a week after D-Day; my father, Austin Ruddy, another war baby and his sister, Pamela; my paternal grandfather, also Austin Ruddy, Royal Engineers Sapper 1929–40, invalided through war injury with the BEF in France; my grandmother, Edith Ruddy, a wartime housewife; my maternal grandfather, Frank Leslie Tagg, draughtsman on the Hawker Typhoon aircraft at D. Napier & Son Ltd and member of their 7th (Acton) Battalion, Middlesex Home Guard platoon; great uncle John Oliver Smith, Company Sergeant Major of 5th (St Marylebone) Battalion, County of London Home Guard; great uncle Edward Sidney Smith, AFS/NFS Fireman, 75X Station, Torriano Avenue School, Kentish Town, London 1939–45, plus Charles Cooper, Corporal of the 1st Airlanding Brigade, 1st British Airborne Division: to those who have passed on, I hope I have told your stories well enough – I still have many questions I wish I had asked!

Grateful thanks go to my parents, Austin and Stephanie, plus the rest of my family, for nurturing my interest in history, to the various militaria dealers who have fed my thirst, particularly Roger Miles, and fellow historians who have shared their knowledge.

My partner, Kerry, must be due some sort of long-service medal for putting up with all of this.

I'd also like to thank my friend, photographer Andy Baker, who photographed all the objects, together with the staff at Frontline Books, including publisher Martin Mace, contact Lisa Hooson and my editor Paul Middleton. Thanks must also go to aviation historian Andy Saunders, who first commissioned me to write a similar series of articles in *Britain at War* magazine.

Abbreviations

AA	Anti-Aircraft
AFS	Auxiliary Fire Service (1938–41)
ARP	Air Raid Precautions
ATS	Auxiliary Territorial Service (female Army)
BBC	British Broadcasting Company
BD	Bomb Disposal
BDS	Bomb Disposal Squad
BEM	British Empire Medal
CD	Civil Defence
CO	Conscientious Objector
CWGC	Commonwealth War Graves Commission
d	Pence
Do 17	Dornier 17 Luftwaffe medium bomber
Do 217	Dornier 217 Luftwaffe medium bomber
FB	Fire Brigade
FG	Fire Guard
GI	US Government Issue
HAA	Heavy Anti-Aircraft (3.7in–5.25in calibre)
HE	High Explosive
He 111	Heinkel 111 Luftwaffe medium bomber
HG	Home Guard (July 1940–December 1944)
HO	Home Office
IB	Incendiary Bomb
IRA	Irish Republican Army
ITMA	*It's that Man Again* BBC radio show
Ju 88	Junkers 88 Luftwaffe medium bomber
Ju 188	Junkers 188 Luftwaffe medium bomber
KG	Kampfgeschwader (Luftwaffe bomber unit)
kg	Kilogram
LAA	Light Anti-Aircraft (.303in-40mm calibre)
LDV	Local Defence Volunteers (May–July 1940)
LMS	London Midland & Scottish Railway
LNER	London North East Railway
MAP	Ministry of Aircraft Production
MBE	Member of the Order of the British Empire
MoF	Ministry of Food
MoH	Ministry of Health

MoHS	Ministry of Home Security
MoT	Ministry of Transport
NARPAC	National ARP Animals Committee
NFS	National Fire Service (1941–48)
OBE	Order of the British Empire
oz	Ounce
PoW	Prisoner of War
RAF	Royal Air Force
RE	Royal Engineers
ROC	Royal Observer Corps
ROF	Royal Ordnance Factory
s	Shilling
SC	Sprengcylindrische German thin-cased, higher explosive bomb
SD	Sprengdickwande German thick-walled, armour-piercing, lower-explosive bomb
USAAF	United States Army Air Force
USSR	Union of Soviet Socialist Republics
UXB	Unexploded Bomb
V	Victory
V1	*Vergeltungswaffe 1* 'Vengeance Weapon 1' (German unmanned flying bomb)
V2	*Vergeltungswaffe 2* 'Vengeance Weapon 2' (German rocket)
VE Day	Victory in Europe Day, 8 May 1945
VJ Day	Victory over Japan Day, 15 August 1945
WLA	Women's Land Army
WVS	Women's Voluntary Service

Cross references to other numbered objects are in [brackets]
Financial figures in [brackets] are the 2018 equivalent.
1in = 2.5cm. 1ft = 30.4cm. 3.2ft = 1m. 1kg = 2.2lb

Introduction

When I was growing up in the 1970s and '80s, every older person had lived through the Second World War. They all had their own interesting and unique 'war stories'. My grandmother recounted tales of dark nights huddled in her Anderson shelter in Queensbury, London, as bombs flattened neighbouring homes, whilst her brother quietly recalled narrow escapes fighting fires in the London docks as an AFS fireman.

I began noticing other fading evidence of the world's largest conflict: an incongruous row of post-war houses wedged in a smart Victorian terrace marking where a V1 flying bomb fell. An overgrown air raid shelter lurking behind a fence, or a crumbling concrete pillbox on the beach amongst holidaymakers, still standing sentry, all those years on.

Aged 15, I started interviewing former ARP wardens and Home Guards about the Blitz in my London neighbourhood of Highgate. These eyewitnesses have now all passed on, but all the above evidence fired my interest: clearly, this was one of the most important episodes in our nation's history.

General history books and documentaries gave a wider but two-dimensional realisation of the period. However, when I was given an old gas mask and stirrup pump, the history instantly burst vividly to life, becoming 3D and tangible: a direct connection to events all those decades past was established. I started spending my pocket money in old junk shops and collector's fairs on wartime memorabilia, each object enhancing my understanding of such a momentous epoch – I haven't stopped since and the following objects you will see are the partial results of over thirty years' research and collecting.

This solid surviving evidence is vital to our comprehension of Britain's war. You can't travel back in time, but these objects allow us a flavour of those turbulent and historic times. Archive photos and film footage give the impression that the war years were monochrome. But, as these objects show, despite restrictions, the period was actually full of vibrant colour.

During the examination of historic objects, the phrase 'If only this could talk …' is often heard: in this book, they almost can. All the objects have a general contextual background history and any specific known associated story has also been included, all in a clear form, with cross-references to related subjects. Fact-packed, with names, dates and statistics, this book is not, however, a potted history of Britain in the Second World War: the main general histories of the subject are listed in the bibliography for further reading. The aim of the book has been to mainly portray the everyday objects that Britons experienced on the Home Front, thus items related to more hidden aspects, such as radar, Bletchley Park or unseen secret operations, are not featured.

However, the following often humble 100 objects are equally historically important. They are both testimony and memorials to the struggle and sacrifices our forebears made to preserve the freedoms we still enjoy today. The objects' everyday simplicity and commonality reflects Churchill's 'This is a war of the unknown warriors' speech, when civilians 'carrying on' with daily life, going to work or even just enjoying themselves was resistance to Hitler and all he espoused.

We will now follow the course of Britain's Home Front in the Second World War via our 100 objects.

Austin J. Ruddy, 2019.

1: If War Should Come...
Leaflets, July 1939

Today, if you have unexpected leaflets pushed through your letterbox, chances are it's junk mail, advertising fast-food outlets or unmissable shopping offers and so on. But back in summer 1939, the British government issued millions of leaflets to 'every household in the kingdom', preparing them 'for the possibility of war'.

This series of six leaflets were issued from July 1939, just two months before the outbreak of war, by the Office of the Lord Privy Seal – an unusual but historic governmental position, a sort of 'minister without portfolio', leading famous wartime Minister of Labour Ernest Bevin (1881–1951) to later drily remark that he was 'neither a Lord, nor a Privy, nor a Seal'.

The first leaflet, *Some Things You Should Know if War Should Come*, had general advice about air raid warnings, gas masks, lighting restrictions, fire precautions, evacuation, identity labels, food, and public announcements. The tone of the advice was concerning, but reassuring – 'The Government are taking all possible measures for the defence of the country, and have made plans for protecting you and helping you to protect yourselves, so far as may be, in the event of war'

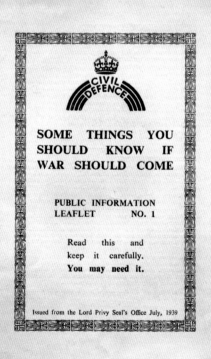

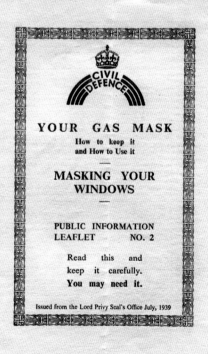

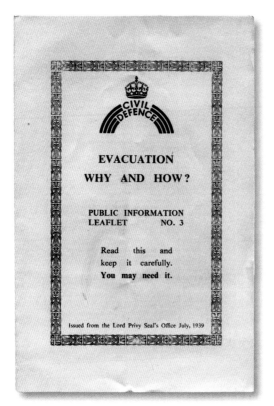

CIVIL DEFENCE

EVACUATION

WHY AND HOW?

PUBLIC INFORMATION
LEAFLET   NO. 3

Read   this   and
keep   it   carefully.
You may need it.

Issued from the Lord Privy Seal's Office July, 1939

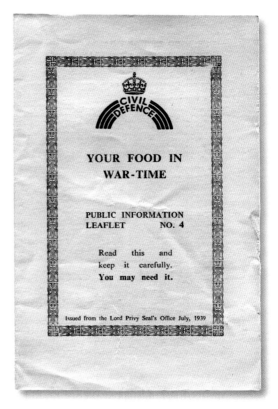

CIVIL DEFENCE

YOUR FOOD IN

WAR-TIME

PUBLIC INFORMATION
LEAFLET   NO. 4

Read   this   and
keep   it   carefully.
You may need it.

Issued from the Lord Privy Seal's Office July, 1939

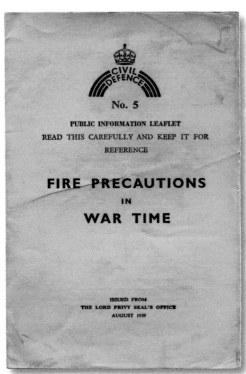

CIVIL DEFENCE

No. 5

PUBLIC INFORMATION LEAFLET

READ THIS CAREFULLY AND KEEP IT FOR
REFERENCE

FIRE PRECAUTIONS

IN

WAR TIME

ISSUED FROM
THE LORD PRIVY SEAL'S OFFICE
AUGUST 1939

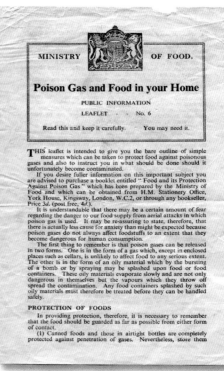

MINISTRY   OF FOOD.

Poison Gas and Food in your Home

PUBLIC INFORMATION
LEAFLET   ·   No. 6

Read this and keep it carefully.   You may need it.

THIS leaflet is intended to give you the bare outline of simple measures which can be taken to protect food against poisonous gases and also to instruct you in what should be done should it unfortunately become contaminated.

If you desire fuller information on this important subject you are advised to purchase a booklet entitled " Food and its Protection Against Poison Gas " which has been prepared by the Ministry of Food and which can be obtained from H.M. Stationery Office, York House, Kingsway, London, W.C.2, or through any bookseller, Price 3d. (post free, 4d.).

It is understandable that there may be a certain amount of fear regarding the danger to our food supply from aerial attacks in which poison gas is used. It may be re-assuring to state, therefore, that there is actually less cause for anxiety than might be expected because poison gases do not always affect foodstuffs to an extent that they become dangerous for human consumption.

The first thing to remember is that poison gases can be released in two forms. One is in the form of a gas which, except in enclosed places such as cellars, is unlikely to affect food to any serious extent. The other is in the form of an oily material which by the bursting of a bomb or by spraying may be splashed upon food or food containers. These oily materials evaporate slowly and are not only dangerous in themselves but the vapours which they throw off spread the contamination. Any food containers splashed by such oily materials must therefore be treated before they can be handled safely.

PROTECTION OF FOODS

In providing protection, therefore, it is necessary to remember that the food should be guarded as far as possible from either form of contact.

(1) Canned foods and those in airtight bottles are completely protected against penetration of gases. Nevertheless, store them

– if, possibly, a tad condescending to the modern reader – 'You, in your turn, can help to make those plans work, if you understand them and act in accordance with them.'

The second leaflet, *Your Gas Mask, How to Keep it and How to Use it. Masking your windows*, addressed what was considered to be the main threat to civilians, chemical warfare: 'Take care of your gas mask and your gas mask will take care of you!', plus the blackout [see Object 4].

The third leaflet, *Evacuation – Why and How?*, stressed the necessity of removing 'children, expectant mothers and the blind' from the bombers' target areas: 'The transport of some 3,000,000 in all is an enormous undertaking ...' [see Object 3].

The fourth leaflet, *Your Food in War-time*, explained how to maintain food stocks and gave notice that rationing would be introduced: 'In war time, there would be no food to waste, but with your care and co-operation we shall have enough.'

The fifth leaflet, *Fire Precautions in War Time*, on orange paper, issued just a month before the outbreak of war, seems almost like a last-minute afterthought. It warned of the dangers of incendiary bombs [see Object 39] and how to tackle them, with the sage words: 'All large fires start as small ones.'

A sixth leaflet, *Poison Gas and Food in Your Home*, apparently issued in much fewer numbers by the Ministry of Food eight months after the outbreak of war in May 1940 during the German invasion of Western Europe, again addressed what many assumed was the greatest threat, chemical warfare.

Unlike the letterbox junk mail of today, the leaflets' cover note – 'Read this and keep it carefully. You may need it' – clearly made their recipients sit up and take notice: these instructions were read and squirreled away in sideboard drawers for future reference – so much so, this series of leaflets is still found quite commonly today.

2: 'LOWIN' ARP Activation Telegram, August 1939

This simple telegram is now a rare historic document, chronicling the communication between central and local authority, when the government ordered city and county councils across Britain to activate their Air Raid Precautions (ARP) plans to protect the public, due to the imminent 'war emergency'.

In an age decades before emails, texts, bleepers or, indeed, widespread radio communications, national and local government made heavy use of the nationwide civilian telephone network, together with hand-delivered telegram notifications.

Dated 23 August 1939, just twelve days before the outbreak of war, this was the first instruction from the Home Office, in Whitehall, London, to local authority ARP Controllers. Codenamed 'LOWIN', the abbreviation stood for 'Local War Instruction'. On receipt, ARP Controllers accessed their previously prepared ARP plans, usually kept locked in a safe, and implemented its contents across their district.

Despite the misconception today that the ARP were an amateur *Dad's Army*/Warden Hodges-type of organisation, this was far from the truth. The key to the success of

Britain's wartime ARP organisation lay in its early pre-war inception in 1924, allowing fifteen years of planning. Often criticised as overly bureaucratic, in this case, governmental organisations acted early enough and in doing so, saved millions of British lives.

At the top of the civil defence pyramid was the Minister of Home Security (also Home Secretary), head of the newly formed Ministry of Home Security, based at the Home Office, London. At the outbreak of war in 1939, this was Sir John Anderson MP (1882–1958), replaced in October 1940 by the successful Herbert Morrison MP (1888–1965), for the war's duration.

From February 1939, Britain was divided into twelve Civil Defence Regions, each headed by a Regional Commissioner. In the event of severance of central control from London, through air raid destruction or even invasion, each of these Regions could become autonomous, operating independently under the authority of the Regional Commissioner. He was the direct link between central and local government and it was his role to implement government policy across his region. In extreme circumstances, such as the breakdown of local authority control due to heavy bombing, the Regional Commissioner could take direct control of a conurbation.

However, although central and local authority bureaucracy may have been fully operational, it was a different story at ground level: there were massive shortages at front-line level. The vast majority of local authority ARP services were understaffed by, in some cases, several thousand personnel. This was due for several reasons, from public reticence and wishful-thinking that it would 'all blow over', through to active opposition by some councils: although the 1937 ARP Act made it mandatory for local authorities to create ARP plans, some, such as London's West Ham and Stepney borough councils, resisted on cost grounds.

After the Germans invaded Western Europe in May 1940 and the threat to Britain became more pressing, the public filled the ARP personnel quotas and any shortfalls were made up throughout the war years by official government conscription or 'direction'.

3: Evacuee Identification Label, September 1939

There are several million people – and their descendants – alive today who can thank a single government ARP policy for their existence: evacuation.

Realising cities would be major air raid targets, plans had been drawn up in 1938 to remove the most vulnerable. Britain was divided into three areas: 'evacuation' or 'danger' zones, mainly larger cities where bombing was expected and the evacuation of children and mothers was highly recommended; 'neutral' zones, such as county towns and cities, which were under some threat but where children could remain, and 'reception areas', such as the countryside, where the threat was believed least.

With the imminent approach of war, on 1 September 1939, under Operation Pied Piper (not the most appropriate name, as in the fable, the Piper abducted the children, who were never seen again), city children gathered at their schools, were identity labelled and escorted in groups to railway stations. In the first three days,

1.5 million Britons were evacuated: 827,000 school children, 524,000 mothers and babies, 13,000 pregnant women, 70,000 disabled people and over 103,000 teachers and helpers.

Generally, though not exclusively, children from working-class families took up the government's scheme, to be billeted with strangers, whereas the middle and upper classes organised their children's evacuation independently, to stay with friends and relatives.

However, unlike as popularly envisaged today, the evacuation was not a mass exodus that left the cities childless: only half of all children were moved from urban areas, instead of the expected 80 per cent, as many parents

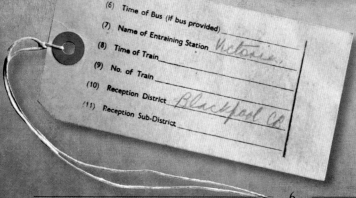

suffered last-minute cold feet. Indeed, when the expected air raids did not materialise, 60 per cent of children returned back to their homes at Christmas 1939.

But as the Phoney War faded and became real, there were several more evacuations. In summer 1940, when Germany occupied France and invasion threatened, 100,000 people were moved inland from coastal towns. Likewise, just months later, when the air raids started, the cities were once again evacuated.

Children were also evacuated abroad. From June 1940, the Children's Overseas Reception Board evacuated over 2,500 youngsters by ship to Canada, Australia, South Africa and New Zealand. The scheme ended abruptly on 17 September 1940, when German submarine U-48 sunk the City of Benares ship, with the loss of seventy-seven of the ninety child evacuees aboard.

A final, sometimes forgotten evacuation took place in summer 1944, when over a million evacuees left southern England to get away from the new V-weapons menace.

It is estimated that a total 3.5 million Britons were evacuated during the war. The experience proved to be mixed. Many generous hosts opened their doors, whilst other doors were only opened by the threat of compulsory billeting orders.

Some evacuees were welcomed into warm, caring homes, making new 'family' and friends, better than their previous inner-city lives and did not want to return in 1945. Other evacuees entered into cold, resentful or even abusive households. In turn, evacuees also varied: some were polite and grateful, others, the opposite. One Midlands resident recalled: 'The evacuees were strange, wild creatures, with a different tongue and were invariably very tough – as we found to our cost.' Either way, the evacuation experience, for evacuees and their hosts, would never be forgotten.

As Manchester was a potential bombing target, 172,000 children from 236 schools were evacuated from the city. This evacuation identity label was for a 14-year-old schoolgirl who lived in Prestwich, just 3 miles north of Manchester. Not all the details on her label were filled in, but it appears that around 1939 she was evacuated with her classmates of Notre Dame High School, via train from Manchester's Victoria Station, to Blackpool, about 50 miles away – not too distant from her home and by the sea. The coastal resort became home to 35,000 evacuees, mostly from Manchester, but also Merseyside and even London. I wonder how this girl's wartime evacuation experience proved?

4: Blackout Car Headlamp, September 1939

'Light pollution' means that all Britain's cities can now be clearly seen from space as areas bearing a bright tell-tale glow, surrounded by countryside darkness. However, in 1939, the lights went out across Britain – and would not pierce the veil of the blackout for another five years.

Although the Luftwaffe had the world's most sophisticated electronic beam navigation systems, air crews still relied on visual targeting to aim their bombs. So, at the start of 1938, the Air Defence Research Council conducted several blackout experiments in Midland cities to see the efficacy of dousing all lights, in a bid to hide conurbations at night and hinder enemy bombers.

Britain's blackout regulations were introduced on 1 September 1939, two days before the

THE HARTLEY HEADLAMP DEVICE

Instructions for correct fitting to ensure compliance with the War Time Lighting Restrictions laid down by the Ministry of Home Security

outbreak of war. A variety of compulsory measures were introduced: windows and doors had to be 'blacked out' with dark material or boards, street lights were doused and car headlights fitted with metal filters, such as this Hartley headlamp device, to reduce the spread of their beams. Small, low-power hand torches were sold, but there was a shortage of their batteries.

The blackout was strictly enforced by ARP wardens and police, shouting 'Put that light out!' In 1940, 300,000 Britons were prosecuted for breaching the blackout, the fines being the equivalent of just under a week's wages.

But, ironically, this mass safety measure caused widespread problems. Under the cover of darkness, crime rose, with muggings and smash-and-grab shop robberies widely reported. Pedestrians walked into lamp posts, tripped over kerbs or fell down steps. Worse still, there was a drastic rise in car accidents: in the first four months of the war, 4,133 people were killed on Britain's roads, 2,657 of whom were pedestrians – and this was in the Phoney War lull, before the Luftwaffe had even dropped a single bomb.

When the night Blitz began, despite the blackout being overwhelmingly adhered to, its effectiveness proved debatable. A 'bomber's moon' aided the Luftwaffe, with moonlight reflected on and illuminating railway lines, rivers, even rain-soaked streets. Unfortunately, it was also reported that anti-aircraft searchlight beams sometimes reflected off low clouds and illuminated the very cities they were supposed to be protecting. In turn, Luftwaffe bombers initiated their raids with parachute flares that, according to witnesses, 'turned night into day'.

The blackout's 'stygian gloom' proved antisocial, restricting nightlife in cities and lowering morale, causing much grumbling. Some MPs even campaigned for its lifting. Attempting a compromise, many urban councils introduced reduced power 'star light' street lamps. However, they cast a dreary glow on the streets and despite their low light, many residents feared they could still aid the bombers.

With the turning tide of the war and disappearance of the Luftwaffe, on 17 September 1944, the 'dim-out' was introduced, allowing slight measures, such as shop windows to be mildly illuminated. It wasn't until 30 April 1945, the day of Hitler's suicide and just a week before the war's end in Europe, that the blackout was finally lifted. Reports in local newspapers testify that crowds gathered to 'bathe' in the lights in town centres or had 'illumination parties', with curtains wide open.

Now, over seventy years on, some councils create their own mini-blackouts, switching off street lights after a certain hour as an austerity measure in a time of pressured finances and environmental concerns.

5: *Your Courage... Poster, September 1939*

At 11.15 am, on Sunday, 3 September 1939, Britain's Prime Minister Neville Chamberlain (1869–1940) announced to the nation that for the second time in just over twenty years, Britain was once again at war. Despite sincere – on his part, at least – attempts to avoid international conflict and bloodshed, his fascist counterparts, Germany's Adolf Hitler (1889–1945) and Italy's Benito Mussolini (1883–1945), had no real interest in negotiation: thus, Chamberlain, in tired tones, broadcast some of the most famous and unfortunate words in twentieth-century British history: '... consequently this country is at war with Germany.'

Though Chamberlain's policy of appeasing the aggressors proved controversial, it did bide enough time for Britain to rearm and prepare the nation's infrastructure for the struggle to come.

Many governmental departments used this time to plan – with the exception of one of the most important agencies, the Ministry of Information, which was only officially formed the day *after* the outbreak of war – and it showed.

Headed by Minister of Information Hugh Macmillan (1873–1952), as its name suggests, the Ministry was also responsible for propaganda, in film, radio and print. Perhaps due to its inexperience and rushed nature, although civil servants had started preparations in April 1939, the Ministry's first poster campaign backfired, becoming an abject lesson in how *not* to make friends and influence people.

The Ministry issued a series of four posters, all of the same, simple design and tone, bearing a royal crown and commands in capital letters. The very first poster of the war, *Your Courage, Your Cheerfulness, Your Resolution, Will Bring Us Victory*, created by civil servant A. P. Waterfield, was meant to steady nerves and boost public morale: in surveys, it was found to do the opposite. Read in another way, it suggested that the British people's struggle – and worse still, by implication, their sacrifice – would simply consolidate the powers-that-be. *The Times* called the poster 'an insipid and patronising invocation'.

Indeed, the other three posters in the series, *Freedom is in Peril, Defend it With All Your Might; Don't Help the Enemy! Careless Talk May Give Away Vital Secrets;* and *Keep Calm and Carry On* were no more appealing. They looked like something more out of authoritarian Stalinist Russia than a free democracy. Indeed, their style of 'Newspeak' seems to have been mimicked in

the apocryphal 1949 novel, *Nineteen Eighty-Four*, by George Orwell (1903–50), as was the Ministry's headquarters, at the impressive but overbearing 1937 art deco Senate House, in Bloomsbury, central London, on which Orwell based his Ministry of Truth building.

Ironically, the most famous of these posters, *Keep Calm and Carry On*, although 2.5 million were printed, was never officially at least, issued. Intended for use only after devastating mass air raids, it was only after one was found in a Northumberland second-hand bookshop in 2000 that the poster was actually widely consumed by the public, via a savvy private commercial entrepreneur.

But, back in 1939, the campaign's own goal led to political admonishment, removal of the Ministry's Press Relations Group and the reduction of the Ministry's staff by a third. However, lessons were learned. From then on, it is noticeable that British propaganda posters became more subtle and sophisticated, using professional artists and designers. The finger-pointing was replaced by less officious, generalised, third-person invocations, such as *Dig for Victory, Salute the Soldier, Beware the Squander Bug*. The information war had only just begun …

6: General Civilian Respirator, September 1939

Gas masks are perhaps the most symbolic and evocative objects of the British Home Front, produced in their millions, yet ironically – and fortunately – never needed during the six years of conflict.

The fear of chemical warfare was a lasting legacy from the previous world war, which worried both the government and populace. As such, the first ARP measures largely concentrated on countering this grim menace.

The Chemical Defence Experimental Station (now the Defence Science and Technology Laboratory) at Porton Down, Wiltshire, was tasked with developing gas masks – officially, respirators – that were economical to manufacture, yet effective. Fortunately, the vast majority of respirators were produced before the war, when rubber supplies from the Far East were still available.

By the Munich Crisis of September 1938, some thirty-eight million general civilian respirators had been issued. However, by the war's end, a staggering ninety-seven million had been made, explaining their commonality today. With a doctor's certificate, those with asthma could obtain the respirator with a nose outlet valve to aid breathing. Only 350,000 of this rare variant were produced.

However, there were actually several different types of respirator produced. A rather strange-looking device, with a large viewing panel and side bellows, called a baby helmet, involved placing the top half of the baby inside it and the mother pumping air into the chamber. Some two million helmets were produced.

Around three million small child's respirators, for infants aged around two to five, were

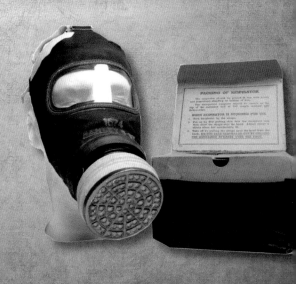

manufactured, with a bright red rubber face piece and blue filter, designed to be less intimidating to young children. Mysteriously, it was known as a 'Mickey Mouse gas mask', even though it bore no resemblance to the Disney character. Later, a war economy version, with a plain, black rubber face piece, known as a 'Pluto gas mask', named after the Disney dog, was produced from 1942.

For the ARP services, such as wardens and ambulance drivers, 4.5 million civilian duty respirators were issued, essentially a chunkier version of the general civilian respirator. A version was even produced with a built-in microphone for telephone switchboard operators. Those ARP personnel operating in tougher conditions, such as rescue workers or decontamination squads, were issued with the standard military service respirator, with an air tube and separate, bagged filter.

For the elderly and those with breathing difficulties, 50,000 helmet or 'invalid' respirators were issued, with a framework headpiece and air bellows on the front. Similarly, 36,000 hospital respirators, the rarest of the civilian series, were produced. Both were similar in design and principle to the baby helmet respirator, requiring the wearer or an assistant to manually pump air into the headpiece.

Businesses were quick to produce a variety of carriers for the general civilian respirator, from simple cloth covers to decorated tin containers, even special handbags with a storage pouch.

Later in the war, despite the obvious risk, it became a sign of bravado not to carry your gas mask in public. Fortunately, Hitler never used poison gas against Britain: there is one theory that, aside from the fear of retaliation, the widespread issuing of respirators potentially nullified the viability of poison gas as an offensive weapon of choice.

Over seventy years on, wartime gas masks still turn up today in attics or collectors' fairs. Though interesting and important, poignant relics, they should never be worn, as their filters contain harmful asbestos.

This general civilian respirator is an early June 1937-dated example, with a rubber face piece made by the Henley Tyre and Rubber Company of London. The white head strap indicates it is a 'large' size. The white cotton tape holds an additional Contex filter that was added to respirators from May 1940 against Arsine smoke gases. Its original cardboard box of issue has been protected by the addition of a leatherette-strapped carrier. Also discovered in the container was this small snapshot of two boys wearing their general civilian respirators in their back garden around summer 1939 or 1940!

A group of school children during a gas mask drill, circa 1941. (*Historic Military Press*)

7: Petrol Ration Coupons, September 1939

The interwar years had seen a gradual growth in car ownership as 'pleasure motoring' grew in popularity. However, within a year of the outbreak of war, British car production had decreased to a small proportion of its pre-war numbers, as the great British motor manufacturers, such as Austin, Bentley, Hillman, Humber, Jaguar, Morris, Rolls-Royce and Wolseley, turned over their production lines to the manufacture of military vehicles and engines. Thus, many of the cars seen on the roads during wartime were pre-war models, or even earlier.

The government had already made detailed plans for motoring restrictions before war began. Whilst private motoring would not be banned,

petrol rationing was soon introduced on 23 September 1939, just three weeks after the war's outbreak. Those who tried to pre-empt rationing by hoarding petrol, if caught, were heavily fined.

Petrol coupons were issued, the amount varying to the car's horse-power: initially, 200 miles-worth of petrol was allowed per month – meaning long-distance journeys largely disappeared overnight. Here's an example of a motor fuel ration book for a motorcycle from November 1941.

Branded petrol was replaced by 'pool', a medium-quality fuel, so-called because the petrol companies pooled their resources together for the war effort. However, in actual fact, despite the pressure on Britain's supply lines, in the summer of 1940 the nation's fuel stocks were surprisingly plentiful: careful pre-war planning by the oil companies meant that, although targeted by the Luftwaffe, the nation's oil tank farms still held enough fuel: so much so, it was even considered using oil as an anti-invasion weapon to set the beaches and sea on fire. In the event of a German invasion, the Home Guard had confidential orders to destroy petrol stations to prevent their use by invaders, as such supplies would be a key factor in their advance.

While the construction of German autobahn motorways continued until 1943, in Britain, many of the new roads and bypasses planned in the 1930s were suddenly kicked into the long grass as the road construction companies and materials were diverted into building airfield runways. Thus, road travel was often long and exhaustive, along the old B-roads, passing through many towns and villages – sometimes further delayed by Home Guard roadblock checks and the removal of location signs.

However, the toll on tankers inflicted by U-boats in the Battle of the Atlantic bit hard. When a tanker was torpedoed, there was little chance of survival for its brave merchant seamen. The crisis peaked in July 1942, when the basic petrol ration was banned altogether, except for those on essential business. At this point, many cars were simply put up on blocks in the garage under dustsheets 'for the duration'.

Alternatives, such as gas, coal and even wood-powered vehicles were introduced, but proved of limited popularity. Once again, the black market filled the gap – if you were willing to pay up to five times the price of a gallon of petrol. To try and catch illicit fuel usage, petrol for commercial or agricultural use was dyed red. However, it was commonly known that the dye could be strained out simply by pouring it through a gas mask filter.

However, to most Britons in the 1940s, all this made little difference: cars were still a luxury that most families could not afford – archive photographs show whole residential streets empty of parked cars, unlike today.

Petrol rationing finally ended on 26 May 1950, five years after the war's end. In today's age, with a variety of petrol stations to freely pull in and fill up with as much fuel as you want, petrol ration coupons such as these seem a strange and distant concept.

8: Identity Card, September 1939

I f you were stopped in the street by the police, could you prove who you are? Indeed, would you object to having to prove who you are? In wartime Britain, government legislation ensured the carrying of identity cards was compulsory, to safeguard the nation from spies and criminals.

Way before biometrics, microchips, holograms or even widespread colour photography, very simple folded cards were issued in their millions to Britons as their number one form of identity. On this one document depended everything, from your employment, food supply, even your daily freedom.

The National Registration Act, passed two days before the outbreak of war, on 1 September

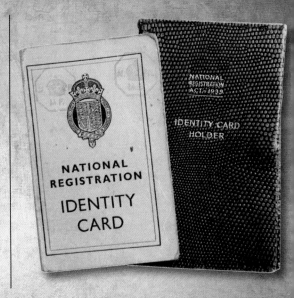

NATIONAL REGISTRATION

KTYE 169 —

RUDDY

AUSTIN

1. This Identity Card must be carefully preserved. You may need it under conditions of national emergency for important purposes. You must not lose it or allow it to be stolen. If, nevertheless, it is stolen or completely lost, you must report the fact in person at any local National Registration Office.

2. You may have to show your Identity Card to persons who are authorised by law to ask you to produce it.

3. You must not allow your Identity Card to pass into the hands of unauthorised persons or strangers. Every grown up person should be responsible for the keeping of his or her Identity Card. The Identity Card of a child should be kept by the parent or guardian or person in charge of the child for the time being.

4. Anyone finding this Card must hand it in at a Police Station or National Registration Office.

51-4766

NATIONAL REGISTRATION

KTYE 169 —

RUDDY

AUSTIN

Born 13/5/42

Registered Address of Above Person

8 BEDFORD ROAD

MILL HILL N.W.Y

OFFICIAL STAMP   BKA

51-6325.

H.B.LTD.   N.R.101.

(Signed) Austin Ruddy

Date 23. 5. 42.

1939, made it compulsory for all Britons to carry an identity card. On National Registration Day, 29 September 1939, every household in Britain had to complete a survey listing every occupant. These forms were collected and processed, leading to the issue of forty-six million identity cards.

Initially, all identity cards were buff coloured, but after March 1943, cards for adults were of light blue card, while those issued to children under sixteen remained buff. Your card carried details of your marital status, name, age, gender, occupation and address and, most importantly, your individual National Registration number. This was the 'smart' part of the card. Rather than just a random long number assigned to your name, your number identified your family household, even which locality you lived in.

The card was really more designed for administration purposes and form filling: you could not obtain food or, later, clothing ration books without the card. You needed it when applying for work, to see if you were applicable for a reserved occupation or liable to join the armed services. These were all applications that took days to process and were reference number-based.

However, despite the relative sophistication of the number identification system, it had major flaws. As an immediate form of identification, it was seriously lacking. Most identity cards did not possess a photograph of the bearer, so if stopped by a policeman and you were in possession of somebody else's card, it was difficult to prove you really were (or were not) 'John Smith'. Likewise, although they did have some fine print detail, it was still possible to forge these simple documents.

Identity cards were not the only form of official recognition. If you served in the ARP, Home Guard, or, indeed, any of the Home Front services, you often had an identity card for that specific organisation.

Many factories and businesses produced enamel lapel badges bearing their company name with the words 'On National Service', enabling their employees to access important restricted works. These badges were also issued to avoid the debacle of the previous world war, when working men in civilian clothes were issued with white feathers by those who accused them of cowardice, believing they were not playing their part in the war effort.

Although the war ended in 1945, the identity card scheme remained in force for another seven years, in an attempt to counter the black market and those avoiding National Service. In December 1950, Liberal councillor Clarence Willcock (1896–1952) refused to show his identity card when stopped for speeding in north London. He was prosecuted under the National Registration Act 1939, but successfully appealed, arguing that the national emergency that led to the act had expired. The second Churchill government repealed the act on 22 May 1952, but every few decades the issue of identity cards is still debated in Parliament.

Not my identity card, but my father's! My grandfather, Sapper 1867956 Austin Ruddy, of the Royal Engineers, was wounded during the 1940 campaign in France. Invalided out of active service, he became base staff at the Royal Engineers barracks in Ripon, North Yorkshire. He also moved his wife, Edith, and daughter, Pamela, away from the Blitz in London to be with him. My father, also Austin, was born in 1942 and ten days later was issued this buff identity card, bearing his own National Registration number. Just to confuse matters, the card was signed by his father – also Austin! Around 1951, the family moved back to London, hence the white change of address sticker.

9: 'War Against Hitlerism' Teapot, December 1939

For over 200 years now, the British have been known the world over for their love of tea. Originally an expensive luxury drink for the upper classes kept safely locked away in tea caddies, it became popular with all Britons in the middle of the eighteenth century when the government removed a tax on it. However, during the Second World War tea took on a whole new significance as a reassuring and refreshing pep to morale.

Tea was served from mobile canteens to bombed-out residents and tired ARP workers at the scene of an incident or in thousands of mugs from factory canteens. But tea was an overseas product, not grown in Britain, which had to be imported from the other side of the world – a big operation, even in peacetime, made all the more complicated in time of war.

So, how did the government ensure that tea-loving Britons could still enjoy their daily cuppa? The answer is, with a great deal of help from the tea industry, at home and thousands of miles away in India and Africa.

Rectangular teabags were not invented until 1944, and even then loose tea was still the norm. Britain's first foods were rationed in January 1940, but tea was left alone for another six months. Lord Woolton, Minister of Food, later recalled: 'Rationing tea was more than a bit of a risk. My experienced political friends told me that any minister who interfered with the nation's tea committed political suicide.' Perhaps that was the reason why the tea ration was comparatively generous: 2oz of tea per person per week, enough to make three cups a day (later, it even went up to 4oz).

Officialdom took precautions to guard this valued commodity. Tea was stored outside the capital, away from London's bombed warehouses. In 1941, the Empire Tea Bureau even produced a ten-minute film called *Tea Making Tips*, which included 'a few simple rules' on the preservation of tea and the best way to make it. To conserve rations, the Ministry of Food advised 'one spoonful of tea for each person and none for the pot'.

Even so, emergency 'Pool tea', a single, government emergency brand, was almost introduced three times when tea supplies were threatened: packages and labels were even printed. In 1942, on the north-east Indian frontier with Burma, tea plantations were threatened with being overrun by the advancing Japanese. The Ministry of Food's Tea Division brought up all extra tea stocks in India, indeed, anywhere it could find it, including Africa.

The workers of the India Tea Association were working 'all-out' to provide a maximum yield of crop, but thousands of the tea planters and pickers were also called up for military service, creating a serious labour shortage. The tea producers in southern India also increased production and eventually half the tea ration came from Ceylon (now Sri Lanka).

There was also competition for tea stocks from the armed services abroad, who valued a quick brew-up during a lull in the fighting. Also, each of the twenty million Red Cross parcels sent to British prisoners of war contained a quarter-pound package of Twinings tea.

Then, it was up to the brave sailors of the Merchant Navy [see Object 84] to traverse treacherous U-boat infested seas to bring the tea to Britain, which, incidentally, was no easy cargo: dried tea leaves contain fannings or dust particles, which, when mixed with air in the form of a dust cloud, can cause an explosion if sparked.

Britons would have to wait over seven years after the war, on 3 October 1952, before tea rationing ended – then they could drink as much tea as they liked.

This fancy earthenware teapot was made by the pottery of A. G. Richardson & Co. Ltd, of Tunstall and Cobridge, Staffordshire, for their Crown Ducal range. As written on one side, it was made for sale in the Christmas 1939 catalogue of the mail order firm, Dyson & Horsfall, of Aqueduct Street, Preston. It is decorated with the flags of the Allied and Commonwealth countries, with the words 'Liberty and Freedom' on one side and the inscription: 'War Against Hitlerism – This souvenir teapot was made for Dyson & Horsfall of Preston to replace aluminium stocks taken over for Allied armaments, 1939', with the added wording, 'That right shall prevail'. The teapot still surfaces in antiques and militaria fairs, so it must have been a popular wartime Christmas present. This particular example is still heavily tea-stained – I wonder how many cups it served throughout the war?

Tea and refreshments being served by ARP personnel in an air raid shelter. (*Historic Military Press*)

10: Lord Haw-Haw Postcard, 1940

'Jarmany calling, Jarmany calling ...' grated the sinister, sneering voice through big box wirelesses into Britain's homes. But who was the mysterious English-sounding propagandist with haughty tones, broadcasting from Germany?

Nicknamed 'Lord Haw-Haw' soon after the outbreak of war by newspaper critic Jonah Barrington (really Cyril Carr Dalmaine, 1904–86) as this postcard shows, his background was surmised upon: a disgruntled toff? A two-dimensional movie villain? In actual fact, he was neither: he was a convicted street-fighting thug who climbed the greasy ladder of fascism to become its international mouthpiece. Yet, Haw-Haw's notoriety became a draw to millions of Britons, as much a radio celebrity and mentioned in the same breath as 'Big-hearted' Arthur Askey and Richard 'Stinker' Murdoch, comic entertainers of the popular BBC radio show, *Band Waggon*.

Although Britain's secret home intelligence organisation MI5 already quietly knew his identity, it was Haw-Haw who revealed his name, live on air, in April 1940. Born to Anglo–Irish parents on 24 April 1906, in New York, USA, William Joyce attended school in Galway, Ireland. As a teenager, during the Irish War of Independence he assisted the British Army against the IRA.

Fleeing possible repercussions, Joyce came to England around 1922, living in south London. It was here that his interest in fascism grew. In 1932, he joined the British Union of Fascists (BUF), becoming its Director of Propaganda within two years, and later, its deputy leader.

THIS IS NOT BIG-HEARTED ARTHUR, NOR IS IT OLD STINKER---OH, NO! IT'S THE DONKEY THAT'S BRAYING FROM HAMBURG, LORD HAW-HAW, HEE-HAW,-HAW, HEE-HAW!

However, BUF leader, Sir Oswald Mosley (1896–1980) sacked Joyce in 1937, who went on to form the more German-leaning and short-lived National Socialist League.

Just before the outbreak of war, Joyce fled with his wife, Margaret, to Germany. Within weeks, he was broadcasting Nazi propaganda to Britain on the medium-wave station, Reichssender Hamburg.

Today, with so many forms of communication, it is difficult to appreciate how influential and powerful radio was [see Object 86]. By 1940, Joyce was attracting six million regular British listeners. Ironically, some Britons did Joyce's work for him. Rumours spread that Joyce announced a specific town was going to be bombed on a certain date. But, although the Luftwaffe had night air superiority, they were not invincible enough to tip off British defences when and where they would be raiding. Indeed, after monitoring his broadcasts, the Ministry of Information stated: 'It cannot be too often repeated Haw-Haw has made no such threats.'

In actual fact, there were several other temporary Lord Haw-Haws and 'black' propaganda radio programmes, but Joyce's was the most infamous.

As the Nazis began to falter, so did Joyce's diatribes: his last broadcast, on 30 April 1945, in the ruins of the Reich, was an arrogant, drunken, self-pitying rant.

Three weeks after VE Day, Joyce was apprehended in woods near the German–Danish border by British troops. During his arrest, he was shot through the buttocks. Joyce was sent to London's Old Bailey for trial. Although born in America, it was noted that he had travelled to and worked for Germany while a British passport holder – technically, treason. Despite an appeal, on 3 January 1946, unrepentant, Joyce ended his thirty-nine years at the end of a rope in Wandsworth Prison, hanged like a common criminal. Though millions of Britons had listened to his broadcasts, few mourned his passing.

11: Food Ration Book, January 1940

In twenty-first-century Britain, bulging waistlines reveal that food is so widely available and affordable there is now an 'obesity epidemic'. And, according to the Food Standards Agency, in 2017, over 7 million tonnes of food was wasted. By comparison, in 1940, wasting food became an imprisonable offence, for, as a wartime poster stated, food was a valuable 'munition of war'.

Being an island has defensive benefits, but it also had drawbacks. In the First World War, Germany used its U-boat submarines to blockade Britain, limiting imports and food supplies. In 1917, food rationing was introduced.

As the clouds of war once again developed, the government began to plan rationing in 1936, printing and stockpiling ration books two years later. They were also far quicker to implement a programme of rationing. On 8 January 1940, bacon, butter and sugar were rationed. Meat,

tea, jam, biscuits, cheese, egg, lard, milk and canned and dried fruit rationing followed.

Fresh vegetables and fruit were not rationed, but supplies were limited. Some types of imported fruit became rare: oranges, lemons and bananas attained almost mythical status – there was even a 1943 hit song called *When Can I Have a Banana Again?*

There were three different-coloured cover ration books: buff for adults, blue for children aged five to sixteen and green for pregnant women and children under five, which entitled the holder to extra fruit, a daily pint of milk and twice the egg ration.

A typical weekly ration for an adult was 50g butter, 100g of bacon and ham, 100g of margarine, 225g of sugar, 1s 6d [£3.75] of meat, 50g of cheese, one fresh egg, three pints of milk and 50g of tea. Additional entitlement included 450g (one jar) of jam every two months, one

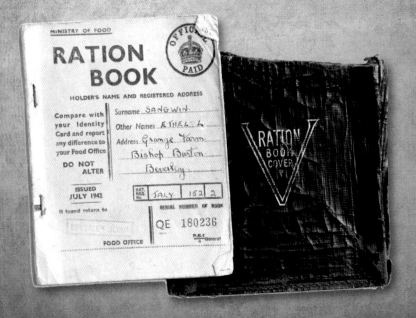

packet or can of dried eggs and 350g of sweets per month. From December 1941, points rationing was introduced, giving more choice for certain foods, such as tinned goods, dried fruit, cereals and biscuits. From 1942, a national wholemeal loaf was introduced, due to a shortage of white flour. Technically, it was nutritious, but it was not popular – rather like rationing itself.

It became common to see housewives queuing outside their registered grocers following rumours that a supply of off-ration pears, for example, had been delivered.

Unrationed cheap and cheerful meals, such as soup, mince, boiled potatoes, cabbage, followed by sponge pudding and custard, was served from 2,160 wartime British Restaurants, under the auspices of the Ministry of Food and run by local authorities in church halls and such buildings.

Rationing was also a great leveller, attempting to ensure that everybody, no matter their income,

received the same nutrition. However, the system only worked if everyone abided by it: 'under the counter' or black market extras obviated its equality and fairness.

It may not have been universally popular but, despite the scarcity of food, the nation's nutritionally balanced ration diet meant that Britons were healthier and fitter than they've ever been.

Ration books were issued annually. The first editions required shopkeepers to remove small coupons from the ration book with the purchase of rationed food. However, this became so laborious that instead from 1941 coupons were stamped by the retailer. The ration book cover also changed each year. This 1942–43 example from Beverley, East Yorkshire, has been well-preserved in a leatherette 'Ration Book Cover', which bears the V for Victory symbol [see Object 52].

The first Lend-Lease food supplies arrive in the UK. The original caption, dated 1941, states that the group is 'meeting the first American food ship to arrive under lend-lease to Britain'. Among those present are Kathleen Harriman, Lord Woolton (Minister of Food), Averill Harriman (US Lend-Lease representative), and Robert H. Hinkley (US Assistant Secretary of Commerce). (*Historic Military Press*)

12: Conscientious Objector's Application Form, February 1940

In a free democracy, can you force someone, against their conscience, to fight? Then again, is it right to have the privilege of free choice not to take up arms while others fight and die for that freedom? It was a moral and practical question that was asked by both the individual and the state in the war.

Under the National Service (Armed Forces) Act 1939, men and women of varying ages were called up or conscripted into the army, air force or navy. The individual could object on the registration form, usually due to religious, moral, ideological or political reasons: such people were known as conscientious objectors (COs). From this point, their relationship with the state – and other Britons – changed.

In the First World War, some 16,000 British COs faced tribunal boards. Those who were not exempted for military service and still dissented, found themselves imprisoned. Some committed suicide. Many who were exempted were publicly shamed and presented with white feathers, a symbol of cowardice, by street assailants.

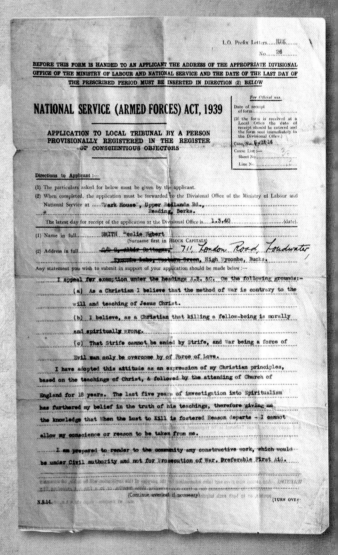

Come the Second World War, 59,192 Britons claimed exemption, almost four times that in the previous world war. Only 3,577 were given unconditional exemption. Nearly half (28,720) were given conditional exemption on the agreement that they took up approved work in agriculture, mining, ARP or hospital work.

Some 14,691 were registered for non-combatant duties in the armed forces, with 350 serving in the highly dangerous work of bomb disposal [see Object 38].

Some 12,204 COs were rejected, becoming liable to conscription. However, 5,550 'absolutists' still refused to serve and, following military court-martial, were sent to detention barracks or civil prisons.

The tribunals were not easy to face. Composed of a panel of five adjudicators, the questions were often barbed or framed in such a way as to be unanswerable.

There was a small support network for COs, chiefly the Peace Pledge Union (PPU), which had been founded in 1934, by the canon of St Paul's Cathedral, Dick Sheppard (1880–1937). The group produced newsletters and offered advice to those facing tribunals.

For those who maintained their freedom of choice in wartime British society, it must be said that they had not necessarily attained an easy option or 'skive'. COs faced shaming, rejection, isolation even harassment and violence from former friends, family, neighbours and even local authorities. Indeed, in 1940, 119 councils dismissed COs from their employment.

For critics of conscientious objection, Nazism and all that it stood for had to be fought: refusing to fight Hitler and facing him with a pacifist response would simply have offered an open door that would have been exploited, resulting in an end to almost 1,000 years of national freedom.

Nevertheless, compared to the First World War, the state was more tolerant and accommodating of those who chose not to fight.

On 15 May, 1994 – International Conscientious Objectors Day – Michael Tippett, composer and PPU president (1958–98), unveiled a memorial to COs in London's Tavistock Square.

Here is a National Service (Armed Forces) Act 1939 application form to be registered as a conscientious objector by a man from Loudwater, near High Wycombe, Buckinghamshire, dated February 1940. His application was based on his Christian beliefs, including that 'war is contrary to the will and teaching of Jesus Christ' and that 'killing a fellow-being is morally and spiritually wrong'. He stated that he was 'prepared to render to the community any constructive work … not for the Prosecution of War. Preferable First Aid.' The tribunal ordered that he was conditionally exempted in the Register of Conscientious Objectors. Associated papers reveal he joined Slough's National Fire Service, attaining both his National Civil Defence Safe Driving Award Certificate of Merit and St John Ambulance Association First Aid to the Injured courses in 1943. He was released from the terms of his National Service condition in May 1946.

13: Mass Observation Journal, March 1940

Do the government, newspapers or news channels really reflect what the people of Britain think, or do they just broadcast what they *think* we think – even, what they *want* us to think? In the late 1930s, these were the questions pondered by the sociologists of a new independent organisation, Mass Observation.

We now live in the age of social media, where nearly everybody seems to publish their thoughts for all to read. However, back in the 1940s, not only were people often more guarded and reserved, but, if you did want to publicly express an opinion there were fewer ways to do so: maybe a conversation in the queue for the bus, down the pub over a pint or in a formal correspondence to a newspaper's letters page.

In 1937, three Cambridge University graduates, anthropologist Tom Harrison (1911–76), poet Charles Madge (1912–96) and filmmaker Humphrey Jennings (1907–50), questioned the official pronouncements on national matters such as the abdication of

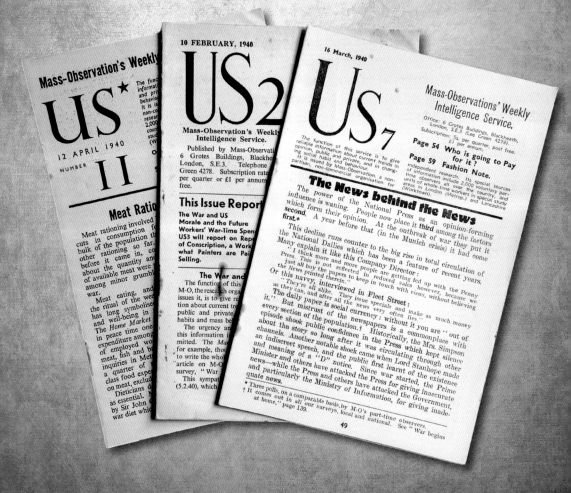

Edward VIII and the coronation of George VI – did the public agree with the government line, or were they being fed 'spin', as it is termed today?

Such nationwide research would obviously be expensive, but with no budget the founders had to fund the project themselves and rely on benefactors and the work of volunteer amateur contributors, who observed and recorded public opinions in diaries and questionnaires. Private investigators were also paid to listen in on conversations in public places.

The coming war would be their biggest project to date. In August 1939, they invited the public to record their lives and thoughts via personal diaries that were sent to Mass Observation for interpretation. Some 480 diarists responded, forming part of the 2,000 other volunteer observers, who, throughout the war, provided Mass Observation with interesting grassroots thoughts on everything from air raids and rationing to world events and teacup gossip.

However, the government fought back and it could be argued, compromised Mass Observation's independence. Soon after the war's outbreak, Mass Observation publicly criticised the Ministry of Information's first efforts at propaganda posters [see Object 5]. The government heeded Mass Observation's advice – and went a step further: they recruited and commissioned the organisation to carry out research on their behalf. Not only that, but were Mass Observation not just an *unofficial* prying version of authority anyway? Snooping was generally viewed as quite 'un-British'. Mass

Observation's Orwellian authoritarian name did not help matters.

After the war, the organisation's independence could be further questioned when, in 1949, the project became a private market research firm, Mass Observation (UK) Ltd, merging with advertising agency BMRB in the 1990s.

Nonetheless, now under the auspices of the University of Sussex, Brighton, Mass Observation continues today to gather the thoughts of the nation via correspondents. Their contributors' wartime diaries are held in a modern archive called The Keep and make interesting reading and grounds for local research. However, it should be remembered that as the observers were all volunteers, they did not represent a balanced cross-section of society and were mostly middle class, educated and left-thinking. Similarly, their thoughts were not necessarily an accurate interpretation of reality, but largely based on rumours and opinion.

It may prove surprising to know that the wartime findings of Mass Observation were not kept secret till after the conflict. For an annual subscription of £1 [£50], you could receive the organisation's 'Intelligence Service' bulletin 'Us'. Published weekly from London, as the journal's introduction stated, 'The function of this service is to give reliable information about current trends in opinion, public and private, and in changing social habits and behaviour.' This small bulletin also prepared the way for today's giant market research industry. The Mass Observation Bulletin is still published to this day.

14: Refugee 'Thank You' Card, 1940

For centuries, Britain has offered sanctuary to the persecuted. Perhaps it's the traditional British sense of fairness and goodwill; the axiom of 'treat other people as you would wish to be treated'. The Second World War was no different.

Indeed, even before the war had begun, individuals and non-governmental organisations tried their best to rescue children from war zones. As the Spanish Civil War (1936–39) raged between the Nationalists and Republicans, the Basque Children's Committee organised the evacuation of just under 4,000 children, who arrived at Southampton Docks on 23 May 1937. Initially, they were housed at a large refugee camp near Eastleigh, Hampshire, before being rehomed throughout Britain.

Following the violent Nazi Kristallnacht pogrom against German Jews in November 1938, the following month the British government eased immigration restrictions for those fleeing the torment. Jewish refugees first arrived in Harwich, Essex, in December 1938. Some 10,000 children of the Kindertransport were saved. Stockbroker Nicholas Winton MBE (1909–2015) organised the rescue of 669 Czech children, for which he was knighted in 2003. Many who managed to escape Germany never heard from their relatives again. The last they heard was a telegram from the Red Cross that their loved ones had been deported 'to the east' – a cruel euphemism that usually meant the concentration or extermination camps.

Following the outbreak of war, and more so after the German invasion of Western Europe, Britain became home to over 30,000 refugees, mostly from Poland and Belgium. Similarly, around 29,000 refugees fled from the Channel Islands, around a third of the population, who were mainly billeted in the north of England.

However, with the rapid fall of Europe, spy, or 'fifth column', fever hit Britain. Had the enemy infiltrated the nation amongst the refugees? Under Defence Regulation 18B, some 22,000 Austrian and German 'enemy aliens' were interned. But it was not just foreign suspects: some 750 British fascists were also arrested, their leader, Sir Oswald Mosley following suit on 23 May 1940, with his British Union of Fascists organisation, was banned a week later.

As a consequence of Italy's entry into the war on the Axis side on 10 June 1940, Italian restaurants and ice cream parlours in Britain were attacked by mobs. Some 4,000 Italians with less than twenty years' residency were also interned.

The main destination for internees was the Isle of Man, in moderate comfort. Here, they sat out most of the war. The irony was not lost on many who had come to Britain to flee captivity. However, for Britain it was difficult to tell friend from foe. In retrospect, Churchill came to lament the use of internment, which was in his words, 'in the highest degree odious'.

This simple, hand-painted token of appreciation, showing a ship escaping a red swastika to London, charts the path to freedom from the Nazis. It is dated 1940 and is signed by ten refugees, including at least one from Czechoslovakia and several others whose names possibly indicate they were German or Austrian Jews. They were billeted in a 'refugee house', in Crescent Road, Chingford, north-east London. Their moving statement: 'We came down-hearted and you gave us new hope,' says it all. This illustrated page from a notepad is probably all these refugees had with which to thank their British hosts for their sanctuary and, possibly, their lives.

15: Wartime Wedding Photo, Spring 1940

In a time of uncertainty, when wealth, health and the future were all threatened, it might have seemed logical to put any long-term plans on hold: but not to thousands of Britons, who carried on and tied the knot. Indeed, for many couples, a wartime wedding was the brightest highlight in those dark days. Nowadays, thousands of pounds and a full year's planning are spent on a wedding. But back then, there was no such luxury: organising a marriage under Blitz conditions was no easy task and proved a battle in itself.

In 1939, as Britain faced the unknown, there was a slight hesitation among couples to marry. But love soon found the Bulldog spirit – in 1938, there were 409,000 weddings: two years later, as Britain faced her darkest hour, the figure jumped to 534,000.

Often, one or both partners were serving in the forces and the best they could hope for was a forty-eight-hour leave pass. The moment they left their barracks, the clock started ticking. At first, white weddings brought some 'carry on as before' spirit to wartime. However, as Britain struggled and utility measures bit, it was considered by some as unpatriotic to have a white wedding, so many brides just wore smart formal clothing on their big day. Later, couples defiantly tried to revert back to pre-war white weddings. A serving groom could wear his military uniform, but for the bride, sorting the trousseau was a struggle. No extra clothing coupons were available, so make do and mend [see Object 54] prevailed. Some brides wore or adapted their mother's or even their grandmother's wedding dress. Others even fashioned dresses from parachute silk, old lace curtains or dyed bedsheets! The government showed some sympathy by allowing the production of thin, 9-carat (instead of 22-carat) gold utility wedding rings, but these were in short supply and second-hand family jewellery was often worn.

Despite being the centrepiece of the wedding, the ceremony was often a drab affair. It was not unusual to stand in a cold, draughty, bomb-blasted church (due to their size, many ecclesiastical buildings were hit), with boarded windows or even part of the roof missing. Photographic materials were in short supply, so many couples simply had just one or two photographs, instead of the hundreds taken today. To cap it all, the war on waste meant it was illegal to manufacture confetti, so many made do with a nicer, more romantic, sprinkling of rose petals.

The reception was a little more cheerful. A permit to buy extra food could be obtained by a visit to the local food office and a quiet word with the local shopkeeper might provide something from under the counter. The odd bottle of something alcoholic would also appear, no questions asked. For the wedding cake, wartime camouflage and deception came to the fore. On the face of it, impressive three-tiered cakes were still seen. But in July 1940, restrictions on the usage of sugar placed a ban on the making or selling of iced confectionaries. Instead, bakers supplied reusable cardboard cake covers, which were lifted to reveal a small, disappointing, plain, dark cake! As for wedding presents, utility was paramount. There was a shortage of luxury goods, so instead of cutlery sets and toasters, everyday practical gifts, such as soap powder or money, were given. There was no flight to somewhere hot and sunny: an overnight stay at a local hotel – or even the in-laws home – was the next best thing to a honeymoon. But it could be worse:

many a honeymoon night was spent shivering in a damp Anderson shelter, cursing Hitler.

With many men away serving abroad, there was a decline in marriages. However, when the troops returned in 1945, the figure jumped up to 457,000 weddings – with a baby boom to boot [see Object 57].

The bane of researchers today, like many wartime photographs, this image was never captioned. However, with a bit of detective work, the groom's chest insignia reveals he was a member of the Beckenham AFS, so this view of a traditional firemen's guard of honour axe archway was probably taken around spring/summer 1940. The Borough of Beckenham, in south-east London, was on the bombers' flightpath to the capital and as such, although on the outskirts, had a tough Blitz. Its fire service suffered particularly heavily in 1941, with thirty Beckenham AFS men killed. The highest loss of life occurred at 1.53 am on 19/20 April 1941 – a heavy London night raid known as 'The Saturday' – when four Beckenham crews were ordered to the AFS station in Old Palace School, Leonard Street, Bow, East London. Just twenty minutes after they arrived, a parachute mine made a direct hit on the school, killing all twenty-one firemen outright. This remains the largest single loss of fire brigade personnel in English history. Today, there are two plaques to their memory, one at the site of the school, the other at Beckenham fire station – I wonder if any of those firemen are pictured here during this happier moment?

16: Luftwaffe Air-Drop Churchill 'Gangster' Leaflet, May 1940

'Cometh the hour, cometh the man' goes the old adage – and in 1940, that man was Winston Churchill. He did not win the war single-handedly, but, it could be argued, his words and actions played a great part in the eventual victory. Yet, despite the simplified two-dimensional caricature of Homburg hat, cigar and 'V' sign, Churchill was a far more complicated character.

Winston Leonard Spencer Churchill was born on 30 November 1874 into an aristocratic Oxfordshire family. Both his father and grandfather had served as Conservative politicians. The young Winston was schooled 'in the right way', at several private schools including Harrow, where, although academically he did well, his mind was elsewhere: this is perhaps the first signs of his characteristic bulldog stubbornness.

As a young man, he joined the army, seeing action in Cuba, India and Africa. Later, he became a journalist and, during the Boer War, was captured but escaped. He then became an MP – first for the Conservative party, then the Liberals. He saw high office as Home Secretary and First Lord of the Admiralty, though he developed a reputation with his peers as an adventurer during the First World War Dardanelles debacle of 1915–16.

The interwar years were a time of political wilderness for Churchill. Although he warned of the growing threat from Hitler, his calls for rearmament during a time of appeasement kept him isolated. But it was the outbreak of the

WANTED

FOR INCITEMENT TO

MURDER

This gangster, who you see in his element in the picture, incites you by his example to participate in a form of warfare in which women, children and ordinary civilians shall take leading parts.

This absolutely criminal form of warfare which is forbidden by the

HAGUE CONVENTION

will be punished

according to military law

Save at least your families from the horrors of war!

Second World War that thrust Churchill back into the political limelight, again becoming the First Lord of the Admiralty.

Prime Minister Neville Chamberlain's appeasement delayed the German threat pre-war, but on 10 May 1940, Hitler invaded Western Europe and Churchill was the man chosen to lead the nation in the face of this crisis.

It should be noted that aged sixty-five, he took the job on, an age when most men are thinking of retirement. Yet those who surrounded him noted his energy and drive. This was the making of Churchill: he was later to say: 'I felt as if I were walking with destiny and that all my past life had been but a preparation for this hour and for this trial.'

For the next five years, Churchill would lead the nation through victory and disaster, with a series of highly eloquent, inspiring speeches and public appearances. He was a war leader who managed to draw the support of Britons of all political persuasions – a rare thing, compared to today's binary politics.

However, for historical balance, Churchill was not perfect. An imperialist, his views on race and religion, while not untypical of the time, were sometimes xenophobic, even racist. His military

and political decisions were also not always successful. But he was a patriotic pragmatist who realised the importance of his prime ministerial position meant that the nation always came first – at all costs.

Yet, the war years changed Churchill's outlook: his post-war writings express regrets and a new appreciation of others. As well as a national victory, for Churchill, the Second World War was a personal victory. A legendary sharp wit and speaker, he became one of the nation's greatest orators: his words were weapons, each letter a bullet. He was a one-man national morale booster, and remains to this day widely regarded as our Greatest Briton.

This press photo of Churchill with a Thompson sub-machine gun was taken while he was inspecting anti-invasion defences near Hartlepool, County Durham, on 31 July 1940. Two weeks later, the German propaganda machine regurgitated it across East Anglia, in the form of an aircraft-dropped leaflet, comparing Churchill to an American gangster and warning Britons not to resist invasion. It backfired: the British people wanted a war leader who would offer 'blood, toil, tears and sweat' to take on the Nazi menace – and in Churchill, they had one.

Winston Churchill is pictured with the West Ham Town Clerk, Charles E. Cranfield, on the corner of Winchester Street and Factory Road inspecting the smouldering ruin of the Silvertown Rubber Company, 8 September 1940. (*Historic Military Press*)

17: LDV Armlet, May 1940

The black German arrows advancing across the map of France were heading straight for the Channel. Many believed Britain was next in line. The white cliffs of Dover, visible from the French coast and separated by only 21 miles of calm summer sea, would be the next goal for the mighty German army, which was steaming through all the armies it encountered. Yet, for this very British problem came a very British solution – the Local Defence Volunteers.

" I've laid your uniform out, my Lord."

The speed with which German Blitzkrieg tactics had routed all before them led many to believe that a 'Fifth Column' of enemy spies and saboteurs had helped undermine the recently vanquished Continental nations. A growing public volunteer spirit, kindled by the national press, put pressure on the government to 'arm the people'. Although there were official concerns about dishing out firearms to whoever requested them, the government realised that such volunteers could relieve the stretched regular army from comparatively mundane but essential tasks, such as standing guard at vital points or manning roadblocks.

At 9 pm, on 14 May 1940, Anthony Eden, the Secretary of State for War broadcast to Britain:

Now is your opportunity. We want large numbers of men, who are British subjects, between the ages of seventeen and sixty-five, to come forward now and offer their services in order to make assurance doubly sure. The name of the new force which is to be raised will be the Local Defence Volunteers. This name describes its duties in three words. In order to volunteer, give in your name at your local Police Station … Your loyal help, added to the arrangements which already exist, will keep our country safe.

Following the broadcast, men queued at their local police stations to enlist. Enthusiasm for the Local Defence Volunteers (LDV) took the government by surprise, with 250,000 men volunteering in the first week. By July, the LDV was 1.5 million strong. However, such was the

speed of its formation, there were no uniforms or arms to immediately equip the new force.

The idea of a British volunteer force in times of the nation's greatest need was not new. Such militias can be traced back a thousand years to Anglo–Saxon times and every major conflict since. Indeed, during the First World War, 590,000 men served in the home defence Volunteer Training Corps (VTC). They wore armbands bearing the initials 'G.R.' ('Georgius Rex' – King George), but wags joked that it stood for 'George's Wrecks', 'Genuine Relics,' even 'Government Rejects'. This line of parody would follow the VTC's successor.

Upon their formation, the LDV's initials became satirised as standing for 'Long Dentured Veterans', 'Last Desperate Venture' and 'Look, Duck and Vanish': however, in truth, the final moniker was actually an accurate assessment of their observational role during an invasion.

Initially, the only 'uniform' issued to the volunteers was a khaki armband, or in military terms, armlet, bearing the initials 'LDV' – and even this took some weeks to arrive. There was also another pressing reason for such an official identifying feature: the Germans had warned they would shoot armed civilians without uniform as 'franc tireurs' ('free shooters'), under the terms of the 1899 Hague Convention. Whether this meagre strip of cloth would have placated the invader and saved the life of its wearer, thankfully, was never put to the test.

This simple cotton armlet reflects the desperate nature of that invasion summer in 1940 and the spontaneous, but very British, public response in the face of an overwhelming, looming threat.

18: *If The Invader Comes* Leaflet, June 1940

Most promotional material that's pushed through our letterboxes often goes straight into the recycling without even a glance. However, back in summer 1940, a leaflet was delivered that was designed to make its recipients sit up and take note – but did it?

The government and military had made their plans to resist invasion – but what about the nation's fifty million population?

Issued by the Ministry of Information in co-operation with the War Office and the Ministry of Home Security.

If the
INVADER
comes

WHAT TO DO — AND HOW TO DO IT

THE Germans threaten to invade Great Britain. If they do so they will be driven out by our Navy, our Army and our Air Force. Yet the ordinary men and women of the civilian population will also have their part to play. Hitler's invasions of Poland, Holland and Belgium were greatly helped by the fact that the civilian population was taken by surprise. They did not know what to do when the moment came. *You must not be taken by surprise.* This leaflet tells you what general line you should take. More detailed instructions will be given you when the danger comes nearer. Meanwhile, read these instructions carefully and be prepared to carry them out.

I

When Holland and Belgium were invaded, the civilian population fled from their homes. They crowded on the roads, in cars, in carts, on bicycles and on foot, and so helped the enemy by preventing their own armies from advancing against the invaders. You must not allow that to happen here. Your first rule, therefore, is :—

(1) IF THE GERMANS COME, BY PARACHUTE, AEROPLANE OR SHIP, YOU MUST REMAIN WHERE YOU ARE. THE ORDER IS "STAY PUT ".

If the Commander in Chief decides that the place where you live must be evacuated, he will tell you when and how to leave. Until you

receive such orders you must remain where you are. If you run away, you will be exposed to far greater danger because you will be machine-gunned from the air as were civilians in Holland and Belgium, and you will also block the roads by which our own armies will advance to turn the Germans out.

II

There is another method which the Germans adopt in their invasion. They make use of the civilian population in order to create confusion and panic. They spread false rumours and issue false instructions. In order to prevent this, you should obey the second rule, which is as follows :—

(2) DO NOT BELIEVE RUMOURS AND DO NOT SPREAD THEM. WHEN YOU RECEIVE AN ORDER, MAKE QUITE SURE THAT IT IS A TRUE ORDER AND NOT A FAKED ORDER. MOST OF YOU KNOW YOUR POLICEMEN AND YOUR A.R.P. WARDENS BY SIGHT, YOU CAN TRUST THEM. IF YOU KEEP YOUR HEADS, YOU CAN ALSO TELL WHETHER A MILITARY OFFICER IS REALLY BRITISH OR ONLY PRETENDING TO BE SO. IF IN DOUBT ASK THE POLICE-MAN OR THE A.R.P. WARDEN. USE YOUR COMMON SENSE.

Although there were radio and cinema newsreels, television broadcasts had been suspended for the duration, so the distribution of government messages was by hard copy – leaflets. The Ministry of Information was largely responsible for the production and distribution of such messages, but as the invasion would mostly be challenged by the military, it co-operated with the Home Defence Executive of the War Office and the Home Office in the production of a public leaflet.

But what could the populace do, if anything? It would seem that the three parties behind the leaflet were divided. During the Battle for France, the Allied armies had been obstructed by roads clogged with refugees, who also became targets for marauding German aircraft. To avoid such a repeat, the Home Office wanted the population to 'stay put'. Meanwhile, the military wanted mass evacuations out of the landing areas, whilst, ironically, the Ministry of Information wanted the public to actively resist! The fudged compromise and rather puzzling term agreed upon and used in the finished leaflet was: 'Think before you act. But think always of your country before you think of yourself.'

On 18 June 1940, fifteen million copies of the *If the Invader Comes* leaflet was printed and every household in Britain received a copy over the following three days.

The Ministry of Information follow-up survey found that the public's reaction to the leaflet was mixed. Despite its tone, many did not take the leaflet very seriously, while findings by the public

research group Mass Observation [see Object 13] discovered the public thought they were being treated as 'blithering idiots'. Perhaps the 'If' in the title diminished the leaflet's immediacy and impact.

Almost as an afterthought, at the end of the following month, a further fifteen million copies of a shorter follow-up leaflet, *Stay Where You Are*, were also distributed. Whilst the focus remained on 'staying put', the leaflet attempted to clarify what its predecessor's 'think before you act' statement meant: 'You have the right of every man and woman to do what you can to protect yourself, your family, and your home.' But again, what did this mean? Civilians taking up arms against troops was contrary to the 1907 Hague Convention and could have led to reprisals, as on the Continent, something the government could not be seen to endorse.

The following year, as the summer invasion season again approached, fourteen million copies of a further leaflet, *Beating the Invader*, was distributed in May 1941. Opening with a statement by the Prime Minister, the leaflet listed ways civilians could passively resist the invaders, such as sabotaging their own cars, and suggested Britons 'carry on' and 'stand firm' – again, whatever that meant.

As the pendulum of war turned against the Germans and the invasion threat dwindled, the Ministry of Information would produce no further anti-invasion leaflets – probably a relief for all concerned.

19: Luftwaffe Air-Drop Last Appeal To Reason Leaflet, August 1940

While the British were battening down the hatches for possible invasion, Hitler went on an uncharacteristic charm offensive.

On 19 July 1940, before the German Reichstag, Hitler gave a triumphant three-hour speech trumpeting his forces' victories in the capture of Western Europe. Never one to undersell himself, Hitler claimed he had been 'chosen by Providence' and even that he was a 'prophet':

A LAST APPEAL TO REASON

BY

ADOLF HITLER

Speech before the Reichstag, 19th July, 1940

... Mr Churchill should make an exception and place trust in me when as a prophet, I now proclaim: A great world empire will be destroyed ... Mr Churchill may believe this to be Germany. I know it to be England. In this hour I feel compelled, standing before my conscience, to direct yet another appeal to reason in England. I believe I can do this as I am not asking for something as the vanquished, but rather, as the victor, I am speaking in the name of reason. I see no compelling reason which could force the continuation of this war.

To the uninitiated ear, all this may have sounded relatively reasonable, but Churchill and the British people were only too aware of Hitler's previous guarantees: his word meant nothing. The Führer's bloodied hand of friendship would not be embraced. In the House of Commons, the Prime Minister was asked what response he would be making to Hitler's 'appeal': with his noted dry wit, Churchill said he would not be responding, as they were 'not on speaking terms'.

Hitler's Reichstag speech was publicised worldwide, on radio and in the press, even reprinted in British newspapers. Nonetheless, Britain's lack of an official response to Hitler's apparent magnanimous offer seems to have sidestepped the dictator.

A fortnight later, in response, a tabloid-sized, four-page transcription of his speech, entitled *A Last Appeal to Reason by Adolf Hitler* was air-dropped across England and Wales. Over a ten-day period, starting on 1 August 1940, these leaflets were disseminated by both German bombers and balloons, reaching as far west as Swansea and as far north as Manchester, plus the Midlands and the south.

But the response was not what Hitler intended. The leaflets were treated with derision, being auctioned off for the Red Cross or even ending up torn into squares and used as toilet paper! The greatest impact the leaflet had was when a few faulty unopened bundles smashed through the roof of an office building.

Undeterred, the Germans continued to attempt to influence the British public several more times during the war with air-dropped leaflets, such as *The Battle of the Atlantic is Being Lost!* and *The Lost War in the Air* (July 1941), *Dieppe – We and the British Invade France* (September 1942), *Here is the Reason Why the British Government Says Nothing about the Shipping Losses* (March 1943) and *Why Die for Stalin?* (March 1944).

However, the Luftwaffe's output paled into insignificance compared to the millions of air-dropped propaganda leaflets distributed over Germany by the RAF and USAAF. As the Luftwaffe lost free range over Britain, Germany's solution to this conundrum was unmanned science. Between August and December 1944, V1 flying bombs distributed fifteen different types of leaflet across England, including one series called *V1 P.O.W Post*, which attempted to trick recipients into helping the Germans discover where the missile had landed – 'phishing', 1940s-style!

All this German effort in the war of the printed word was to no avail. All it resulted in was the diversion and destruction of increasingly valuable resources, manpower and aircraft. For the British, it provided a source of derision, charitable fundraising – and free toilet paper.

20: Pillbox, Summer 1940

Y ou might have spotted one nestling in a hedgerow or partially buried in a sand dune: a weathered, crumbling, concrete remnant of the Second World War – the humble pillbox. But, actually, these hardened fortifications were far from passive: in 1940, they would have been the first line – and in many cases, the last line – of defence against invasion and as such, should be viewed as Britain's castles of the twentieth century.

These small concrete bunkers gained their name during the First World War after their resemblance to contemporary tablet containers. However, it was the Second World War that saw their greatest use as defensive positions. On the Continent, thousands were built pre-war. However, following the invasion of Western Europe, a massive programme of pillbox construction started in Britain.

In six months, around 28,000 pillboxes were built, mostly in the coastal counties, in the biggest defence building programme Britain has ever seen. The reason can be traced back to the wreckage-strewn roads of Europe: the British Army lost half their tank force in France

and so the pillboxes that we see today were the rather desperate static alternative to the infantry support tank.

Pillboxes are commonly thought of as hexagonal concrete structures. However, in reality, there was not just one design, but an almost infinite number of variations, dependent on local defence needs, designs and materials available.

Another myth is that pillboxes were randomly dotted about, often in obscure locations. Each pillbox was carefully placed by a Royal Engineers officer as part of a wider defence strategy. However, as the more remote examples tend to be the only survivors of this plan today, pillboxes often seem isolated in the landscape.

Indeed, pillboxes were a key part of the 'stop lines' that divided up Britain, together with anti-tank ditches, obstacles, road blocks, weapons pits and trenches – all designed to slow the invader down, allowing time for mobile army units to arrive, engage and, hopefully, either destroy or repulse the invader back into the sea.

During 1940 and 1941, civilian builders and army units put a lot of hard work and long hours into the programme of anti-invasion

defence construction. On their completion, these defences were manned by army infantry units and the Home Guard. However, as Britain moved back on to the offensive, such static defence was soon seen as obsolete and by February 1942 they were declared redundant. Ironically, come 1944, some were now used as targets to train attacking Allied troops for the D-Day invasion of France.

In the intervening seventy-plus years since the war's end, the Council for British Archaeology estimates that about three-quarters of Britain's pillboxes have been demolished, leaving around 6,500 surviving examples. Today, many pillboxes lie abandoned, covered with graffiti and filled with rubbish – or worse: an ignominious and irreverent end to what are, essentially, symbols of struggle.

However, after decades of research and re-evaluation, some pillboxes have been preserved and listed, with information boards: some even form centrepieces on new housing estates. But they are a minority, and these monuments to Britain's most recent darkest hour are still demolished.

Britain's pillboxes are, effectively, war memorials and an important reminder of what almost came to pass. They would have been steadfastly held 'to the last man and the last round'. Had they become surrounded or overcome with flamethrowers, these pillboxes would also have become the final horrific stand for many brave men.

This 1940 pillbox, officially designated by the War Office's Directorate of Fortifications and Works (FW3) as a Type 28A, held around seven men and is the largest and only anti-tank type. One of two such pillboxes that guarded the approach from the beach at Heacham, Norfolk, its 2-pounder anti-tank gun would fire through the large embrasure, left, whilst a .303in Bren machine gun, in a separate chamber, fired from the other loophole, right. An adjoining Home Guard 29mm Blacker Bombard spigot anti-tank mortar pedestal, an anti-tank ditch, roadblock and mined bridge from the beach can still be seen today.

Throughout 1940 and 1941 building of anti-invasion defences continued apace throughout the UK. 'Concrete barriers are ready on the roads, blockhouses have been built, barbed wire barricades are waiting' notes the original caption to this picture, dated 22 August 1940, of a soldier on duty by a pillbox. (*Historic Military Press*)

21: Home Guard Instruction, Summer 1940

On 16 July 1940, Hitler issued Führer Directive No. 16, proposing the potential invasion of Britain, 'to eliminate the English Motherland as a base from which the war against Germany can be continued, and, if necessary, to occupy the country completely'. The designated name for the invasion was Operation Sea Lion.

Britain, following the evacuation of its troops from France, had been rearming and rebuilding its military forces, in readiness for the expected invasion.

On 14 July 1940, Churchill referred to the Local Defence Volunteers as the 'Home Guard'. Churchill had previously used the term in 1939, however, he did not invent it: Confederate Home Guard militia units had been founded in 1862 and participated in the American Civil War. The LDV officially became the Home Guard on 23 July 1940. The new name was an improvement on the officious and nondescript-sounding 'Local Defence Volunteers', which Churchill thought 'uninspiring'.

Nazi Propaganda Minister Doctor Joseph Goebbels (1897–1945) mockingly responded, although his vituperation was slightly lost in translation: 'Churchill has spoken of Home Guards under arms. We ask what arms? Broomsticks or the arms of the local pub, with pots of beer and darts in their hands?'

The not-so-good doctor, however, did have a point. Although British arms production grew steadily, most Home Guards had no personal weapon. Official requests were made for souvenir firearms from previous conflicts, the donation of shotguns and even museum pieces. Some lucky Home Guards were issued the dependable British .303in Lee-Enfield service

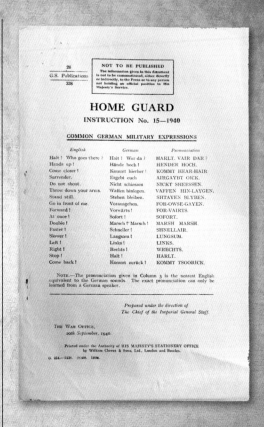

rifle, but soon most were taken away to re-equip the army.

Despite America's neutrality, the British government used the 'special relationship' to buy 500,000 First World War US .300in M1917 rifles, which were safely shipped across the Atlantic in July 1940. Unofficially, by 1942, the civilian-organised American Committee for the Defense of British Homes donated 25,343 firearms, too. Canada also supplied 75,000 Ross rifles. Slowly, Britain's Home Guard was developing teeth – though, in that perilous summer the only anti-tank weapon they had were 'Molotov Cocktails' – crude petrol bombs.

Over the coming weeks, further small but important morale-boosting improvements were made, such as the issue of some denim uniforms, albeit often ill-fitting. Similarly, in August, the Home Guard were affiliated to their local regiments and allowed to wear the regimental badge, imbuing a further sense of military bearing and esprit de corps.

Over the summer, Home Guard sections patrolled from dusk till dawn, watching, often from sand-bagged observation posts in the countryside, for saboteurs or parachutes blossoming in the sky.

The volunteers were taught defensive warfare at their local church hall or at regional training schools, the most famous being Osterley Park,

west London. Here, left-wing Spanish Civil War veteran Tom Wintringham (1898–1949), with the support of *Picture Post* publisher Lord Hulton (1906–88) [See Object 45], set up a private battle school for Home Guards from all over Britain, who would then go back to their battalions and pass on what they had learned.

The War Office also issued a total of sixty-eight Home Guard official Instructions over the course of the war, such as this one, No. 15, dated September 1940, with such potentially useful common German phrases as '*Hande hoch!*' (Hands up!) and, possibly, more realistically, '*Kommt zuruck!*' (Come back!)

Members of the Waterlooville, Hampshire, Home Guard parading for the National Day of Prayer, held on 8 September 1940. (*Historic Military Press*)

22: Unofficial Home Guard Training Booklet, 1940

One thing the Home Guard were not short of was training advice – and it wasn't all just from official sources. Over 200 colourful – both visually and in literary terms – instruction booklets were commercially produced during the war. Most were based on existing official military manuals, often with the author's own commentary, extolling everything from old school 'Colonel Blimp' First World War tactics to downright suicidal guerrilla terrorism.

Many of the early unofficial manuals were written by those with more recent experience of modern warfare, such as Spanish Civil War veterans Tom Wintringham (*New Ways of War*, Penguin Special), Bert 'Yank' Levy (*Guerrilla Warfare*, Penguin Special) and John Langdon-Davies (*Home Guard Warfare*, George Routledge & Sons Ltd), or John Brophy, who had served in the First World War (*Home Guard – A Handbook for the LDV*, Hodder & Stoughton) and leading surrealist artist Roland Penrose (*Home Guard Manual of Camouflage*, George Routledge & Sons).

However, as early as November 1940, official Home Guard Instruction No. 20 warned:

A considerable number of unofficial books, pamphlets and newspaper articles are now being published on the training of the Home Guard. Although these unofficial publications often contain much that is useful … others will be found in which the arguments are based on false assumptions and the criticisms on misrepresentation. No unofficial publications will be used as a substitute for official training instructions and pamphlets.

Indeed, there seems to have been little to stop any author or publisher publishing books full of suggestions, no matter their credibility. One such 1942 publication, *Manual of Guerilla Tactics*, by Bernards, who published several such 'Key to Victory' flip books, suggested 'destroying track of enemy tank by means of crowbar', with an illustration of a Home Guard eagerly thrusting said tool into a rather fanciful small panzer's drive wheel. No accompanying German troops or other tanks were pictured and this mythical method of anti-tank warfare would most likely have proven suicidal.

But, it seems it was precisely the unavailability of official military pamphlets that made the unofficial training publications so attractive, the variety of new titles reaching a peak in 1942, with well-known commercial military manual publisher Gale and Polden the main producer.

By this date, the titles had become more gung-ho (*Bloody Bayonets*, *Rough Stuff for Home Guards*, *Harrying the Hun*), with cover illustrations and the advertised contents – 'Sniping, silent killing, booby traps, detonators, destroying supplies and communications with a special section on the preparation and use of explosive' – becoming more extravagant and desperate as the war developed.

Warfare was becoming more unconventional and these manuals reflected this. However, they also answered a growing anxiety among some sections of the Home Guard. In truth, by the middle war years, the tide was turning: the German invasion threat was receding – as was the Home Guard's raison d'être. This anticlimax proved frustrating for many Home Guards who had spent hundreds of hours of their own time training and patrolling in readiness, all on top of exhausting long hours of war work.

The Home Guard in training during the summer of 1940. The original caption, dated 7 August that year, states this image shows 'members of the fast-growing British Home Guard training for the expected Nazi invasion, sighting at a low-flying airplane from behind a sandbag barricade "somewhere in England". This practise is to prepare them for real action against airplane troops.' (*Historic Military Press*)

In line with the dwindling threat, only a handful of new titles were published in the final three years of the war. Likewise, sales also dipped: the publishers tried to stretch the appeal of these publications, sometimes completely leaving out the words 'Home Guard' from covers or adding the names of other services – 'For H.G., RAF, Army and Navy Use' – to broaden their commercial reach.

While these colourful unofficial booklets make interesting and sometimes doubtful reading today, their purpose was to imbue, encourage and develop a fighting spirit among their Home Guard readership. Fortunately, we shall never know if their contents would have proved practical.

This 108-page manual, *Field-Craft for the Home Guard*, is quite an early one, dating from September 1940, at the height of the invasion threat. It was written and published by A. T.

Walker, a veteran of the Argyll & Sutherland Highlanders, who had 'personal experience of Sniping in France during the last war' and trained field craft to army officers and Home Guards in the next. It was stated that a 'substantial percentage' of the proceeds from the book would fund Home Guards with 'special sniping equipment', such as 'field glasses, snipers' suits, camouflaged face masks, etc'. In the introduction, Colonel P. J. Blair DSO TD, the Honorary Area Organiser of Edinburgh Home Guard, noted:

The Home Guard are determined to take their part to the full in restoring decency in the world and in saving liberty and civilisation. Their enthusiasm is firmly founded in faith in their crusade against the greatest evil which has ever assailed humanity. They will do everything to defend their country and their homes.

23: Occupied Channel Islands Identity Card, June 1940

Hitler may have called off his invasion of the British mainland, but that didn't mean he left empty-handed, for he still captured and occupied British territory – the Channel Islands. Located just 15 miles from the French mainland and 60 miles from Britain, the Channel Islands – comprising Jersey, Guernsey, Alderney, Sark and Herm – were the only part of Britain ever to fall under Nazi rule.

By late May, it was clear that the Battle of France was lost. Located so close to France and with minimal defences, Britain could not guarantee the security of the Channel Islands, so on 15 June 1940, evacuated its troops, leaving the islands demilitarised. Between 30 June and 4 July 1940, 25,000 islanders were also evacuated to the British mainland, leaving around 66,000 resident.

Unaware the islands had been demilitarised, on 28 June 1940, the Luftwaffe bombed the harbours of Jersey and Guernsey, killing forty-four islanders. The Germans had planned a military invasion, Operation Grünpfeil (Green Arrow), but soon realised the islands were

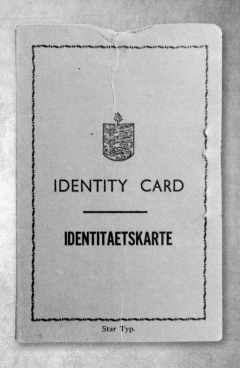

undefended. Guernsey surrendered on 30 June 1940, Jersey the following day, Alderney the day after and Sark on 4 July. A long five years of occupation was about to begin.

Initially, things did not change too much. Radios were confiscated, curfews introduced, cars had to drive on the other side of the road, but the Germans kept the civilian government in place, albeit under close control. German propaganda showed a British bobby talking awkwardly to a Luftwaffe officer in Jersey or military bands jack booting past Lloyds Bank in Guernsey. But this uncomfortable civility was not to last.

The Germans began to fortify all the islands against British counterattacks: many of the imposing concrete bunkers remain today. In Jersey alone, 65,718 land mines were laid. In

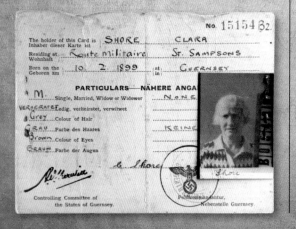

Alderney, the entire population, save six islanders, were evacuated, while two labour camps and two SS-run concentration camps – the only Nazi concentration camps on British soil – were built to house European forced labourers who worked on the fortifications, 700 of whom died. As the war went on, the occupation became harsher. Over 2,000 islanders were deported to Europe, with twenty-five dying in Continental concentration camps.

It was a fine line between existing and collaboration. Some did aid the Germans and denounce their fellow islanders. Due to the islands' small size and the risk of reprisals by the large German garrison that made up half of the population, there was no active resistance as on the European mainland. There was, however, passive resistance, such as defiant public graffiti or covert news distribution.

However, for the Germans, the Channel Islands were a token victory, indeed, a military hindrance. Their occupation diverted thousands of much-needed troops away from other fronts and cost valuable resources. Conditions became dire, particularly after D-Day, when the Allies blockaded the Islands. The final occupation Christmas of 1944 saw severe shortages and both islanders and occupiers came close to starvation, with German soldiers stealing and eating pets. The only respite came from the Red Cross aid supply ship, SS *Vega*.

By VE Day on 8 May 1945, all on the islands were relieved the occupation was over (although the German garrison on Alderney did not surrender until eight days later). On 9 May 1945, HMS *Bulldog* arrived in St Peter Port, Guernsey and the German forces surrendered unconditionally. British troops landed shortly afterwards, greeted by crowds of jubilant but exhausted islanders.

In 1941, all Channel Islanders were required to carry new German identity cards. Every resident was photographed, one photo affixed to their identity card, another kept in a German police file. The cards, which had to be carried at all times when outside, showed the bearer's details in both English and German for security checks. The obligatory Nazi eagle and swastika, stamped over the photo of a British citizen, is particularly disconcerting.

German troops marching through the centre of St Helier, Jersey, following their occupation of the Channel Islands. (*Coloured by Jon Wilkinson*)

24: Spitfire Fund Fundraising Card of Honour, Summer 1940

There are certain iconic historical objects from the Second World War that not only came to represent the conflict, but also the nation: arguably, at the top of Britain's list is the Vickers Supermarine Spitfire.

The legendary, high-performance, single-seat fighter, designed by Reginald Joseph Mitchell (1895–1937), was introduced into service in August 1938, just a year before war. Its sleek, graceful but potent presence instantly made it popular with both pilots and the public alike. With a top speed of 367mph, it certainly was a much-needed improvement on the RAF's previous biplane fighters.

Following the Dunkirk debacle, it was clear which nation was next in Hitler's sights. On 18 June 1940, Prime Minister Winston Churchill famously announced: 'What General Weygand has called the Battle of France is over. The Battle of Britain is about to begin.' Eight days later, the first stages of this crucial battle began. Luftwaffe aircraft probed Britain's defences, with scattered bombing raids. From 4 July, the Luftwaffe started bombing British coastal supply convoys, ratcheting up further pressure on besieged Britain.

The press played a key part in highlighting the developing threat. Step forward Lord Beaverbrook, Max Aitken (1879–1964), the Anglo–Canadian media tycoon and Minister of Aircraft Production. In the coming battle, the Spitfire would be portrayed as Britain's defending sword. Beaverbrook engaged the public, firstly, by requesting aluminium for a salvage scrap drive, to be melted down and made into fighter aircraft. Secondly, he encouraged

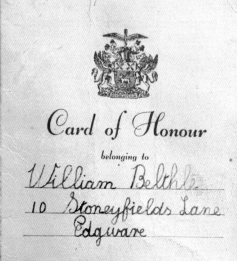

the foundation of regional Spitfire Funds, where the public could fundraise £5,000 to 'buy' their own fighter and have it named after their town or city. (Of course, the money didn't really 'buy' an individual Spitfire, but went straight into the government coffers and funded the war effort as a whole).

Nonetheless, the appeal was an immediate success, with many areas funding not just one, but several fighters, such as Liverpool, which paid for five Spitfires. To encourage and promote the scheme, donors could buy a celluloid Spitfire Fund badge for sixpence. Shot down German aircraft were also publicly displayed to attract donations. Group savers, such as a factory, were sometimes presented with a small plaque commemorating their total. Wealthy benefactors also paid for aircraft themselves, such as potato merchant Mr W. D. Cook of Donington, Lincolnshire, who paid for a Spitfire named the 'Doningtonian'.

Not all Spitfire Funds were UK-based. The African country Gold Coast raised £25,000, a large sum for a poor country, which paid for five Spitfires, while Assam, in India, bought eleven and the Persian Gulf Fighter Fund bought six fighters named 'Bahrain'. Indeed, Uruguay – officially neutral – fundraised seventeen RAF aircraft.

The fundraising continued to bear fruit: by the end of 1940, factories were producing up to 350 Spitfires a month. By the time the Spitfire Funds closed, they had paid for around 2,600 fighters, although incomplete records mean only 1,600 can be traced today.

Such was the success of the scheme, not only was it extended to fund most other types of British aircraft, but the wartime National Savings organisation also embarked on annual fundraising drives, similarly encouraging areas to raise money for a chosen cause, such as the 1941–42 Warship Weeks [see Object 77].

In 2015, a recovered and rebuilt Spitfire Mk.I that had crashed on a French beach during the Dunkirk evacuation sold for £3.1 million at auction – the equivalent of 620 wartime-funded Spitfires, in old money!

This colourful 'Card of Honour' for the 'Hendon Four Fighter Fund' belonged to schoolboy William Belthle, of Edgware, who collected the requisite 24 penny fund stamps, attaining a colourful final 'Stamp of Honour'. The card's wording bears poignant resonance today: 'In years to come, when Peace has followed Victory, you will be able to show this Card of Honour to your children's children … you will remember how your effort of to-day supported the amazing performance of our steel-nerved Fighter Crews, who, in 1940, are our gallant representatives in aerial combat.'

25: Battle Of Britain Souvenir Calendar, September 1940

Attacks by Luftwaffe aircraft had been increasing in the preceding weeks, but the official start of the Battle of Britain is generally credited as 10 July 1940. It was to be the first battle Britons could see on their doorstep, just by simply looking up into the skies. Much of the time, all that could be seen was the criss-crossing of white contrails against the bluest of skies. But thousands of feet up, young men in their twenties were twisting and turning in a mortal battle to the death for their nation.

The RAF had 1,963 serviceable aircraft, the Luftwaffe, 2,550. Defending Britain were 2,353 British RAF pilots. However, there were also 574 pilots from other countries, including Poland, New Zealand, Canada, Czechoslovakia, Belgium, Australia, South Africa, France, Ireland, USA, Southern Rhodesia, Jamaica, Barbados,

Newfoundland and Northern Rhodesia. The top-scoring ace in the Battle of Britain was Czech pilot Josef František, of 303 (Polish) Squadron, who downed at least seventeen enemy aircraft before his death a month later. Though less well known, both the RAF's Bomber and Coastal Command also took the war to the enemy, attacking their ports and airfields.

The Luftwaffe launched their main offensive on 13 August 1940. Attacks moved inland. Luftwaffe Commander-in-Chief Hermann Göring's (1893–1946) answer to the RAF's continued dogged resistance was to increase the weight of the attacks. At the end of August and early September, the battle entered its critical phase, with Britain's south coast airfields being pummelled by heavy air attacks. But the Luftwaffe was overestimating its successes.

Despite his 'Stuffy' nickname, Air Officer Commanding Hugh Dowding (1882–1970), Commander of RAF Fighter Command, was a visionary who, pre-war, developed Britain's integrated air defence system. Radar was a key part of this ground control interception organisation, known as the Dowding System. Based on Britain's telephone cable network, essentially, it was an early version of the internet and, similarly, proved extremely difficult to knock out.

The Luftwaffe had other disadvantages. Their main fighter, the Messerschmitt Bf 109, had a range of 435 miles, but only fifteen minutes' fuel over England, with London its maximum range. If a Bf 109 pilot was shot down, he was captured and out of the war, whereas RAF pilots were on home soil and could fight again.

The battle reached its crux on 15 September 1940, when 630 RAF fighters took on 1,120 Luftwaffe aircraft. The RAF lost twenty-nine aircraft with fourteen pilots killed: the Luftwaffe lost sixty-one aircraft, with eighty-one killed and sixty-five captured. Realising the folly of continuing, two days later, Hitler postponed Operation Sea Lion – indefinitely.

The battle officially ended on 31 October 1940. In total, the Luftwaffe lost 1,700 aircraft, with 2,662 casualties. The RAF lost 1,250 aircraft and 544 air crew.

Although the 1940 Battle of Britain was just over three months long, the date has entered the pantheon of Britain's long history, alongside other such crucial dates as 1066 or 1805. Had Britain lost the battle, we could have been open to invasion. Its importance is still commemorated today, every 15 September marked as Battle of Britain Day.

Ever the master orator, Churchill perfectly captured the battle in his speech to the House of Commons on 20 August 1940, stating: 'Never in the field of human conflict was so much owed by so many to so few.'

This lucky horseshoe-shaped ceramic perpetual desk calendar, produced soon after the battle by Osborne Ivorex, bears the premier's quote, with three Spitfires above the English Channel, a church tower and rooftops in the foreground. Fittingly, it bears the date of Sunday, 15 September – Battle of Britain Day.

The wreckage of a Heinkel He 111 of III/KG1, werke 5376 V4+C, which was shot down in the Battle of Britain and crashed at 21 Manor Avenue, Caterham, Surrey on 27 August 1940. (*Historic Military Press*)

26: Battle Of Britain Official History Booklet, September 1940

The victory in the Battle of Britain was essential on several levels, not only for the British people. Churchill had been trying to prove to America that Britain was worth backing and supporting. With the industrial might of this powerhouse of democracy, Britain would be better able to protect herself and eventually move on to the offensive. Thus, the conflict was also a battle of hearts and minds. But it was also a battle of myth and reality.

The campaign was largely about perception, both then and now. With almost eighty years' reflection and the release of records, historians have been able to separate fact from fiction. Past depictions of the battle in films, while persuasive, were not always accurate. For example, not all RAF fighter pilots were from public schools or spoke with a plummy accent; they were from all sorts of different backgrounds. Similarly, while long dogfight scenes may be good cinematically, in reality, the Spitfire only had enough ammunition for fifteen seconds' gunfire, so had to fire in short bursts.

Focus on its enduring impressive image has also led many to believe that the Spitfire was the RAF's main fighter. That accolade could equally belong to the RAF's other fighter, the Hawker Hurricane. It is true that Spitfire squadrons had a lower attrition rate and a higher victory-to-loss ratio than those flying Hurricanes. Due to the Spitfire's higher performance, it was tasked with intercepting enemy fighters, whereas the 30mph slower Hurricane was primarily tasked to destroy the Luftwaffe's slower bomber force. However, not only did more Hurricanes (2,309) take part in the battle compared to Spitfires (1,400), but,

in total, Hurricanes outscored Spitfires, the former credited with 55 per cent of Luftwaffe losses, compared to 45 per cent by the Spitfire.

That said, at the time, the victory claims were dubious. On 15 September 1940, the Air Ministry released a statement to the press stating that '175–185 German aircraft had been shot down in one day'. In the fog of battle, pilots on both sides often overestimated their kills. However, the actual figure was 66 per cent fewer. Nonetheless, when the newspapers published these figures, they acted as a fillip to morale.

Some aspects of the campaign have also been forgotten. Following his defining role in the victory, Dowding was dismissed just three weeks after the battle due to disagreements and his command's inability to stop Luftwaffe night raids.

Indeed, some historians have also questioned how close-run the battle was, suggesting that Fighter Command was not in as parlous a state as popular history records. New appraisals argue bombed RAF aerodromes were often repaired quickly and easily, and that Britain's efficient supply system meant both aircraft and pilots were replaced rapidly.

The portrayal of the battle as a twentieth-century David versus Goliath was vital to the morale of the British people, showing that the German juggernaut could be stopped and the nation was not as weak as many believed. Nonetheless, the significance and achievement of this British victory should not be understated: up to that point, every other nation the Germans attacked, they conquered.

The battle was, effectively, won by a British sword: the main blade's edge was the 2,927 RAF airmen who fought the Luftwaffe. The hand on the sword's handle was the government and military commanders who directed the battle. But the body of the blade was also made up of the Royal Navy and British Army, plus the millions of Britons, from the workers in aircraft factories who made the fighters, to the RAF ground crews

who ensured the aircraft could be flown, as well as the Women's Auxiliary Air Force radar operators and operations room plotters, plus all the Home Front services and civilians who backed and funded the battle – this was a national victory.

Less than six months later, in March 1941, the Air Ministry/Ministry of Information published their official history of the battle. Written by author Hilary Aiden St George Saunders (1898–1951), it was one of around sixty-five such official histories that would be published by His Majesty's Stationery Office. Initially published as a plain text-only booklet, it was hurriedly reissued with photos. There are interesting differences to today's historical accounts: the booklet gives the battle's starting date as 8 August 1940 (as opposed to 10 July 1940), while Air Chief Marshal Dowding is completely written out of the history: indeed, only Churchill and Göring are mentioned. Nonetheless, it would be HMSO's most successful publication, selling fifteen million copies.

Spitfire Mk.Ia, of 602 (City of Glasgow) Squadron, at RAF Westhampnett, Sussex, in September 1940. It was flown by Pilot Officer Osgood V. Hanbury, who shot down four Luftwaffe aircraft during the battle and damaged several others. Tragically, Hanbury was posted missing after a transport aircraft he was travelling in was shot down on 3 June 1943. He was aged 25. (*Public Domain*)

27: Air Raid 'Shelter' Enamel Sign, September 1940

Without warning, on the sunny afternoon of 7 September 1940, Göring's Luftwaffe made a historic and crucial change of direction, both literally and strategically. For the RAF's airfields, it would bring some relief – but for the citizens of London, it would herald the start of fifty-seven nights of death and destruction.

Up until this point, despite its size, London had largely been excluded from Luftwaffe bombing. On the night of 24 August 1940, off-course Luftwaffe bombers accidentally bombed the British capital, causing token retaliation by RAF Bomber Command the following night and several times afterwards. Easily provoked, with his Nazi pride pricked, on 4 September 1940, a furious Hitler publicly ranted in Berlin: 'When the British air force drops two or three or four thousand kilograms of bombs, then we will in one night drop 150, 230, 300 or 400

thousand kilograms – we will raze their cities to the ground.' Just three days later, Hitler attempted to put his words into action.

Despite Hitler's warning, RAF Fighter Command were puzzled when they noticed 300 Luftwaffe bombers deviating from their usual airfield targets and heading up the Thames, bound for the capital. The RAF were unable to stop the huge aerial armada and by the day's end, much of the docks and East End were ablaze, leaving 430 civilians dead and 1,600 seriously injured. So surprised by this attack, GHQ Home Forces believed a German invasion was imminent and, under the code word 'Cromwell', the nation's defences were put on high alert. The London Blitz had begun.

How Britain's population was to be protected from aerial bombardment had been a subject of much debate, between scientists, politicians and the public, almost since the end of the First

World War. The government estimated that fifty casualties, about a third fatal, would result for every tonne of bombs dropped on London. Theorists prophesised significantly higher fatalities.

The most obvious precaution was to simply remove civilians from the urban target areas, which the government did under the evacuation scheme [see Object 3]. Unlike in Germany, where shelter policy was to build expensive, giant, hardened bunker air raid shelters accommodating hundreds, British government shelter policy was of dispersal: lots of smaller air raid shelters, based on the probability that although more may be hit by bombs, fewer civilians would be killed than if huge shelters were hit.

By the outbreak of war, Britain's shelter-building programme was under way, but far from complete: thankfully, the Phoney War allowed a period of catch-up in time for the onset of the Blitz. Implementing government policy, local councils built a variety of brick and concrete communal surface shelters in streets plus covered trench shelters, both types holding around fifty shelterers. Neither type were bomb-proof and the former developed a bad reputation for collapsing on its occupants, though both shelters were safer than staying in bed, sheltering at home, as many civilians did.

Political groups of the left demanded deep shelters. Initially, due to the cost, the government refused. Although forbidden, from September 1940, crowds began to seek shelter in the London Underground. The authorities relented and bunks were installed for overnight shelterers. In 1944, the government introduced eight deep tube shelters in the capital, providing civilian protection against the new German V-weapons. Pre-war government fears that urban populations would become troglodyte dwellers, psychologically damaged and unwilling to come to the surface, were overwhelmingly unfounded.

If the sirens suddenly sounded while you were out in the streets, this sign could have saved your life. With white writing on a black background to aid visibility in the blackout, directional signs to the nearest air raid shelter were affixed to walls and lamp posts. Measuring 2ft by 1ft and made of enamel – crushed glass on a metal backing – various similar signs were produced during the war, including 'Gas Cleansing Station', 'First Aid Post' and 'ARP Report Centre'. They are now hotly collected by militaria, enamel sign and design enthusiasts.

28: Anderson Shelter Stove, Autumn 1940

For those families who wished to shelter at home, the government introduced a new type– the Anderson shelter. Cheap, simple and easy to produce, the Anderson was a unique British design classic, which saved the lives of thousands of Britons.

The Anderson shelter was actually quite a late, last-minute invention, only designed in 1938 by engineers William Paterson (1874–1956) and Oscar Carl Kerrison in response to a request from the Home Office for an easily mass-produced domestic shelter. Its name derived from Sir John Anderson (1882–1958), the Lord Privy Seal, who, pre-war, had been responsible for overseeing Britain's air raid precautions. It might well also have been named after Dr David Anderson, who, alongside Bertram Hurst and Sir Henry Jupp, of the Institution of Civil Engineers, approved the shelter's design.

A total of 3.6 million Anderson shelters were produced, with the first delivered to households in February 1939. The basic shelter comprised of fourteen corrugated galvanised sheet steel panels. The 6.5ft-long structure was made up of six arched 6ft-high upright panels, bolted together where they joined at the top. The 4.5ft-wide front was made up of four panels, comprising an entrance with a further four panels as the rear, featuring a removable emergency exit panel. The whole shelter was partially buried 4ft deep, with a 15in soil covering added for further protection. Some owners grew vegetables on this top cover as part of the Dig for Victory campaign. The Anderson was designed for up to six shelterers, although more could be accommodated by adding extra upright panels. Wooden bunks were specially designed for the shelters.

The key to the Anderson's strength was its arched profile, a design feature recognised since Roman times and incorporated in bridges and viaducts since then. Even though it was only partially buried with just over a foot of earth cover, its profile offered little resistance to blast, which just travelled over it, as opposed to the unprotected flat sides of surface shelters, which could either collapse or be pierced by an explosion. However, for full efficiency, Anderson shelters had to have an earth blast wall protecting the entrance – a detail often forgotten or ignored: post-raid ARP photos record sobering images

of unprotected shelters with their front metal panels punctured by bomb splinters.

As the Blitz occurred over winter 1940/41, doorless Andersons were not hospitable places to retreat into during the night. Whatever insulation was offered by the earth covering was negated by the open entrance, which at best, was often just covered by a sack or crude wooden door. The shelter's 4ft depth meant they sometimes penetrated high water tables or springs and soon filled knee-deep with water. Councils tried to waterproof the shelters with an impervious lining, but there was a concrete shortage, so few attained this addition. Add to that the fact the shelters also acted as spider farms, then it's relatively understandable why many residents chose to 'risk it' and stay in bed instead!

The government understood the Anderson's inhospitality and towards the end of the Blitz, in March 1941, announced the introduction of a new indoor shelter, the Morrison, named after the Minister of Home Security/Home Secretary, Herbert Morrison. Designed by Professor John Fleetwood Baker (1901–85), the Morrison was table shaped, 2ft-high, by 6.6ft-long and 4ft-wide. Comprising 359 parts, it was mostly made of steel plate, with wire mesh sides. It could hold three adults and was, essentially, issued free to working-class families, although due to the shortage of steel, very few were issued before the end of the Blitz. Produced in fewer numbers than the Anderson (around a million), the shelters were designed to withstand the weight of a collapsed house: raid experience proved the Morrison shelter was a relatively effective lifesaver.

At the war's end, councils collected both types of shelter. Morrison shelters were reused as industrial workbenches or warehouse stacked storage. Some Anderson shelter sections were sold on for use as bus stop shelters or cycle shelters. A greater number of the curved sections were reused as garden or allotment sheds. As such, few 'true' complete Anderson shelters remain in situ today and they are now rare structures, with increasing historical significance.

In winter 1940, the Ministry of Home Security advised that an upturned flower pot with a candle in it could be used as a heater in cold Anderson shelters. However, some manufacturers went one step further and produced stoves that not only heated the shelter, but could be used to fry food or boil a kettle! This example, marked 'W & M Shelter Stove', belonged to a Sunderland docker. Apparently, it was quite common for the stoves to be taken into the shipyard, polished and painted, for that extra smart shelter look!

An Anderson shelter remains intact amidst destruction in Latham Street, Poplar, London, during 1941, after a parachute mine fell a few yards away. The three people that had been inside the shelter were unhurt. The effects of air raids in this area of London can be clearly seen. (*Public Domain*)

29: Air Raid Siren Magazine Cover Illustration, September 1940

Despite the advent of air raids, during the First World War, there had been no official ARP organisation, let alone a national air raid warning system. Instead, policemen on bicycles wore signs stating 'Take Cover' and maroons were fired from tall buildings. Boy Scouts signalled the end of air raids, roaming the streets blowing bugles. Clearly, in the next war, with an even greater threat from the air, a more efficient warning system was needed.

In 1938, backed by Britain's unique early warning radar and Observer Corps organisation, it was decided that RAF Fighter Command would be responsible for initiating air raid warnings to threatened areas.

There were four warning states – Yellow: a preliminary warning, telephoned to ARP Control Rooms and Report Centres, giving twenty-two minutes' warning before the arrival of enemy aircraft; Red: the 'action' or 'alert', warning 'Raiders Approaching/ Imminent', on receipt of which, ARP Control would alert the police, who, centrally, would sound local air raid sirens, with their two-minute, fluctuating or warbling varying pitch, supposedly giving twelve minutes' warning of the enemy's arrival. Green was the 'Raiders Passed/ All Clear': a slightly calmer sounding, single, continuous siren, again lasting two minutes. Finally, there was White: a message to the ARP organisation indicating all precautions could be relaxed (this was abandoned in July 1940).

Gent and Co Ltd, of Leicester, had been producing electrical goods since 1872, specialising in clocks and alarms. They started to develop their Tangent Electro-Motor Syren during the First World War and with this experience, in the run up to the next war applied and won the sole Home Office grant contract to manufacture air raid sirens, beating Lancashire rivals Carter sirens. Such was the huge order, a new block had to be built at their factory to enable the increased production.

Gents' standard siren, often seen in wartime newsreels, was advertised in their May 1939 trade catalogue as a 4hp, double-ended siren – as pictured on the cover of this November 1941 edition of *Newnes Practical Mechanics* – that could be heard for 4 miles. Weighing 348lb/158kg, they cost £50 [£3,000], although they also produced other variants. The siren was designed by Mr J. George Evatt, of Leicester. An associate member of the Institute of Electrical Engineers, he also designed a luminous call system used on ships, including the *Queen Mary* and the *Queen Elizabeth*, and in hospitals and hotels, plus fire alarm systems for factories and care homes.

By the war's end, Gent had produced 4,500 4hp sirens, as well as 1,000 smaller sirens, plus 6,000 hand-operated sirens for the military. Gents' sirens provided warnings for all parts of Britain, plus Cyprus, Egypt, Gibraltar, Malta and South Africa, and, following D-Day, to France and Belgium.

Britain's air raid warning system was not perfect. In some cases, the siren – or 'sy-reen', as some mysteriously called it – didn't sound until after the raid had started and lives were lost. By September 1940, so many hours of work were lost due to the disruption caused by too broad an alert area that the system had to be more localised. Indeed, many Britons nonchalantly ignored the siren – at their peril. But many thousands, if not millions, of lives were saved by the warning the system gave.

This was not the end of the siren story. During the Cold War, smaller sirens, made by Carters of Lancashire, gave a four-minute warning of nuclear oblivion: this warning's value was debateable. Many were also used as flood warnings or to call firemen to their fire stations.

During the war, there were recorded instances of people collapsing and dying at the siren's sound. All these years on, those who can remember testify that the simple sound of the wartime air raid siren on TV programmes still causes anxiety and the hairs on the back of their neck to rise. But that is what the sirens were designed to do.

Back in September 1940, although the Luftwaffe had lost their ability to roam freely across Britain in the daytime, they now began to use the cover of darkness to continue their assault. The 'banshee wail' of the nation's air raid sirens would now pierce the still night on a daily basis … The following objects explain the anatomy of a Luftwaffe air raid.

30: German Target Identification Map Of Coventry, Autumn 1940

It's often been commonly thought that the Luftwaffe just arrived over a city, dumped their bombs, then flitted off into the night. The reality is that air raids were generally more sophisticated than that.

Germany had started the aerial reconnaissance of Britain in 1936, three years before the war. German civil aircraft, carrying secret cameras, photographed military and urban centres. So thorough was their secret work that it proved to be the first complete aerial photographic survey of Britain. In the early years of the war, these spy flights continued via specialist Luftwaffe *aufklärer* (aerial reconnaissance) units.

Analysing, identifying and annotating these photographs, the Luftwaffe's 5 Abteilung 95th Branch (Foreign Powers Section) of the Operations Staff, compiled individual target files. Additional sources of information about the targets were freely available from pre-war British company trade brochures, even bribed international salesman.

Maps of British cities were also compiled, identifying important features such as railway stations, utility works and factories. Sometimes today called 'bombing target maps' or 'invasion maps', this is incorrect: they were general military geographical survey maps that could be used for any purpose – target acquisition one of them. Compiled from 1939 up to 1942, they were simply copies of pre-war British Ordnance Survey maps, overprinted in German.

However, such was the speed of the German advance, the Luftwaffe target analysts had a huge task with very limited time to compile their work. These maps could be inaccurate, missing new roads, factories, even whole housing estates. Nonetheless, this is what the Luftwaffe based their bombing operations on and it is interesting to note that often, bombing plots accurately fell within the target areas marked on these photos and maps.

Following the initial incendiary and flare target marking by Luftwaffe pathfinder aircraft, soon after the main bomber force would approach the target singly, moving on parallel paths confined to a belt some 15 miles wide. These 'crocodile' paths were quite different from the 'bomber stream' tactics later employed by the

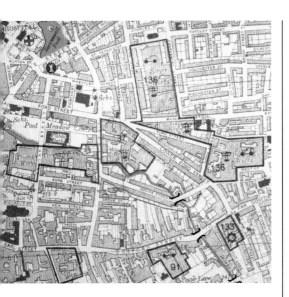

RAF Bomber Command. Luftwaffe bombers were spread out, with only one raider per 180 square miles, making it difficult for RAF night fighters to locate them. This flight pattern also drew out the duration of the raid, feeding the fires and disrupting the sleep of workers, in an attempt to impede their production rate.

Although the Luftwaffe highlighted key targets (*zielgebiete*), bombing was not pinpoint accurate, so targets were sometimes grouped together into a target area (*zielräum*), such as an industrial estate containing several factories or a station and sidings that could be attacked with a stick of bombs.

The bombers would try to remain over the target for as long as possible, circling, identifying and aligning their bombing run. Bombs would often be released individually every few minutes to cause maximum disruption and further draw out the raid. Even over such major targets as London, bombers showed their contempt for the ineffectual defences by circling for twenty-five minutes over the capital.

There is debate among historians as to what extent the Luftwaffe deliberately targeted civilians. Some point out that, apart from a handful of accidental or minor bombings, the Luftwaffe did not start to deliberately target London until 7 September 1940. Also, much of the Luftwaffe's bombing was what is termed today 'collateral damage', where neighbouring housing was hit while aiming at industrial targets. Additionally, despite having the most advanced electronic navigation systems of the time, 1940s technology was not as accurate as the laser-guided weapons of today – and even now, there are still collateral casualties.

However, others point to the deliberate daylight machine-gunning of trains, buses and civilians in the street. Indiscriminate parachute mines and later the V1 and V2 rockets were also used as blast weapons, while incendiary bomb attacks caused rapidly spreading firestorms – which the Germans were later to protest against themselves. But by then, Germany was openly engaging and encouraging what Hitler's propaganda minister, Joseph Goebbels, called 'Total War'; unrestricted combat against all targets – including civilians.

This section of the target identification map for Coventry, Warwickshire, was published after December 1941, by which time much of the city centre had been devastated in the famous raid of the previous year. Interestingly, it shows that Coventry Cathedral (marked 'CATH', bottom left), which was destroyed in the infamous raid of 14 November 1940, was sandwiched between the purple highlighted factories of the Standard Motor works, Singer Motors, Morris Motors, plus the Triumph and Gloria Company – founded by German industrialist Siegfried Bettmann in 1896 – and also destroyed by his countrymen.

31: Luftwaffe Bomb Shrapnel Collection, September 1940

Often, an unnerving period of silence would follow the air raid siren's warning call, only punctuated by the tip-tap of last-minute shelterers running for cover. ARP wardens would keep an ear to the skies as they patrolled the city's empty streets, made more eerie by the blackout and shadows cast by the white light of a bombers' moon. Then it would come: the low, undulating rumble of desynchronised German aero engines. Hitler's Luftwaffe were approaching …

Searchlights would pierce the darkness to try and pick out the enemy bombers for British anti-aircraft guns, who would engage the night raiders with a fusillade of shells.

A clatter and fizzing would suddenly echo around the bombers' chief target area, as the initial hail of incendiary bombs hit the streets and ignited, lighting them up in a piercing white glow, illuminating and firing buildings for all to see – including the follow-up bombers.

Then, the main bomber force would arrive and drop its high-explosive (HE) bombload. Occasionally, flutes, called 'Trumpets of Jericho' or 'screamers', were fitted to HE bomb tail units, causing a screeching whistle to create further fear on the ground, adding to the night's fearful cacophony.

The Luftwaffe employed two types of HE bombs: about 80 per cent were SC (*Sprengbombe-Cylindrisch*) bombs, thin-cased, general purpose demolition bombs, with a high charge ratio of up to 55 per cent HE for maximum blast effect. They varied in size from 50kg, 250kg, 500kg, 1,000kg 'Hermann', 1,800kg 'Satan' and the largest, the 2,500kg 'Max'. Fortunately, the Luftwaffe used its smallest bomb, the 50kg, the most and the largest, 'Max' only a handful of times. The other type of HE bomb type, SD (*Sprengbombe-Dickwandig*), were thick-cased, semi-armoured piercing, fragmentation bombs. They only had a 35 per cent explosive filling, but had greater penetration qualities and were used as anti-personnel bombs or against hardened buildings, such as factories. Their weight range was slightly different: 50kg, 250kg, 500kg, 1,400kg 'Esau' and 1,700kg. Added to the mix, from September 1940, 500kg and 1,000kg cylindrical naval mines were dropped by parachute. Intended to sink shipping, their heavy HE component made them ideal blast weapons, sometimes levelling half a street. They were hard to aim as they were at the mercy of the prevailing wind, and thus were largely inaccurate.

After the all clear had sounded, both local council ARP officials and regional Ministry of Home Security scientists would soon arrive to assess bomb damage. From the destruction caused and the size of bomb craters, they could estimate the total bombload dropped during the raid.

In total, during the Blitz, it is estimated that the Luftwaffe dropped 16,593 tonnes of bombs on Britain. In 1940–41, Germany had the most technologically advanced bomber force in the world. The Luftwaffe employed three main twin-engine medium bombers, the excellent Junkers Ju 88, the ageing Dornier Do 17 and its main workhorse, the Heinkel He 111. However, all were built for tactical operations, supporting short Blitzkrieg ('lightning war') attacks against rival armies, rather than long-term strategic bombing campaigns. The Heinkel could carry a bombload of 2.5 tonnes, the others less. Compare this with the RAF's four-engine Avro Lancaster of 1942, which had a 10-tonne bombload – four times that of the Heinkel. The Luftwaffe had nothing comparable.

Although extensive and widespread damage was caused to London and other British cities, the Luftwaffe were unable to deliver enough devastation to cause a breakdown in society or halt industrial production. Ultimately, the Blitz against Britain failed because the Luftwaffe did not have the equipment to enable a sufficiently heavy bombing campaign.

One glance at this shrapnel – or, to give its correct name, bomb splinters – from a Luftwaffe 500kg HE bomb instantly shows why it would prove lethal to any living being caught in its path. The jagged metal (pictured right), still with its dark green paint, is from the bomb's tail section. The fused detonation would cause the bomb's HE contents to explode, and its explosive weight would determine how great was the explosion. The bomb casing would also shatter into hundreds, if not thousands, of pieces of red-hot metal splinters (pictured left). These splinters were blasted at the same speed as the gas from the explosion expanded. This detonation velocity is alarming – up to 10,300m per second, meaning those in the way would have little chance of taking avoiding action …

32: Anti-Aircraft Shell Nosecap And Shrapnel, September 1940

Pre-war films and books, such as H. G. Wells' 1933 *The Shape of Things to Come*, predicted that in any future war, the skies would amass with bombers and cities would be reduced to rubble. Just the previous year, Conservative politician Stanley Baldwin (1867–1947) had warned the nation: 'I think it is well also for the man in the street to realise that there is no power on earth that can protect him from being bombed. Whatever people may tell him, the bomber will always get through.' And invariably they did.

Thankfully, however, the sky did not turn black with Nazi bombers, but those that came were still an unstoppable force. Britain's meagre anti-aircraft (AA) defences were shockingly powerless during the Blitz: in September 1940, on average, it took 20,000 AA shells to shoot down one bomber. Scientist Professor A. V. Hill (1886–1977) explained that the odds of downing an attacking bomber were stacked against the defenders: 'One cubic mile of space contains 5,500,000,000 cubic yards. The lethal zone of a 3.7in AA shell is only a few thousand cubic yards and exists for only one-fiftieth of a second.'

To be fair, whilst it was the ideal, downing the enemy was not the sole purpose of Britain's AA defences. Distracting bombers on their bombing run towards the target would disrupt their aim (though, uncomfortably, this could also explain why some German bombs missed their industrial targets and hit neighbouring homes).

Although the largest element, guns were one part of Britain's AA defence network, working in conjunction with RAF fighters, barrage balloons, decoy ground sites and radio jamming countermeasures.

Britain had a variety of weaponry with which to engage the enemy. Light AA defences started with the .303in Lewis and Bren machine guns, 20mm Oerlikon/Polsten cannon and the 40mm Bofors AA gun. While of limited range (6,000ft), they had a rapid rate of fire. Heavy AA defences included the First World War Vickers 3in gun, the new and predominant Vickers 3.7in gun, plus, in limited numbers, Vickers 4.5in and 5.25in guns. While these heavier guns had a lower rate of fire, they had a longer range

(30,000ft), meaning they could engage higher-flying bombers and drive them further away from targets.

The AA guns did not simply point at the sky and blaze away. Heavy AA guns were grouped on a site, in a battery of four, plus a command post, with adjoining height-finding and flightpath-predicting equipment. Targets were often acquired with rudimentary site radar, spotter crews, plus information from RAF Fighter Command, gathered from coastal radar and the Observer Corps. Neighbouring searchlight sites also illuminated enemy aircraft at night.

The problem was, there were simply not enough AA guns: in July 1940, there were only 1,200 heavy and 549 light AA guns available for deployment in the whole of Britain (later, Germany had 9,000 heavy and 30,000 light AA guns). Coupled with basic technology, Anti-Aircraft Command's Blitz performance was not good. On 14 November 1940, the night of the Coventry Blitz, the Midland city's thirty-six AA guns fired over 6,700 shells, downing just one enemy aircraft out of 515. With such free range, no wonder Luftwaffe aircrews were rarely bothered by the puffs of smoke they saw.

In a dark irony, not only did faulty unexploded AA shells crash down and kill British civilians, but during the Blitz, Britain's AA guns seem to have had more of a passive than active defence role – in morale: Britons, unaware of the guns' inefficiency, heard the noisy barrage and assumed 'we were giving it back to them'.

Commander-in-Chief of Anti-Aircraft Command, General Sir Frederick Pile (1884–1976), gradually overhauled the nation's AA defences. By the end of the Blitz, while still a third short, there were double the number of heavy AA guns the previous summer. From 1942, women Auxiliary Territorial Service (ATS) and Home Guards also served at gun sites. Better

technology, in the form of advanced gun-laying radar, automatic gun-loading and tracking, and even, proximity shells, which automatically detonated when they were near their target, were introduced. By August 1944, Britain's AA defences were downing 74 per cent of V1 flying bombs, saving thousands of lives.

This battered aluminium object was the desired favourite of every schoolboy shrapnel collector – the nosecone from a 3.7in AA shell fuse! Technically, a 1939-dated No. 207 mechanical fuse, the blue letter 'T' (for 'time') is still just visible, indicating it was designed to explode up to forty-five seconds after firing. The fuse caused the rest of the shell to explode, shattering it into these lethal shards to puncture Luftwaffe aircraft from Britain's skies. Widely used during the Blitz, we shall never know if this particular example helped down an enemy bomber – statistics suggest it probably didn't!

Members of the public watch as a QF 3.7-inch anti-aircraft gun crew goes through its paces in London's Hyde Park on the eve of war in the summer of 1939. (*NARA*)

33: Civilian War Death Certificate, October 1940

Despite the best efforts of the ARP and fire services, together with the anti-aircraft defences and RAF night fighters, enemy bombers did 'get through' – and claimed a dreadful toll of civilian lives: some 40,000 Britons were killed during the Blitz.

Packed close together in cellars, air raid shelters or even underground stations, when struck by a high-explosive bomb, the enclosed area confined the bomb blast and caused many fatalities, such as on 14 October 1940, when, at 8.02 pm, a 1,400kg 'Esau' semi-armour-piercing HE bomb penetrated 32ft underground and exploded in Balham underground station. The blast burst a water main and sewer, causing a mudslide that killed sixty-eight shelterers.

It was the job of the ARP to enter such conditions, then attempt to rescue any survivors and recover bodies – or what was left of them. Unproven ghoulish rumours that bodies were just left at bad incidents and the site filled in continue to this day. In reality, the ARP services were more professional than that: where possible, relatives wanted remains to bury. Some fatalities simply appeared to be asleep, without a scratch, the blast having collapsed their lungs. Others were only fragmented remains, which were collected in a 'bits bag'. Either way, they were sent to the ARP mortuary.

Pre-war statisticians had theorised that for every ton of bombs dropped, seventeen people would be killed. They also predicted the Luftwaffe would drop up to 600 tons of bombs per day, indicating mass fatalities would ensue and additional mortuary facilities would be needed. In response, the Emergency Mortuary Service was created, with the personnel recruited from medical staff and local undertakers.

A temporary information label was affixed to the body by the ARP Rescue or First Aid Party at the incident. A mortuary van would then take the body to the mortuary, where on receipt the body would be given a reference number. ARP mortuary procedure followed official Ministry of Health guidelines. The body would then be stripped and the clothing and personal belongings itemised. A Civilian War Death form would then be filled in and signed off by the mortuary superintendent in charge. The body would then be prepared (tidied), put in a white shroud and placed on a metal ARP stretcher to await official identification, if possible, by a relative, friend or acquaintance. From July 1940, it was stipulated that, where practical, photographs should be taken of unidentified bodies to help in the identification process.

Unusually, ARP mortuaries were often in drained local public swimming baths, which could hold large numbers of bodies, if need be, with the sub-level cold tiling temporarily helping preservation. There were also 'overflow' and reserve mortuaries. Extra preparation for mass casualties saw the purchase of fibre coffins, at 11/5d [£30] each and children's shrouds, in three sizes. After heavy air raids, there were, indeed, mass burials at several cities, including Coventry, Plymouth, Belfast, Liverpool and Bristol, among others.

ARP mortuary staff are the most forgotten and unrecognised of the ARP services, yet they had the most harrowing and disturbing role of all. They may have been experienced in dealing with the dead, but not in these numbers. They had to register, photograph and record scores of bodies brought to them, in all states. Their most harrowing task must surely have been dealing with child fatalities. They did this professionally and one wonders, with the sights they saw, what sleep they had and what long-term memories they harboured. The Commonwealth War Graves Commission lists a total of 67,092 civilian war deaths through enemy action.

This Civilian War Death form brings home the reality of the Home Front behind the sing-songs and Blitz spirit stereotypes. It is the ARP mortuary form of Gladys Worboys, aged eleven. Her father, Sidney, aged forty-nine; her mother, Alice; her sisters Lilian, aged seventeen, and Eileen, fourteen, were all also killed at Dame Alice Owens Girls' School, in Goswell Road, Finsbury, London, on 15 October 1940. They were five of the 143 people sheltering there when a large parachute mine demolished the building above them, sealing the exits. The pipeline carrying the New River ruptured, flooding the shelter. A 2005 memorial to the 109 victims of this bombing stands in Owen's Fields, on Goswell Road. This object is published in their memory.

A woman is assisted across a London street, after she was rescued from the debris of a building damaged by a German bomb during a daylight raid on 23 October 1940. (*Historic Military Press*)

34: Chief Air Raid Warden's Helmet, Autumn 1940

New headwear was seen across wartime Britain and it proved popular – but this was no fashionable hat: it was a protective steel helmet, designed to save the lives of those working during an air raid.

This helmet, with a wide brim to protect from falling objects, was called a Mark II and was based on a very similar-looking design invented in 1915 during the First World War, called the Mark I helmet, or, unofficially, a Brodie, after

its creator, John Leopold Brodie (1873–1945). However, the basic design can be traced back as far as the medieval fourteenth-century kettle helmet, perhaps even earlier.

From summer 1940, an economy version of the helmet, called a Mark II, Number 2, was introduced, comprising of substandard or milder steel, identified by up to four holes punched in either side of the rim, indicating its composition.

Although retaining the same basic shape and design as its predecessor, the Mark II helmet had an improved liner and sprung webbing chinstrap. It could protect the wearer from some shrapnel, debris and blast, but was not bulletproof. Indeed, the famous German equivalent, the *Stahlhelm*, with a flatter rim, offered better direct neck protection.

Nevertheless, produced in their millions, the Mark II was issued not only to Britain's military, but also its ARP, police and fire services. The initial issue to the ARP was in plain military khaki paint, however, by the start of the war, many were painted black.

Not long after, various initials, representing the wearer's branch of the ARP, were added to the front, such as 'W' for Warden, 'R' for Rescue, 'A' for Ambulance, 'M' for Messenger and 'FAP' for First Aid Post/Party, although a plethora of variations exist.

From June 1940, the London Region introduced blackout-visible white helmets plus black bands to denote higher ranks. Outside London, ranks were indicated by up to three black painted diamonds, replaced in 1942 by the London scheme. The example pictured belonged to John Merrifield, who was the thirty-year-old Chief Warden of the Earlsdon Division,

Coventry. The double black bands indicate his senior supervisory rank.

Indeed, air raid wardens were the linchpin of the whole ARP service. Formed in March 1937, the warden's main role was to patrol his or her allotted sector and, if a bomb fell, briefly assess the incident, fill in a damage form, and run back to their wardens' post to report the incident to the control service. However, through necessity, the job developed into multifarious important tasks: wardens took part in rescue, first aid, unexploded bomb reconnaissance and organising the other ARP services at an incident.

At local level, wardens also became the public face of the ARP organisation, advising residents on civil defence matters and training them in firefighting, and as well as conducting gas mask and shelter censuses, even, at times, having to break bad news to relatives. However, their public duties were not always appreciated: their maintenance of the blackout, with the cry of 'put that light out', sometimes made them unpopular, accused of being 'little Hitlers', with numerous reported cases of wardens being assaulted by disgruntled citizens.

Wardens were often more mature in years and mostly male, although around a seventh were female, often much younger in age.

Although, as with most of the front-line ARP personnel, they were an amateur army, and despite their now relatively light-hearted popular image, they were mostly dedicated and professional, having to know their local sectors and its residents inside out. They had extensive training, sitting courses and examinations in ARP matters and attaining qualifications. They were local guardians who earned their place in wartime history.

35: ARP Bluette Uniform, Autumn 1940

As well as the Wardens service, there were various different branches of the ARP organisation. At the top of the local chain was the Report and Control service. Usually based in a bunker or hardened basement, sometimes under the town hall or council offices, the ARP Controller observed as the air raid unfolded and with the help of a large plotting map of his area, directed the necessary ARP services to the various incidents. He was updated on how the bombing was developing by the Report service, based in district report centres, who received telephone situation messages from the Wardens organisation.

Based in district ARP depots, the first raid service called upon were the Rescue service. Drawn from the building trade for their knowledge of house construction, some of the most physical, yet also careful, ARP work was carried out by the men of this service. Their job was to rescue people trapped in their bombed homes. To do this, they could call upon cranes to shift rubble, but the vast majority of their skilful work was painstaking as they had to delicately remove rubble without it collapsing on the casualty. Rescue personnel carried out the most dangerous ARP work, tunnelling under debris to reach casualties trapped in flooded, gas-filled cellars or working beneath teetering walls, often as the bombs fell.

Also at the incident were elements of the ARP casualty services. Arriving in cars laden with metal stretchers were the First Aid Parties, or in the London Region, Stretcher Parties. They provided immediate

preliminary aid, before ferrying casualties to either a waiting ambulance or the local ARP first aid post, where nurses, under the direction of a Medical Officer, would treat the patient. If injuries were severe, casualties were forwarded to the local hospital for surgery. This system of treatment was based on and developed from First World War casualty clearing stations, associated with the trench warfare of the Western Front.

One major pre-war branch of the ARP services was, fortunately, never needed. The Decontamination service comprised of council refuse personnel who, if poison gas was used, would don gas-proof suits and respirators, then decontaminate streets and homes with bleach powder and water. It would have been a huge manual undertaking, made further complicated by their restrictive anti-gas outfits. To help understand what poison gas they were dealing with, local chemists were appointed as Gas Identification Officers. Again in gas-proof clothing, they would use specialist testing equipment to identify the chemical or biological agent. From 1941, specialist Food Treatment Squads were introduced to decontaminate tinned foods and other salvageable food stuffs.

Despite all the ARP preparations that went into the pre- and actual raid contingencies, surprisingly, little thought had been put into post-raid organisation. Initially, some councils had suggested those bombed out of their homes simply gathered in local parks. The experience of the Blitz suggested far greater support services were needed and so rest centres, emergency feeding stations, salvage squads, advice offices, clothing and furniture aid, plus rehousing were all expanded from 1941.

The final element of the ARP organisation was the police force. There at the birth and training of the ARP organisation, the police were also responsible for a certain amount of its administrative and reporting work.

Despite fifteen years of pre-war planning, the subject of what the ARP services were going to wear seems to have been largely overlooked until the last minute. Initially, ARP personnel were issued with simple armlets to be worn with civilian clothing, identifying their branch of service. However, by the time of the 1940–41 Blitz, the main uniform of the ARP services was this denim bluette combination boiler suit, (officially designated ARP 41), seen here with the area title of 'Lambeth'. There were also overcoat variants for women wardens (ARP 42) and women drivers (ARP 43). The ARP 41 overall is commonly seen in newsreels and photos of the time, often covered in rubble dust – or, perhaps, worse.

36: Unofficial ARP Advice Booklet, Autumn 1940

There was no shortage of ARP advice for citizens, both officially and unofficially. Leaflets, articles, books and pamphlets, both before the war and during, provided potentially life-saving information. Eighty years on, this literature makes fascinating reading: it is also clear how pre-war theory changed to actuality gain from Blitz experience.

The Home Office had published official ARP literature since 1935, with *ARP Handbook No. 2: Anti-Gas Precautions & First Aid for Air Raid Casualties* (about turn, *Handbook No. 1: Personal Protection against Gas* was published the following year). Over the next decade, they also published a raft of official ARP circulars, manuals, memoranda, pamphlets and bulletins.

However, these works were really meant for the ARP services, not the wider public. To the layman, they must have appeared quite dry, word heavy, with few pictures and no colour. Commercial publishers saw a gap in the market and began producing their own more reader-friendly publications. The Home Office does not seem to have opposed or viewed these as rival publications – indeed, some state permission had been granted to quote from official works – so perhaps officialdom just viewed *un*officialdom as helping spread the ARP word.

Some unofficial ARP booklets even date back a decade *before* officialdom started publishing works on the subject. However, both showed an early main focus on countering gas warfare.

Ironically, one of the chief writers on ARP matters, scientist (later Professor) John Burdon Sanderson (J. B. S.) Haldane (1892–1964) wrote the *pro*-gas warfare monologue *Callinicus: A Defence of Chemical Warfare* (Kegan, Paul, Trench, Trubner & Co. Ltd, 1925). Thirteen years later, he wrote one of the leading precautionary books *against* air raids, *A.R.P.* (Victor Gollancz, 1938).

Those such as straight-talking Major-General C. H. Foulkes wrote from previous military experience, with *Commonsense and A.R.P.* (C.

Arthur Pearson Ltd, 1939). Others, such as architectural firm Tecton, used their trade expertise to suggest designs for large air raid shelters in *Planned ARP* (Architectural Press, 1939). Even political groups got in on the act, making their tracts appear like ARP advice, such as the Communist Party of Great Britain's *A.R.P. The Practical Air Raid Protection Britain Needs!* (1938).

Some publishers, such as Jordan & Sons, specialised in ARP, producing at least fifteen booklets on the subject. But it wasn't just publishing houses spreading the word: Dr S. Evelyn Thomas, of St Albans, Hertfordshire, produced five top-selling ARP books, some self-published.

Commercial enterprises also recognised the market, such as Odham's Press, advertising in Sunday newspapers, for their book *The Complete First-Aid Outfit Book and A.R.P.* (1939), which even included a fourteen-piece mini first aid kit inside the front cover (though the small pieces look more of novelty value).

By this time, theory began to give way to observations of reality, via the Japanese bombing of China or the Spanish Civil War, with journalist John Langdon-Davies (1897–1971), later author of unofficial Home Guard training booklets,

publishing *Air Raid* (George Routledge & Sons, 1938).

During the war, fewer unofficial ARP booklets were published, probably due to paper rationing and the amount of official publications being produced. However, they focused more on specific subjects, such as first aid, or specialisms for Civil Defence personnel, such as *Tactical Exercises in Incident Control* (Gordon & Gotch, 1942) or *Practical Rescue Training* (Pitman & Sons, 1943) by Eric C. Claxton, a Surrey ARP worker who, in 1942, founded the Casualties Union.

In total, around 150 known unofficial ARP booklets were published. From the amount that have survived today, it appears their owners took these little booklets seriously – the knowledge imparted by their words and pictures may even have saved lives.

One of John Langdon-Davies' most popular works was *Air Raid Precautions – What to do in an Emergency – A Comprehensive Guide* (George Newnes, 1939). Published in photo-heavy magazine format with a colourful cover, he explained ARP via 'an ordinary family' in the fictional story 'The Jones Family Sees it Through'. Within a year of publication, this shattered suburban cover scene would prove only too real.

37: NARPAC Pet Collar Tag, Autumn 1940

They are our faithful friends who, through thick and thin, stick with us and offer joy and companionship. So, when war came, it was natural to think of their welfare, just as with any other member of the family. It may have been a conflict between the human species, but wartime hardships such as rationing, finding shelter and evacuation were all shared by our domestic animals: pets struggled along with their owners, too.

The pre-war fear of air raids led to evacuation plans for women and children, but British compassion (or enterprise) did not end there. In 1939, it was estimated that there were seven million cats and dogs in Britain. Businesses offered country refuges for dogs at 10s [£30] per week – or a penny [50p] a day for budgerigars! London Zoo evacuated two giant pandas, two orang-utans, four chimpanzees, three Asian elephants and an ostrich to Whipsnade Zoo in Bedfordshire. As a precaution, the zoo's venomous animals were killed, in case a bomb hit their enclosures and they escaped.

Such was the fear of air raids and because many people could not afford to board their pets, sadly, in the first four days of the war, some 400,000 cats were euthanized. In a bitter irony, as the Phoney War developed, this proved an unnecessarily drastic measure.

The Home Office had not overlooked Britain's domestic and farm animals. In August 1939, they published *ARP Handbook No. 12: Air Raid Precautions for Animals*, with the introduction: 'Animals, like human beings, will be exposed to the risks of air attack in a modern war and everyone will wish, both from practical and humane motives, to do what is possible to protect them and alleviate their sufferings.' In truth, essentially,

the booklet said, apart from evacuation, there was very little that could be done and animals had to take their chances like the rest of the population. More disturbingly, the final chapter explained, with illustrations, how the captive bolt pistol could be used for the 'destruction of incurably injured animals', including horses, cattle, sheep, goats, pigs, cats and dogs.

Soon, however, cats and dogs learned the meaning of the air raid siren and trundled off to the Anderson shelter with their owners. Bizarrely, some pets even seemed to be able to 'predict' air raids, becoming restless or barking: it is likely that, with their better hearing, they could detect the bombers' drone before humans, or because the raids occurred regularly, so as soon as dusk came, they expected trouble. One London family trembled in terror in their Anderson shelter as they heard the faint distant noise of a V1 Doodlebug [see Object 87] – only to discover that it was their cat purring loudly! Indeed, domestic shelters were the only refuge available for pets, as they were banned from public shelters.

Certain types of animals proved especially vulnerable. Goldfish were in constant danger because their glass bowls were susceptible to blast. Horses also proved a problem, as they were highly strung and easily frightened, proving difficult and dangerous to rescue from burning stables. Not all bombs dropped on the cities: many Luftwaffe bombers dumped their bombs in the countryside, with sheep and cows exposed in open fields often as unfortunate casualties.

Like their owners, pets also suffered from food shortages. Hay for horses was unrationed, but the meat shortage made it difficult to feed carnivores such as cats and dogs. Due to the metal shortage, canned pet food was a rarity and dog biscuits were almost unobtainable, so owners fed their pets scraps of meat and leftovers, even though, technically, it was an illegal waste of human food. However, the Ministry of Food released a small amount of dried milk for cats because of the valuable part they played in keeping down rats and mice in homes, warehouses and farms.

Although pets continued to rely on their owners and must have been an added worry in wartime, they played an important part in the battle of morale. The family who lost their home and all their possessions to bombing could be cheered if their much-loved pet was pulled alive from the rubble.

As with humans, there was even a civil defence organisation for our four-legged friends. Pre-war, on the suggestion of the Home Office's ARP department, vets, working with the RSPCA and PDSA, established the National ARP Animals Committee (NARPAC) in August 1939. Its initial *Advice to Animal Owners* leaflet suggested evacuating pets to the countryside, but 'if you cannot place them in the care of neighbours, it really is kindest to have them destroyed' – so, ironically, their first act of the war helped lead to the euthanasia of up to 750,000 pets. However, NARPAC also compiled a National Register of pets and farm animals that were enrolled for an annual fee of 1s [£2.50]. Registered animals were given a numbered metal or plastic disc that helped reunite them with their owners if lost after an air raid. A series of local volunteer Animal Guards and Stewards were responsible for registration and the welfare of pets. As this NARPAC leaflet noted: 'Unidentifiable dogs found straying may be destroyed after 72 hours, under a general Order from the Ministry of Home Security. Cats unregistered can be destroyed immediately but registered animals are taken over by NARPAC Officials, housed and fed until arrangements are made for their return home' – at the very least, some peace of mind in troubled times.

38: Unexploded Bomb Warning Sign, Autumn 1940

Bomb disposal: it was probably the most dangerous job on the Home Front. Instead of the bomb coming to you, you went to the bomb. Nerves of steel and a steady hand were needed for this knife-edge job, where life was measured in milliseconds. Personnel had been 'reassured' by scientists, who calculated that the human body's nervous system was slower than a bomb explosion, so you wouldn't feel or know anything about it if it did explode. Indeed, there would be very little, if anything, of the bomb's challenger to bury.

Despite Germany's use of delayed action fuses during the Spanish Civil War, surprisingly, next to no preparations were made in Britain for dealing with unexploded bombs (UXBs). Initially, it was thought local civilian services could just pick up UXBs from the surface and stack them up for collection by the military.

Fortunately, albeit at the last moment, army Royal Engineer (RE) bomb disposal (BD) parties were formed in May 1940. Each RE BD Section was composed of an officer, who defused the bomb, a sergeant who assisted him, a lance sergeant, four corporals and between fourteen and twenty-five other ranks, who dug down to the bomb and later removed it after defusal. Giant German parachute mines were defused by Royal Naval Rendering Mines Safe squads. So started a lethal, unseen war, between German scientists, who developed increasingly deadlier bombs and fuses, and British scientists, who had to find ways to develop countermeasures, and the BD personnel who had to defuse the bombs.

Some 10 per cent of all Luftwaffe bombs [see Object 31] dropped on Britain failed to detonate. Sometimes, this was deliberate, to cause widespread disruption in cities, which would have to be evacuated and war production halted. Other times, it was because the sensitive fuzes had been damaged by the bomb's high-speed impact. Either way, this unexploded ordnance had to be located, defused and removed.

While most nations still used clockwork fuses, from 1926 Germany was the world leader in advanced electrical fuzes: yet, when the Blitz started, Britain's BD squads had only the most basic training and equipment – a spanner, hammer and stethoscope. But, as the war developed, the BD Sections became better equipped: from the simple Crabtree Discharger, to drain the charge of the German No. 15 impact fuze, through to BD discharger fluid, which destroyed the fuze condensers of Nos. 25, 38 and 50 fuses, through to the electro-magnet Clock-Stopper and, later, the Stevens Stopper sugar solution, for use on the No. 17 time-delay fuse.

Nonetheless, even with this specialist equipment, some fuses were highly dangerous, designed especially to kill BD personnel: the No. 50 was a highly sensitive anti-handling fuze, which could detonate the bomb with even just the force of a pencil tapped against it. The Germans also sometimes added a hidden Zus

40 anti-withdrawal booby trap beneath fuzes, again to kill BD officers. Later, in 1943, they even introduced an extra sensitive mercury-tilt device, called the Y fuze. That same year, the Luftwaffe dropped thousands of small, deadly SD2 anti-personnel 'butterfly bombs' along the East Coast: BD squads had to search and clear miles of town and countryside. Later, they also had to deal with unexploded V-weapons.

BD personnel underwent some of the most stressful experiences on the Home Front. By the war's end, they had defused around 40,000 unexploded bombs in Britain: around 750 BD lost their lives in the process. Even now, seventy-five years after the war's end, unexploded ordnance from the conflict is still being discovered and cleared by today's bomb disposers – the lethal legacy of the Blitz on Britain.

This large red enamel sign was placed by an RE BD squad in the vicinity of the UXB to keep the public away from the danger zone if the bomb exploded. Placing and removing this sign would be the first and last task the BD squad did at the scene of the UXB – if they survived the defusing process.

Working against time, Royal Engineers dig out an unexploded German 1,000kg bomb, half of which is still embedded at a depth of more than twenty feet, in the grounds of the German Hospital, Dalston, September 1940. All patients had been evacuated and there were no casualties. (*Historic Military Press*)

39: Luftwaffe Incendiary Bomb, Autumn 1940

At just 13in long, compared to far bigger German high-explosive bombs, surely this incendiary bomb (IB) has got to be one of the feeblest-looking weapons in the Luftwaffe's arsenal? Wrong. It was actually one of the most devastating: a post-Blitz survey by the British Air Ministry revealed that for each ton of HE bombs dropped, roughly 1¾ acres was destroyed, whereas for each ton of incendiary bombs dropped, at least 3¼ acres was destroyed.

Its potency was also underestimated by the authorities. The main pre-war ARP concern was against poison gas, followed closely by the threat of HE bombing, meaning there was less focus on attack by fire bombs (indeed, the Auxiliary Fire Service was only formed the year before the outbreak of war).

The basic and most common type of German incendiary bomb was the 1kg B1E Elektron weapon. The Germans had invented it the end of the First World War, but never had the chance to use it – they more than made up for it in the next conflict.

With an inflammable magnesium body and thermite powder filling, the bomb detonated on impact, throwing out molten metal, igniting its surroundings. It burned at 4,500° Fahrenheit, sufficient to melt steel. If unchecked, despite their small size, incendiaries could destroy vast amounts of property.

In the 1940–41 Blitz, IBs were mainly released in clusters of thirty-six from 'Molotov Bread Basket' containers, the idea being to swamp a target, making it harder for firefighters to tackle all the bombs dropped. As the war developed, container sizes grew, meaning by 1944, the Luftwaffe's AB 1000-2 container could distribute 620 IBs.

Special pathfinder bomber units, such as KGr 100, a *Beleuchtergruppe* (Firelighter Group), would be the first over a city, dropping IBs and parachute flares to mark the target area for the later HE bomber waves. It was highly effective and would take another two years before RAF Bomber Command developed and used these tactics themselves.

This concentrated fire-bombing is largely the reason why Britain's city centres have lost many of their most historic buildings: once ignited, their wooden construction was near impossible to save. However, if tackled early enough, individual IBs could be extinguished by householders. As a deterrent, in late 1940, the Germans fitted a small explosive charge in the rear of 10 per cent of IBs. From summer 1942, a larger type, the 20in 2.2kg B2-2E-Z IBEN (IB Explosive Nose), proved lethal against firefighters. Similarly, in 1944, the Luftwaffe deployed the 2kg B2 EZ IBSEN (IB Separating Explosive Nose), the explosive section was blown off and detonated after seven minutes, again, to catch firefighting parties.

In total, there were about seven different variants of IB used against Britain, even captured French stocks. The Luftwaffe also employed other fire weapons, including the larger Flam C250/500 oil bomb, which, fortunately, often failed to ignite. During the 1942 Baedeker Raids, the Luftwaffe introduced the Brand C50/250 phosphorous firebombs and Spreng-Brand C50 Firepot explosive IB. They were more potent than the oil bombs of the Blitz, but thankfully, both were comparatively rarely used.

This inert example of the Luftwaffe B1E incendiary bomb has markings on it indicating it was made in 1941. A good proportion of IBs failed to ignite, as they had a very rudimentary impact pin fuse. Sometimes, the canister they were dropped in also failed to open mid-air and just spilt their IB loads on landing, which were simply collected the morning after the raid by the ARP – or souvenir-hungry schoolboys!

Firemen playing their hoses on dying embers in buildings along Queen Victoria Street after the last and heaviest major raid mounted by the Luftwaffe against the British capital during the Blitz. For six hours on the night of 10-11 May 1941, German aircraft dropped over 1,000 tons of bombs on London, claiming 1,486 lives, destroying 11,000 houses and damaging many important historical buildings. (*Historic Military Press*)

40: AFS Fire Hose, Autumn 1940

Britain's fire brigades were not prepared for the onslaught of nightly air raids. Not only did many towns have just one fire station, but their crew and equipment provision was based on tackling occasional, individual domestic and industrial incidents, not widespread firebombing.

But government was slow to act. As early as 1932, they had known the 1,668 local brigades were insufficient for the task, yet it was not until July 1938 that the Fire Brigades Act reorganised Britain's fire cover, bolstering existing local brigades with the addition of a new Auxiliary Fire Service (AFS) of part-time amateur firemen.

The core of regular firemen at a main fire station were supported by AFS crews at six new sub-stations, often located in evacuated schools or garages. Initially, many of the AFS firemen only had civilian cars, or, as in London, requisitioned taxis, to tow wheeled fire pumps. However, supplies of Fordson, Bedford and Austin fire engines (appliances), with onboard fire pumps, plus Merryweather turntable ladder appliances, became available in time to face the Blitz.

Initial recruitment was slow. The required national establishment was 245,981 firefighters, but just five months before war the figure stood at just 159,360. By December 1939, however, it was only 20,000 short. AFS firefighters came from all backgrounds. Artists and writers seem to have been attracted to the service, too. During the Phoney War, because there was no bombing, AFS firefighters were ridiculed as the 'darts club' or even draft dodgers. All this was to change within six months, when they went from 'zeroes to heroes'.

Though they may have started as amateur firefighters, the AFS had a sharp learning curve. During summer 1940, the Luftwaffe targeted oil farms, such as at Thameshaven or in Pembrokeshire. Then, when the London Blitz started on 7 September 1940, large areas of warehousing, neighbouring domestic property, even dockside shipping, became blazing infernos.

Tackling fires caused by the nightly raids required great physical and mental strength. Matters were not helped when hoses ran dry after water pipes were ruptured by bombing. Sometimes, if a fire took hold, firemen faced an impossible task to extinguish a blazing building. Instead, they hosed property opposite to stop the fire spreading, which was possible in many narrow old city streets. Indeed, where blazes did coalesce and were fanned by the wind, an uncontrollable firestorm could engulf a whole street, igniting property, fire appliances – and firemen.

Once the all-clear sounded, the firemen's job was not necessarily done. Damping down the fireground, to prevent reignitions that could guide bombers the following night, took hours and even days. Then, the heavy, soaked, long lengths of hose would have to be rolled up by the tired, wet and ash-covered firefighters, then cleaned once back at the fire station. They would grab a few hours' sleep – and then it would all start again.

London Fire Brigade's finest hour came on the night of 29 December 1940, when the Luftwaffe launched a huge 600-bomber attack on the City, targeting Britain's business and finance centre, starting what has become known as the Second Great Fire of London. Using incendiaries, the bombers ignited 1,500 fires, destroying vast areas of the City, including eight Sir Christopher Wren churches – but the firemen stopped the fires reaching Wren's greatest creation, St Paul's Cathedral.

During the war, 793 firemen and twenty-five firewomen lost their lives, with another 7,000 seriously injured. Appropriately, the Firefighters Memorial, unveiled by the late Queen Mother in 1991, stands opposite St Pauls, in Carter Lane Gardens.

Nonetheless, Britain's Blitz firefighters are still largely forgotten heroes. They drove out during the height of the raids to the epicentre of the attack. Exposed in the street or up high ladders, the only weapon they had in the face of the enemy were fire hoses, such as this genuine Blitz example. Made of heavy canvas, stencilled with the most recent maintenance date of September 1944, it also has a branch (nozzle) dated May 1939. Branches were made of brass, to stop sparks igniting domestic gas leaks. The lugs either side operate the quick release/instantaneous Morris coupling attachment to the hose. Such was the pressure behind the jet of water created by the pump, two firefighters usually had to direct the branch at the fire. How much property and lives they saved is incalculable.

Firemen spray water on damaged buildings, near London Bridge in the City of London, on 9 September 1940. (*Historic Military Press*)

41: Stirrup Pump, Autumn 1940

The stirrup pump: it doesn't look the greatest of war-winning weapons, but don't be fooled by its humble appearance – this simple hand pump helped save many British homes and one of the nation's finest buildings.

A pump in this form can be traced back to the middle of the nineteenth century, maybe even earlier, when Mr J. Jones, an iron merchant and horticultural engineer, of Southwark, London, advertised the patented Hydropult, 'an invention for throwing water by hand power', in *The Gardeners' Chronicle and Agricultural Gazette* of 1863, 'for washing, watering plants and extinguishing fires'. However, it would be in the next century that such a pump would see its greatest service.

Although potentially devastating, if tackled early enough, incendiary bombs did not need the fire brigade to extinguish them – civilians, with a little basic training, could do the job. As a result, from the war's start, 86,000 stirrup pumps were distributed to local authorities and civilians were trained in their use via firefighting lectures.

Although the pump could be operated by one person, ARP instructions recommended a firefighting team of three: one person pumping the water, a second lying prone on the ground directing the hose at the fire and a third supplying the pump bucket with water.

Unchecked, incendiary bombs could burn for ten to fifteen minutes: however, a spray of water from the stirrup pump encouraged the bomb's magnesium body to smoulder away. A firefighting team could pump 1.5 gallons of water per minute: it took up to 6 gallons to extinguish a single incendiary. Using the pump nozzle's 'jet' setting directly on the bomb was not recommended, as it simply made the molten metal erupt, encouraging the fire to spread. Instead, the jet was used to extinguish ignited surrounding furniture.

There were other 'weapons' in the fire watcher's armoury too, including sandbags, used to muffle the bomb; incendiary pincers, a set of grabs on a long pole to physically move the incendiary away from harm; Redhill equipment, which involved using a hoe to guide a burning incendiary into a scoop and then deposit it in a sand container for removal outside; chemical fire extinguishers, such as the Firex glass grenade, (although when its contents mixed with burning magnesium, it could give off noxious fumes), plus a series of

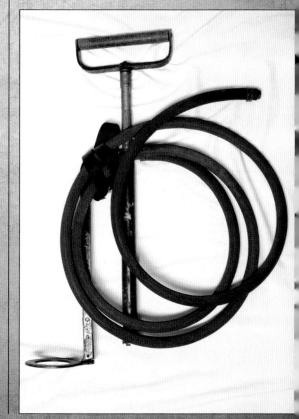

protective eye goggles and fire shields – although a dustbin lid was often handiest!

With the Fire Watchers Order of September 1940, civilians were required to take turns guarding business premises against incendiary attack and it was one such fire watchers' party that saved London's greatest building – with the help of the stirrup pump.

On 29 December 1940, during the Second Great Fire of London, the Luftwaffe dropped 100,000 incendiary bombs on the City – twenty-eight of these struck the domed roof of St Paul's Cathedral. Together with the London Fire Brigade outside, the 200 members of the St Paul's Watch fire parties used stirrup pumps high up inside the dome and on the roof, where fire hoses could not reach, to tackle the sparking incendiaries – and saved one of the nation's most important buildings. Though almost every building around St Paul's burned to the ground, the cathedral survived and became a national symbol of defiance against Hitler and the Luftwaffe during the Blitz.

By the war's end, some 3.8 million stirrup pumps had been produced. Amazingly, many are still in service with the fire brigade today and carried on fire appliances, as they are particularly effective against chimney fires!

A stirrup pump team in action. In this case, these individuals are part of a US Marines fire-fighting squad drilling on the roof of their London Headquarters in 1942. (*Historic Military Press*)

42: Coventry Cathedral Window Glass, November 1940

The historic Midland city of Coventry, in Warwickshire, was truly a great example of English medieval architecture. In the fourteenth century, it was an important centre of the cloth trade. Narrow streets of timber-framed buildings lined the city centre, interspersed with more modern fine Georgian and Victorian properties. But that did not mean the city was an anachronism, frozen in time. It had also developed an internationally renowned motor industry that brought the city employment and prosperity. Ironically, it was this asset that would also bring the city destruction.

Two months into the night Blitz, realising that the sheer size of London's 200 square mile mass was too big a target for his medium bomber force, Hitler sought more manageably sized county cities. So, on the night of 14 November 1940, the Luftwaffe redirected their ire towards the provinces. Under Operation Moonlight Sonata, Coventry would be the first English city to experience concentrated heavy area bombing.

At 7.20 pm, thirteen Luftwaffe pathfinder aircraft, using electronic beam navigation, led a force of around 440 bombers to the city centre, where they dropped 394 tons of HE bombs, plus fifty parachute mines and 36,000 IBs. They caused over 200 fires, developing into a firestorm that overwhelmed the firefighters. The raid reached its peak around midnight, crippling the telephone network, disrupting fire and ARP services.

When the all-clear sounded at 6.15 am, Coventry city centre was unrecognisable, a smoking, rubble-strewn wasteland. One thing that objects, photos, words or newsreel cannot really convey are the smells after a raid: acrid smoke, damp plaster, brick dust, gas, broken

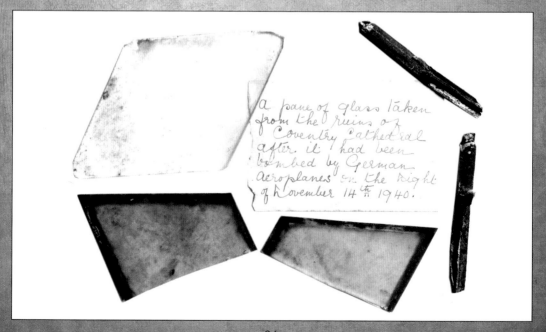

a pane of glass taken from the ruins of Coventry Cathedral after it had been bombed by German aeroplanes on the night of November 14th 1940.

sewers and burning timber – nor the devastating feeling of losing everything: your home, possessions – or loved ones.

Over twenty factories were seriously damaged and around three-quarters of the city's industrial works suffered some damage. Industrial output was disrupted for months. There was a 20 per cent dip in aircraft production. Domestically, over 4,330 homes were destroyed or damaged and around 568 people were killed in the raid, with another 863 badly injured and 393 with minor injuries.

Ghoulishly, the Germans boasted that their Luftwaffe had created a new word '*Coventrieren*', to 'Coventrate' or devastate by heavy bombing. Rather than censor or try to downplay the effectiveness of the Luftwaffe's operation, British and American newsreels openly referred to the raid as 'Coventry's sacrifice', making counter-propaganda of Nazi barbarity, and in turn fuelling civilian calls for retaliatory raids on Germany.

The stand-out symbol that came to represent the devastation of Coventry, indeed, eventually, all bombing, was the ruins of St Michael's Cathedral. At 8 pm, IBs struck the cathedral, but its brave fire watchers managed to extinguish them. However, as the raid developed, the fire parties were overcome and forced to withdraw, leaving this impressive fourteenth-century building to burn.

Such was the devastating nature of the raid, few of Coventry's historic buildings could be saved. However, under the post-war Gibson Plan, Coventry would rise again, with a modernist heart, albeit not to everyone's taste. A new, large pedestrianised shopping precinct, the first in Europe, and in 1962, a new cathedral, designed by Sir Basil Spence (1907–76), alongside its ruinous predecessor, left as a monument, became the city's centrepieces.

Coventry Cathedral was a fourteenth-century medieval masterpiece that any city would be proud to call their own. It contained extraordinary architectural detail. Fortunately, its medieval stained glass by master glass painter John Thornton was removed as an air raid precaution in 1939, however, other stained glass, of several periods up to Victorian, was left in situ – only to be blasted out on to the surrounding streets by the bombing. These poignant objects were found in a wartime Raphael Tuck & Sons [see Object 68] Christmas Auto Stationery Box, with a simple, hand-written note accompanying them: 'A pane of glass taken from the ruins of Coventry Cathedral after it had been bombed by German aeroplanes on the night of November 14th 1940.' No more words are needed.

Inside the ruined nave of Coventry Cathedral, looking west to the tower, after the Luftwaffe bombed it in Operation *Moonlight Sonata*, on the night of 14–15 November 1940. Note the bomb-blasted windows. (*Public Domain*)

43: War-Damaged Blitz Painting, 1941

It seems strange that amidst all the death and destruction of the Second World War, Britain saw a huge creative renaissance among both professional and amateur artists, who drew inspiration from the powerful sights and experiences they saw. In turn, this free expression, through art, music and writing, provided entertainment and escapism for the public, boosting morale.

In Germany, since 1933, the Nazis had been censoring and destroying anything they considered 'degenerate art', whether it was for racial reasons, such as jazz music, because of its association with black performers, or modernist art, which, in 1934, Hitler declared there was no place for in the Reich. Piles of books by Jewish authors were also publicly burned, as were paintings by Salvador Dali (1904–89) and Pablo Picasso (1881–1973), among others. In their place, the Nazis preferred stereotypical Aryan imagery,

of classically inspired strongman sculptures and stern paintings by approved artists.

That said, Britain, too, made use of artists for propaganda, though for the opposite reason: to publicise free expression and the value of democracy. From the war's start, British artists realised their work now took on a new significance and that their skills could be used to contribute towards the war effort.

In 1939, the Director of the National Gallery, Sir Kenneth Clarke (1903–83), suggested the formation of the War Artists Advisory Committee, under the auspices of the Ministry of Information. Selected artists were chosen by the committee as official war artists and they travelled the nation painting war-related scenes on the Home Front, in their own inimitable styles.

Stanley Spencer (1891–1959) painted vivid scenes of Scottish shipbuilders in the Glasgow

docks. Dame Laura Knight (1877–1970) painted lifelike works of women serving, from the barrage balloon site to the industrial lathe. Paul Nash (1889–1946), a war artist in both world wars, just like his brother, John Nash (1893–1977), produced powerful surrealist works, such as *Totes Meer (Dead Sea)*, showing wrecked Luftwaffe aircraft or a swirling, troubled sky in *The Battle of Britain*. Some artists even died for their art: Eric Ravilious (1903–42), a modernist artist who painted dream-like naval scenes, was lost when the search aircraft he was in failed to return. This is just a few of the well-known names who served as war artists, though not all were famous. By the war's end, over 400 war artists had created 5,570 works of art.

Many of these works were exhibited at London's more famous galleries. However, the Council for the Encouragement of Music and Arts (CEMA) also toured Britain with travelling art exhibitions. This, in turn, encouraged the public to turn to the arts. As a medium, painting particularly seems to have attracted firemen and civil defence workers, probably partly as a means of commentary and self-therapy.

Incidentally, Britain's existing art treasures were moved out of the way of Hitler's bombers.

The day before war was declared, six special freight trains, escorted by armed guards, moved artworks from London's National Gallery to limestone quarries at Bradford-on-Avon, Wiltshire. From 1941, Van Dyck paintings and Matisse drawings were stored in bomb-proof, air-conditioned tunnels in a disused slate mine at Manod Quarry, North Wales. Although this left the galleries largely empty, it proved fortuitous: both the British Library and the National Gallery were damaged by bombs.

This dark, dramatic art work, entitled *The Destruction of the City – 29/12/40* was painted in 1941 by north London artist William J. Tucker. The 20in by 13in oil painting shows St Paul's Cathedral, centre left, bordered by a London skyline aflame, with searchlights, anti-aircraft bursts and fire reflected on a night sky. In the foreground, three firemen stand by a fire pump, almost enveloped in flames. One can't help but feel Tucker probably painted this image from his own first-hand experiences in the Blitz. Interestingly, there are four taped repairs in the canvas, with a label to the rear stating: 'N.B. The damage to this picture was inflicted by a flying-bomb which destroyed my home on 1/7/1944 – W. J. Tucker, 2 Berriman Rd, Holloway, London N7.'

An iconic view of St Paul's Cathedral during the Blitz. (*NARA*)

44: Civilian Firefighter's Helmet, January 1941

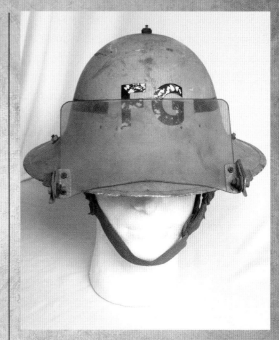

The Fire Guard were Britain's greatest part-time, amateur firefighting army, who helped beat 'Firebomb Fritz'. Yet the vast majority of this overwhelmingly conscripted force had no uniform, just an armlet and strange-looking headgear. Despite its slightly odd appearance, this helmet was the brainchild of three British boffins, offering the latest protective design to millions of Britons.

On the night of 29 December 1940, the City of London was devastated by incendiary bombs. Businesses had been left locked, so firemen had difficulty accessing properties to extinguish fires. It also seems many believed there was still a Christmas lull from bombing. Furthermore, the Minister of Home Security, Herbert Morrison, suggested firewatchers had not turned up for duty, chiding radio listeners: 'Some of you lately, in more cities than one, have failed your country – this must never happen again … You cannot stop a high-explosive bomb from bursting, but you can stop a firebomb from starting a fire … fall-in the firebomb fighters.'

On 18 January 1941, the first Fire Prevention (Business Premises) Order was introduced, making it compulsory for all men aged sixteen to sixty to perform forty-eight hours fire watching a month at their work. However, this did not create enough civilian firefighters and from September, under the CD Duties (Compulsory Enrolment) Order, all males aged eighteen to sixty had to register for fire watching. This order also saw the birth of the more formal Fire Guard organisation. As the war progressed, compulsion was increasingly tightened, and from 1942, women were also conscripted into fire watching.

Originally, the Fire Guard organisation was taken under the auspices of the Wardens service. However, from 1943, it made more sense to have closer links with the NFS, Fire Guards essentially becoming their scouts.

Fire watching was tedious and, after a long day's work, a tiring nocturnal duty. Most of the time, fortunately, nothing happened and the biggest enemy firewatchers faced was boredom. However, where firewatchers carried out their designated duty, they were largely successful, stopping incendiary bombs causing greater fires. Not only that, firewatchers saved millions of pounds worth of vital war materials by spotting and fighting industrial fires.

By the time of the Fire Guard's stand down in September 1944, it was the biggest branch of the Civil Defence services, with a strength of around six million. But this service to the nation came at a cost: over 1,750 Fire Guards died during the course of their duties.

Aside from an identifying armlet, the only other 'uniform' Fire Guards were issued with was a helmet, officially called the Civilian Protective Helmet, but which has become known as a Zuckerman after one of its inventors. The helmet was designed in 1940 by scientists Solly Zuckerman (1904–93) and Derman Christopherson (1915–2000), with Australian neurosurgeon Hugh Cairns (1896–1952). Their design tried to improve on the Mark II military helmet [see Object 34].

Produced by a number of companies, including the Austin and Morris Motor companies, it was made of mild manganese steel. Despite a rather odd and unmilitary appearance, the higher dome allowed a greater space between the metal shell and the wearer's head, allowing greater impact protection. It also had a slightly broader metal brim, offering improved cover from falling debris. Sometimes mistakenly called a 'women's helmet', because it was issued to several of the female Home Front services, it was actually worn by many of the ancillary organisations. It is mostly seen with the pre-September 1941 stencilled titling 'SFP' (Supplementary or Street Fire Party) or the latter 'FG' (Fire Guard).

This rare example is painted white with a black rank band, indicating a Street Party Leader, in charge of a 150-yard street and twenty to thirty Fire Guards. The owner has added a yellow-tinted hinged Perspex visor on aluminium brackets, perhaps suggesting they worked in an aircraft factory where they had access to these materials. Instead of the standard simple liner, which had no chinstrap, it has been upgraded with a liner from a Mark II helmet. Close examination shows the white paint has been dulled with soot, perhaps indicating it saw service during air raids.

45: *Picture Post* Magazine, February 1941

Newspapers are mainly words. But, without television and decades before the internet, one magazine above all others championed and perfected the 'picture story', focusing mainly on high-quality photographs to explain the news as much as the words that accompanied it. *Picture Post* magazine not only led the way in ground-breaking photography and journalism, it also advanced various social causes in Britain and around the world, reflecting on the struggle for democracy and freedom.

Picture Post was first published on 1 October 1938. However, the idea behind this weekly was not particularly new. The popular American magazine *Life*, to which it has been compared, had been launched two years' previously. Indeed, *Picture Post*'s first editor, Hungarian-born filmmaker Stefan Lorant (1901–97) had previously edited *Weekly Illustrated* and founded *Lilliput*, both 1930s photo magazines. But *Picture Post* had been an immediate success, selling 1.7 million copies a week after only two months.

With the coming of war, Lorant failed to gain British citizenship. Fearing his fate in a Nazi invasion, (he had opposed Hitler and had been imprisoned in Germany in 1933), Lorant moved to the US in July 1940. The magazine's second and most successful editor was Tom Hopkinson (1905–90). Although *Picture Post* was officially politically neutral, Hopkinson and his staff's own left-wing views sometimes crept into the magazine's editorial, much to the annoyance of the magazine's publisher, Sir Edward Hulton, a Conservative. Nonetheless, to his credit, Hulton, seeing the magazine's success, allowed Hopkinson to continue in his own style.

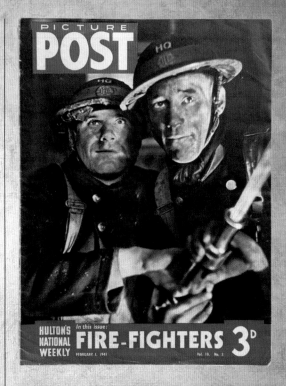

Hopkinson headed a successful and creative editorial team, all driven and at the top of their game. *Picture Post*'s art editor was artist Edgar Ainsworth (1905–75), who, as well as producing impressive work for the magazine himself, commissioned others, such as multi-talented artist and writer Mervyn Peake (1911–68) who drew the suffering of prisoners at Belsen concentration camp. Regular writers also included J. B. Priestley, George Bernard Shaw (1856–1950) and Dorothy Parker (1893–1967). Photographers included Kurt Hutton (1893–1960), Felix H. Man (1893–1985) and Francis Reiss (1927–2017).

Picture Post was a forward-thinking, progressive magazine. Almost two years before the Beveridge Report, on 4 January 1941, while the Blitz was still raging and Britain's victory looked far from assured, *Picture Post* published a special issue entitled *A Plan for Britain*. Distinguished contributors wrote on their proposals for a better society, including minimum wages, full employment, child allowances, a national health service, land usage and education reform. Its editorial stated: 'Our plan for a new Britain is not something outside the war, or something after the war. It is an essential part of our war aim. It is, indeed, our most positive war aim. The new Britain is the country we are fighting for.' Essentially their plan was a blueprint for what was later the Welfare State. It kindled discussions about the nation and the quality of life of future generations, inspiring William Beveridge's 1942 report [see Object 70].

The Second World War was also *Picture Post*'s finest hour: it was estimated that over 80 per cent of the population had read the magazine at some point and sales peaked with nearly two million copies sold in December 1943 alone, a figure that would make magazine owners and TV producers sit up today.

But this was not to last into peacetime. After a disagreement over coverage of the Korean War, Hulton fired Hopkinson in 1950. By June 1952, circulation had fallen to half its wartime sales. Television was the final nail in *Picture Post*'s coffin: despite numerous new editors and even the introduction of colour and 3D photographs, the magazine could not compete with the draw of the goggle-box. *Picture Post*'s final issue was published on 1 June 1957, when its circulation was less than 600,000 copies a week (a figure, nonetheless, many magazine editors could only dream of today).

We are now used to and almost take for granted the fact that we can see scenes in any part of the world in an instant, often live, on television or the internet. But for the wartime generation, the world around them was still largely an unknown quantity. Through its dramatic photography, *Picture Post* brought reality home to readers, from the comfort of their armchair. Colour photography may give us the full spectrum of what the eye sees, but *Picture Post* managed to achieve as powerful a medium with just two colours – black and white. This issue, Volume 10, No. 5, of 1 February 1941 is a great example. For the main feature, their photographer followed the London Fire Brigade over the course of a night Blitz, from the control room to the incident, capturing the drama of silhouetted firemen battling fires, all in striking monochrome. For his troubles, the photographer lost a £50 [£2,300] camera, a tripod, his trousers, and received a burned leg. For this extraordinary effort, the magazine broke its own rule of anonymity and published his name: Bert Hardy (1913–95). Self-taught from a humble background, Hardy became *Picture Post*'s chief photographer, later, from 1942, serving as an official war photographer for the Army Film and Photographic Unit, covering D-Day, the liberation of Paris and the crossing of the Rhine. He was one of the first photographers to enter Belsen concentration camp. Note the painted-on jet of water coming out of the firemen's hose on the posed cover: again, this was long before computer-enhanced imagery was even dreamt of.

46: Local Newspaper Emergency Edition, March 1941

In the following six months after Coventry's heavy air raid, if they hadn't already, all Britain's main industrial cities would receive a punitive visit from the Luftwaffe. By 1941, Luftwaffe operations were focusing more on the ports as part of the Battle of the Atlantic. Populations who thought their distance from London meant they were relatively safe now felt Hitler's fire.

London was such a large, unmistakable target, it was freely mentioned in news headlines. However, such was the vulnerability of these provincial targets, badly blitzed cities such as Hull were just referred to on the BBC radio news as a 'North-East Town'. This censorship became even more bizarre at a regional level when local newspapers, such as the *Leicester Mercury*, could only refer to 'raid damage in a Midland town', but displayed the name of that 'Midland town' above the headline in the newspaper's title.

In the days before regional TV, radio, and the internet, local newspapers were essential information providers and the sole source of local news. However, when war came, not only were they stunted by censorship and the conscription of staff, but the Control of Paper Order reduced their newsprint to as low as 79.7 per cent of pre-war supplies, resulting in fewer pages.

When the provincial Blitz came, city centre local newspaper offices became highly vulnerable. Numerous newspapers, such as the *Coventry Evening Telegraph*, the *Midland Daily Tribune* and *Nuneaton Chronicle*, were bombed out of their premises. The human cost was also high: roof spotters and firewatchers were killed guarding these offices.

It was a badge of pride that no provincial newspaper ever failed to produce an edition during the war, despite the bombing, but it did come close. On 7 December 1940, both the *Bristol Evening Post* and *Bristol Evening World* were reduced to a single, duplicated typed news sheet.

This edition of Plymouth's *Western Morning News*, of 22 March 1941, with its censored headline 'South West Town Badly Attacked', looks like any other wartime edition of the

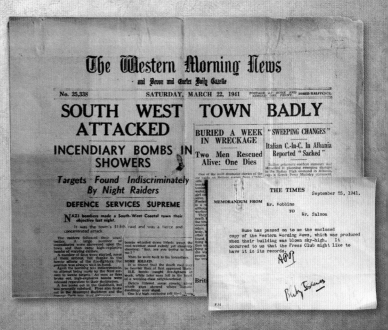

newspaper – but its production was something of a victory over the Luftwaffe.

Two days' previously, the King and Queen [see Object 47] had made a morale-boosting public visit to Plymouth. Two hours after the royals left, the Luftwaffe launched a devastating fire raid, destroying much of the city centre.

Brazenly, the Luftwaffe returned the following night, further adding to the damage, destroying St Andrew's Church, the Guildhall and the council offices. Only two buildings survived in the city centre, the National Westminster Bank and Leicester Harmsworth House, the office of the *Western Morning News*, in Frankfort Street. Although externally Georgian in design, it had been built in 1938 with stronger, modern construction methods.

Only when the raid was at its worst did the newspaper staff move to resume work in the basement shelter. They emerged to find windows blasted and glass scattered over their desks. One block of the building had been destroyed, along with several tons of newsprint and 30,000 images in the newspaper's historic photo library. Encircled by blazing buildings and exploding bombs, firemen played water jets on the newspaper office to stop it combusting. Nonetheless, a four-page edition of the newspaper was published from its blitzed office. It would be some time before they could publish the news that 336 citizens had died in the two-night raid.

The attached typed memorandum, dated 25 September 1941, from *The Times*, reads: 'Bune has passed on to me the enclosed copy of the *Western Morning News*, which was produced when their building was blown sky high.' Well, it didn't quite come to that. The *Western Morning News* continues publication to this day and its former offices, Leicester Harmsworth House, still stand, now converted into shops on Plymouth's New George Street, surrounded by post-Blitz redevelopment.

Civilians and Civil Defence personnel survey the scene in one of Plymouth's main thoroughfares after the Luftwaffe attacks in the so-called 'Plymouth Blitz'. (*Historic Military Press*)

47: The King Is Still In London Song Sheet, March 1941

If, a millennia before, his predecessor Aethelred became known as 'the Unready', then George VI, by his own words, should be known to history as 'the Unprepared'. His older brother, Edward VIII (1894–1972), should have been on the throne throughout the Second World War, but his abdication to marry American divorcee Wallis Simpson (1896–1986), pushed George into monarchy in 1936. Three years later, this quiet, reserved and anxious man with a speech impediment also found himself leading the nation into war.

On 3 September 1939, King George VI (1895–1952) addressed the people of Britain and across the Empire, warning of difficult times ahead and urging his people to stand firm. As well as monarch, the King was Admiral of the Fleet, Army Field Marshal and Marshal of the Royal Air Force, although these latter high-profile roles were more symbolic and ceremonial.

His wife, Queen Elizabeth (1900–2002), stood by his side and publicly refused to leave London or send their children to Canada, as she was advised to by Lord Hailsham, declaring: 'The children won't go without me. I won't leave the King. And the King will never leave.' So it was to be.

King George VI and Elizabeth remained at Buckingham Palace throughout the war, except at weekends, when they visited their daughters, the Princesses Elizabeth (born 1926) and Margaret (1930–2002), at Windsor Castle, Berkshire. Essentially evacuated themselves, in October 1940, the two princesses broadcast a morale-boosting message to other evacuees on the *Children's Hour* radio programme.

When the Blitz broke on London on 7 September 1940, the working-class East End received the heaviest bombing, while the well-off West End saw fewer attacks. The King and Queen toured the East End after raids, occasionally booed by disgruntled locals who thought the smartly dressed royals had arrived as sightseers.

However, at the same time, Buckingham Palace received nine direct hits from the Luftwaffe, with bombs landing in the grounds on 10 September 1940. Three days later, more serious damage was caused by two bombs that destroyed the Royal Chapel. The royal couple were in a small sitting room 80 yards from the explosions. Soon after, Queen Elizabeth said she felt she could now 'look the East End in the face'

– a bit of an exaggeration, but the Luftwaffe's actions boosted the royals' public standing.

There were also special preparations to protect the monarchy in the event of a German invasion. The Coats Mission, under Major James Coats MC, was a secret army unit created in 1940 of 129 Coldstream Guards to defend the Royal Family and help evacuate them in armoured cars, known as the Morris detachment, to remote country houses, including Newby Hall, North Yorkshire; Pitchford Hall, Shropshire and Madresfield Court, Worcestershire. If the invasion had reached the Midlands, the Royal Family would have been evacuated via Liverpool by ship to Canada.

In 1945, aged nineteen, Princess Elizabeth joined the Auxiliary Territorial Service (ATS) as a driver and mechanic, with the rank of second subaltern, later promoted to Junior Commander.

Her future husband, Philip Mountbatten (born 1921), later Prince Philip, the Duke of Edinburgh, served the whole war in the Royal Navy, seeing action in the Mediterranean and Far East.

Meanwhile, King George VI, dressed in military uniform, and Queen Elizabeth made morale-boosting tours around Britain, visiting cities, factories and inspecting troops. The King also toured overseas, visiting Malta and North Africa and, following D-Day, France and Holland.

This song sheet contains the words and music for the bombastic popular tune, *The King is Still in London*, written by Roma Campbell Hunter and Hugh Charles and featured by Billy Cotton and His Band in March 1941. Like many tunes of the time, it draws a fine line between song and propaganda. Lyrics, stressing an egalitarian theme, include: 'The king is with his people, 'cos that's where he wants to be. The King is still in London … and he would be in London Town if London Bridge was falling down … Like Mister Jones and Mister Brown the King is still in London Town.'

King George VI, centre foreground, speaks to residents whilst inspecting bomb damage in London's East End, 10 September 1940. (*Historic Military Press*)

48: 'Blitz Spirit' Bulldog Figurine, 1940–41

You cannot see it, taste it or smell it, but this next object was a war winner, vital to the maintenance of morale on the Home Front – Blitz Spirit. Eighty years on, it still exudes from the objects pictured in this book, but back in 1940–41 it was more vital than ever, for home-grown psychological defiance was a key weapon of war in the defence of Britain.

Before the war, in 1938, a committee of psychiatrists predicted there would be three times as many mental as physical casualties from bombing, suggesting three to four million psychiatric patients. Such statistics were largely driven by the fear of the unknown. The devastation of towns such as Guernica during the Spanish Civil War proved the potency of the Luftwaffe's aerial might. Britain's focus on ARP preparations, while attempting to protect the nation, only further ratcheted up this concern. Future Prime Minister Harold Macmillan (1894–1986) later recalled that many 'thought of air warfare in 1938 rather as people think of nuclear war today'.

But, unlike the pre-war forecasts of the sky going black with bombers and whole cities being levelled, when the Blitz started, while the devastation caused was terrible, it was survivable for the vast majority of urban citizens. The Luftwaffe was not as capable as had been feared. In the words of the now-famous wartime poster, people really did 'Keep Calm and Carry On'.

Whilst the nation may have been short of many commodities in 1940, it was not short of morale-boosting Blitz Spirit. Further kindled by propaganda films such as the GPO Film Unit's *London Can Take it!* and *Britain Can Take it!* (1940), Britons from Prime Minister Winston Churchill and radio broadcaster J. B.

Priestley (1894–1984), to the air raid warden and postman, exhibited this newfound defiance. The ordinary citizen also displayed Blitz Spirit: helping bombed-out neighbours, welcoming strangers to their air raid shelter, opening doors to evacuees, making that extra effort to get to work when public transport was disrupted, working that extra shift for the war effort, and sharing the last of their sugar ration.

Even shop owners displayed their defiance of Hitler's wrath. Bomb-blasted department stores on London's Oxford Street carried witty signs such as 'More open than usual', whilst a windowless Soho barber noted 'A close shave, sir? Never mind the blasted windows, walk right in.'

To be fair, Blitz Spirit was not really a new phenomenon. Indeed, there had been the 'Dunkirk Spirit' just months before the bombing began. But it seems this form of national

bonhomie developed and flowered during the Blitz, flourishing throughout the war years, even finding depiction in art and music. The famous 1942 series of artistic posters by artist Frank Newbould (1887–1951) showed beautiful stirring scenes of the British countryside with the header 'Your Britain, fight for it now'. In the end, it proved inexorable. The benevolence of Blitz Spirit beat the bad faith and hate of Nazism.

But, it seems strange that it took a world war to bring out this spirit among Britons. Today, when many people barely know their neighbours, modern society has become less community-minded and insular. Nonetheless, the 'Spirit of the Blitz' is still sometimes referred to, when knuckling down and facing adversity, such as after a large flood or serious incident. The so-called 'British stiff upper lip' may seem a comic stereotype today, but for six long, desperate years, it was a vital national asset.

This unsigned ceramic British bulldog, *c*.1940, is highly redolent of Blitz Spirit. Standing just 6in tall, sprayed gold on green, this plucky and defiant canine sits sentry with a steel helmet bearing the pugnacious wording 'Hitler's Terror'. Its reminiscence of Churchill's dogged character adds to its appeal – both then and now.

Undaunted by a night of German air raids in which his store front was badly damaged, a shopkeeper opens up the morning after for 'business as usual' in London. (*Historic Military Press*)

49: Looting Warning Poster, April 1941

As has always been the case throughout human history, not everyone adhered to the general ethos of the Blitz Spirit. Those who had not cared for the sanctity of other people's homes, shops and property before the war, did not suddenly change their ways in September 1939. For the criminal minority, the war wasn't about pulling together for the common good: on the contrary, they saw it as a great opportunity for personal illicit rich pickings. Indeed, recorded crime rose by 57 per cent, from 303,771 offences in 1939 to 478,000 in 1945.

The introduction of the blackout brought new cover to burglars and robbers. Decades before CCTV, the police, already stretched by reduced numbers due to conscription, had a real uphill task on their hands.

Gangs, sometimes including army deserters, operated at night, making great profits from smash-and-grab raids on furriers or robbing ration book stores for trading on the black market. Even shop owners were prosecuted for either overcharging for goods or selling underweight produce to con the customer.

There was also a rise in crime committed by the young, from vandalising air raid shelters to roaming in gangs and assaulting or mugging individuals, plus petty theft. In April 1941, Lambeth juvenile court dealt with forty-two children in just one day, including a seven-year-old boy who had stolen five shillings [£14] from a gas meter in a bombed house. In total, juvenile crime accounted for 48 per cent of all arrests during the Blitz. Courts were empowered to send miscreants to borstal or approved schools, even dish out birchings.

Bomb damage provided new avenues for the unscrupulous, whose looting added further misery for those who had lost their homes. Even neighbours looted neighbours. Neither were the emergency services beyond temptation. Following the Coventry Blitz, three firemen were given six-month prison sentences for looting a shop. Fire watchers guarding warehouses overnight were also light fingered with the goods they were meant to be guarding: in fact, it could be argued, some caused more financial damage to the business they were entrusted with than the Luftwaffe.

Looting from bombed properties didn't just occur in residential streets. One of the worst examples of anti-Blitz Spirit occurred on 8 March 1941, when London's famous Cafe de Paris, in Piccadilly, was hit by two bombs, killing thirty-four, including bandleader Ken 'Snakehips' Johnson and members of his band. The nightclub was popular with officers and their partners, and as the dust was still settling, looters moved in, picking over the dead and dying, even cutting off fingers to steal rings.

The government was so concerned about looting that it introduced the death penalty and life sentences as a deterrent, as this Yorkshire

WEST RIDING CONSTABULARY.

WARNING

LOOTING

Looting from Premises damaged by War Operations is punishable by **DEATH or PENAL SERVITUDE FOR LIFE**

G. C. VAUGHAN,
Chief Constable.

warning poster, which was posted on bomb-damaged homes, makes clear. However, this capital punishment was never carried out, perhaps because it was near unenforceable as looting was so widespread – there were 4,584 cases of looting by the end of the Blitz.

The courts, however, could still be severe. Those who complain about light sentences today probably have a point compared to wartime justice. Not only were more criminals imprisoned, but they could also be given additional 'hard labour', such as rock-breaking in a quarry or digging drains.

Even more heinous crimes also flourished. In April 1941, Harry Dodkin murdered his wife and buried her under the rubble of London's bombed Vauxhall Baptist Chapel, hoping she would be discovered and quickly buried as an air raid victim. Her body was discovered a year later, but a pathologist recognised her injuries were due to strangulation. Dobkin met his end at

Wandsworth Prison in January 1943. Similarly, twenty-eight-year-old RAF serviceman Gordon Frederick Cummins, a sexual deviant known as the Blackout Ripper, was convicted of the murder of at least four women in London over a six-day period in February 1942. He accidentally dropped his numbered service gas mask, which led detectives to him – he was hanged at Wandsworth Prison four months later.

So, why is wartime crime so rarely known today and does it make the Blitz Spirit a myth? Inevitably, British war propaganda trumpeted good news over bad. The vast majority of Britons, then as now, were law-abiding and so, on the whole, the phenomenon of Blitz Spirit stands. However, this rare surviving post-raid poster, issued by West Riding Constabulary, reminds us of the less palatable and criminal side of British society that existed on the Home Front throughout the war.

Police Officers assist in evacuating residents after an unexploded bomb was located near University College Hospital, London, in 1941. (*NARA*)

50: Luftwaffe Airman's Parachute Harness Release Device, Spring 1941

With meagre anti-aircraft defences, it may seem that the British were pretty powerless in the face of the Luftwaffe's night Blitz. Although, in 1940–41, the Luftwaffe largely had free range over Britain to fly and bomb wherever they wanted, it did not mean bombing operations always went their own way. Many Luftwaffe aircraft and aircrew never made it back to their airfields in occupied Europe.

Indeed, between 20 June 1940, when heightened German air operations over Britain began, up to 31 March 1941, the Oberkommando der Luftwaffe (Air Force High Command) recorded the loss of 2,265 aircraft over Britain, with at least 3,363 aircrew killed and 2,117 wounded, plus 2,641 missing.

Some of those missing disappeared with their aircraft into the seas around Britain, never to be seen again. This was due to several reasons, from being shot down by an RAF night fighter, being damaged by anti-aircraft fire over Britain and the aircraft failing over the sea, to even running out of fuel and navigational errors. Only the aircrews ever knew how their flight ended.

Other Luftwaffe aircrew managed to bail out of their doomed aircraft by parachute and land on British soil. However, due to Britain's sea 'moat', there was next to no chance of escaping back to the Continent. Luftwaffe parachutists usually landed lost, shocked and often in fear: they had heard rumours that Britons routinely lynched captured aircrew. More often than not, the standard reception they received was a cup

of tea and chair in a farmhouse kitchen, while they waited for the local policeman to arrive. It was rare for Luftwaffe aircrew to try and evade capture: the longest attempt seems to have been by bomber crewman Feldwebel Josef Markl in July 1940, who stayed on the run, hiding in the countryside around Newbury, Berkshire, for eight days, until he surrendered, tired and hungry.

After surrendering, Luftwaffe aircrew were not sent straight to a prisoner of war camp. They would be escorted by British soldiers, or military police, sometimes to a local barracks for temporary holding, before being sent to a 'cage', where they would be interrogated by the Prisoner of War Interrogation Section (PWIS), under the command of Lieutenant Colonel A. P. Scotland (1882–1965). The main interrogation centre was the 'London Cage', at 8 Kensington Palace Gardens, a smart former stately home. The levels of duress employed during interrogation have been contested since the war. Luftwaffe aircrew were also sent to Trent Park, another mansion, just north of London at Cockfosters, under Squadron Leader Denys Felkin, head of the RAF's Air Intelligence 1(k) section, responsible for the interrogation of Luftwaffe prisoners. Asides from questioning, more subtle techniques were used here, including hidden microphones and stool pigeons. It was only after this process that aircrew would be sent to a PoW camp [see Object 88].

Similarly, crashed Luftwaffe aircraft were not just immediately cleared away. Firstly, they were guarded until the RAF's Air Intelligence 1(g) section could arrive and pick over the wreckage, to find any new technology or documents and maps that had survived. Only then would an RAF Maintenance Unit remove the wreckage to their local base, essentially a giant scrapyard. From there, it would be sent to a smelting plant to be made into aluminium ingots, which would be used for making RAF aircraft – to shoot down more Luftwaffe aircraft: recycling, RAF-style!

It may seem surprising, but Luftwaffe airmen killed in battle were buried with full military honours, including a cortege with RAF bearers, often with a swastika flag draped over the coffins and a volley of shots by RAF riflemen. Usually buried at a cemetery local to the crash, from 1967, most were reinterred at the new German military cemetery, at Cannock Chase, Staffordshire.

This is a quick-release device from a Luftwaffe Model 30 parachute harness. The device was actually invented by two Englishmen, with the patent assigned to the Irvin Air Chute Company, an American company, with a factory at Letchworth, Hertfordshire. The company had sold several of these mechanisms to Germany in 1937, who found them to be a better design than their own, so copied them instead. The device held together four parachute harness buckles. When the wearer wanted to release the harness on landing, he rotated the front metal disc 90 degrees and depressed it with a sharp blow: (the German wording reads: 'To release harness: turn then press!'). The word on the side means 'unlocked'. Apparently, it belonged to a member of a Luftwaffe bomber crew who was shot down over Weston-super-Mare, Somerset, in early 1941. He was relieved of the device by a Home Guard who captured him on landing and decided to keep it as a souvenir – a war trophy of the victor over the vanquished!

51: House Of Commons Rubble Souvenir Paperweight, May 1941

Throughout early 1941, with the Luftwaffe's wider focus across Britain, there were fewer raids on London than the previous year. However, the Luftwaffe were determined to let the capital know it had not been forgotten. On the night of Saturday, 10 May 1941, there was a full 'bomber's moon': just after 11 pm, the siren sounded – it would be a night that went down in London's history.

The attack became known as 'The Great Fire Raid', although the use of high-explosive bombs was as much a feature of the night. Some 685 Luftwaffe bombers dropped almost 800 tons of bombs, causing over 2,000 fires. Seven hundred gas mains were fractured and burned through the night, enabling later waves of bombers to visually navigate to their target – indeed, the flames of London could be seen as soon as they took off from their Continental airfields, 150 miles away.

One-third of London's streets were left impassable. All the bridges across the Thames were either blocked or cratered and all the mainline railway stations, bar one, were disrupted for several weeks. Many famous London landmarks were hit, including Buckingham Palace, the Tower of London, Westminster Abbey and the Law Courts. Charred paper floated down from the night sky over central London – the remains of 250,000 valuable historic books that had burned at the British Museum. Some

1,436 Londoners were killed and a further 1,792 injured. Morale was badly affected.

But the most famous badly damaged landmark was Britain's historic cradle of democracy, the House of Commons Chamber, which was destroyed. It was the third major destructive fire in its long history. Located in the Palace of Westminster, the neo-Gothic masterpiece was designed by famous English architects Charles Barry (1795–1860) and Augustus Pugin (1812–52) and built in 1840–76.

During the war, the Palace of Westminster was hit by bombs on fourteen separate occasions. One bomb fell into Old Palace Yard on 26 September 1940, severely damaging the south wall of St Stephen's Porch and the west front. The statue of Richard the Lionheart had also been lifted from its pedestal by the blast and his upheld sword bent. Another bomb destroyed much of the Cloisters on 8 December 1940.

However, the worst damage occurred on the night of 10–11 May 1941, when the Palace was hit by bombs at least twelve times, killing three officials, two policemen and the Resident Superintendent of the House of Lords, Edward Elliott. An incendiary bomb hit the chamber of the House of Commons and set it on fire, while another set the roof of Westminster Hall alight. The firefighters could not save both, and a decision was taken to try to rescue the latter. This attempt was successful – but the abandoned Commons Chamber was destroyed, so too was the Members' Lobby. A bomb also struck the Lords Chamber, penetrating the floor, fortunately, without exploding. The famous Clock Tower was also hit by a small bomb or anti-aircraft shell, badly damaging the roof and blasting out all the glass on the south dial face, though the Great Clock continued to keep time. On visiting the smoking, rubble-strewn House of Commons Chamber the next morning, Churchill was seen to weep, one of the few times in the war.

Elsewhere that night, in a bizarre twist, another unwelcome visitor, Deputy Führer Rudolf Hess (1894–1987) flew to Scotland and landed by parachute in Renfrewshire, ostensibly on a secret peace mission, resulting only in his captivity. But this was to be the last raid of the London Blitz. The Luftwaffe had dropped 30,000 tons of bombs during their campaign, killing 41,000 Britons and injuring 139,000 more. They had disrupted production and affected morale, even hampering Britain's war effort, but it had not caused Britain to sue for peace. Unbeknown to most Britons, this final Blitz raid had also been cover for a major change in direction of the war: just over a month later, on 22 June 1941, Germany would aim eastwards and invade its ally Russia.

Creating a positive out of a negative, London Stonecraft Ltd, of West Green Road, N15, resculpted the sandy-coloured Anston limestone rubble from the Houses of Parliament into several objects, from garden bird baths to letter racks and ash trays to book ends, all sold to raise funds for the Joint Red Cross and St John Fund. Each piece came with an individually numbered certificate of authenticity, dated 13 May 1942. This example is Design No. 200, a paperweight, which cost 10s [£20], bearing a seal, made from the roof lead of the Houses of Parliament, showing the famous Clock Tower, known as Big Ben, dated 'London 1941'. Of note, this piece retains the blackened scorch or soot stains from the Blitz fire of 10–11 May 1941.

A photograph showing the damage caused when a bomb tore a hole in the stonework of Big Ben during the bombing on 10 May 1941. (*Historic Military Press*)

52: Treen V-For-Victory Finger Symbol, July 1941

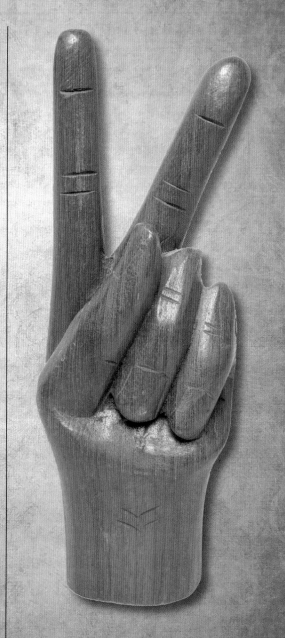

Throughout history, many political leaders have used devices to identity and distinguish themselves, whether it is distinctive catchphrases, clothing or even hand gestures. Hitler used his outstretched right arm as a Nazi salute, while his opponent, Winston Churchill, chose a two-finger V for victory hand gesture. But while Churchill may have become known to history as the V-symbol's most famous proponent, you may be surprised to know that he did not invent it, nor was he the first to use it in the war.

True, on 13 May 1940, in his first major 'blood, toil, tears and sweat' speech on becoming prime minister, Churchill stated: 'You ask, what is our aim? I can answer in one word: victory. Victory at all costs, victory in spite of all terror, victory, however long and hard the road may be, for without victory there is no survival.' However, it would not be until January 1941, when the word was made into a battle cry and symbol of defiance – and not by a Briton.

On 14 January 1941, forty-five-year-old Belgian politician in exile, Victor de Laveleye (1894–1945), broadcast to his occupied homeland on the BBC's Radio Belgique, that, as a symbol of subterfuge and resistance, they should daub the letter 'V' on walls in defiance of their occupiers. The letter was significant, because it stood for the French word for victory (*victoire*) and the Dutch word for freedom (*vrijheid*).

The campaign was an instant success on the Continent and the BBC expanded their 'V for Victory' propaganda. Assistant news editor Douglas Ritchie (1905–67), speaking as 'Colonel V. Britton' on air, also suggested to Belgian listeners tapping out the Morse code letter for V, three dots and a dash (•••-) on tables in cafes as a further act of resistance. It was noted that the opening bars of Beethoven's fifth symphony also had the same rhythm, so the BBC used this as its call sign in its foreign language programmes to occupied Europe.

The V-symbol was also graffitied in the occupied Channel Islands [see Object 23], but the punishment if caught doing so was harsh: arrest and imprisonment. However, there were also more subtle forms of usage. Following a coin shortage on the islands, in April 1941, local artist Edmund Blampied (1886–1966) was commissioned to design new occupation banknotes: ingeniously, Blampied incorporated the V-sign in their design.

It was only after a radio broadcast on 19 July 1941, during which Winston Churchill mentioned the ongoing V campaign, did the prime minister start using his now famous V hand sign. At this point, it also became popular at home, chalked on walls, on the side of air raid shelters and in newsreels – you could even buy lapel badges bearing the letter 'V'.

Churchill sometimes made the symbol with his fingernails facing forwards – also a rude hand gesture. An urban legend suggests that this gesture dates back to defiant English and Welsh longbowmen in the 1415 Battle of Agincourt, but there is no historical evidence to support this. Churchill's private secretary, John Colville, noted that the premier was informed of the offensiveness of this other V-sign, but occasionally continued to use it: perhaps, also, a sign of Churchill's sometimes mischievous sense of humour!

The Germans tried to subvert the campaign by pointing out that the letter V also stood for the German word for victory, *viktoria*, and that the Allies' Morse letter adaptation was derived from composer Beethoven, also German. The Nazis even started their own campaign, erecting a giant 'V' on the side of the Eiffel Tower in occupied Paris, but it did not succeed – everybody knew it was the Allied symbol for the cause of victory.

In the 1960s, the hand gesture was also appropriated by the hippy generation as a symbol for peace during the Vietnam War, its most famous proponent being Beatle John Lennon (1940–80).

This 8in tall piece of treen, nicely carved from a salvaged piece of scrap wood made a handy wartime morale-boosting reminder of the V for Victory campaign. Obviously, when hosting visitors you would have to be careful in which direction you displayed it!

53: NFS Women's Cap, August 1941

The experience of the Blitz had truly been a trial by fire for the Auxiliary Fire Service. Operational duties had revealed many shortcomings of an organisation that had been hurriedly created and based on pre-war local fire brigades, each with their own structures, operating methods and varied equipment, which often caused confusion. For example, the brigades were so divergent that sometimes fire appliances from a neighbouring city would arrive to assist another's brigade, only to find their hoses would not fit the hydrants as there were no standard fittings.

Minister of Home Security Herbert Morrison took forcible action to rectify the situation. On 18 August 1941, the AFS and numerous local fire brigades were nationalised into the National Fire Service (NFS).

Initially, this government action did not go down well with many local fire brigade committees, who felt their independence was being compromised by a centralised authoritarian decision. However, nationalisation was the most logical and efficient solution. The NFS became more organised, with new standardised ranks, uniforms, insignia, training and quasi-military discipline. The move also unified the regular firemen with their AFS cohorts.

Fire appliances, equipment and, most importantly, organisation were also standardised, with Britain divided into forty-three new separate Fire Force Regions, each with its own command, relaying national instruction. Regular printed NFS orders and a series of Manuals of Firemanship became the general texts of the service. A Fire Service College was also started at Saltdean, Sussex, for the training of NFS officers.

Ironically, by the middle of the war, with the lull in air raids, there was far less for the NFS to do. There was some reduction in personnel numbers, while others filled the gap making components for the war effort and, at Christmas, toys from scrap materials for children. However, training remained comprehensive, which was as well as Luftwaffe bombing returned with the Baedeker Raids of 1942 and the Tip-and-Run Raids of 1943.

The final year of the war would be the most diverse one for the NFS. With the build-up of military personnel and materials along the south coast in the preparations for D-Day, under the Colour Scheme, NFS personnel from less vulnerable areas in the Midlands were drafted

to the south as reinforcement in case of enemy attacks.

When the German V-weapon attacks began in June 1944, due to their tremendous blast power, ironically, they often immediately blew out any fires they started, leaving little for the NFS to extinguish. As a result, their role became more of rescue, assisting the CD services.

Following D-Day, the NFS even left Britain's shores. In January 1945, No. 4 Column of the NFS Overseas Contingent was attached to the US Army and advanced through Europe into Germany, facing mines and snipers, but helping control fires caused by the enemy.

With the war's end, true to Morrison's original word, on 1 April 1948, Britain's fire services were denationalised and returned to local authority control, a surprising move in an age of nationalisation. However, even today, Britain's fire service owes much to the reforms of the NFS.

At its peak strength in 1943, the NFS was 370,000 strong. Over 80,000 of these personnel were women, who served in a variety of roles, from canteen or office administration work, to officers or communications staff in control rooms. Others acted as motorcycle despatch riders or drove ancillary vehicles. During the war, twenty-five firewomen lost their lives. One firewoman, twenty-one-year-old Gillian Tanner, was awarded the George Medal for bravery, when she delivered petrol to fire pumps in the London docks at the height of an air raid. Also, twenty-two British Empire Medals and forty-one Kings Commendations for Brave Conduct were awarded to firewomen. This official NFS firewomen's peaked cap, made by the biggest mass-producing hat company in the world, J. Collett & Co. of London, is dated 1944. It reflects both the smart and organised nature of the NFS.

Leicester NFS firewomen try on their new uniform caps, with the firewoman, centre, wearing the flap folded down, tied under her chin.

54: Utility Dress, Summer 1941

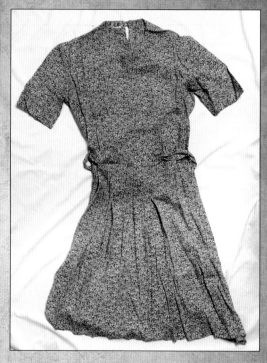

Today, Britons are spoilt for choice for clothes, with many different styles available at cheap prices from several high street retailers. The twenty-first-century penchant for disposable or fast fashion would seem unimaginable to our 1940s forebears, when clothing was made to last. Clothing was also more standardised: women wore a dress or skirt and blouse, men wore a suit and tie and both sexes regularly wore hats: in the case of the latter, usually a cloth cap, trilby or Homburg – and what you wore usually also was a distinguisher of social class. T-shirts were a thing of the future and clothing, no matter your class, was mostly formal.

However, Britain's dress norms were suddenly shook up on 1 June 1941 when clothes rationing was introduced. Initially, Churchill was against the move, as he thought it would be bad for the morale of Britons to be dressed in 'rags and tatters'. However, food rationing had been introduced a year and a half earlier and although many were disappointed, most understood the rationale behind the move.

Each person received a pink 'Clothing Book' (there was no mention of 'ration' on the cover) containing sixty-six coupons, which was the equivalent to one complete new outfit per year. Growing children and factory workers received extra coupons. The amount of coupons needed depended on the garment and the material it was made from, so, for example, a suit required twenty-six to twenty-nine coupons, or women's shoes seven coupons. However, as the war progressed and shortages bit, allocations of coupons were reduced: in 1942, it fell to forty-eight, in 1943 to thirty-six, and in 1945 to twenty-four.

As a further austerity measure, just three months after the introduction of clothes rationing, the Board of Trade introduced Utility clothing. This was a range of simpler clothes, made to stricter limits in materials, including the number of buttons, pockets and pleats allowed. Turn-ups on trousers and double-breasted suits were banned. Nonetheless, leading designers, such as Hardy Amies (1909–2003) and Norman Hartnell (1901–79), were commissioned to create a variety of styles and colours of Utility clothing of satisfactory quality. As an added appeal, the clothing was cheaper, price-controlled and tax-free. However, there were some perceived injustices: those who wore a work, school or Civil Defence uniform were required to surrender precious clothing coupons.

The public also used their ingenuity to bypass clothes rationing. Siblings often wore hand-me-

or a dress from curtains. Patches became quite common on worn garments.

Such was success of the Utility clothing scheme it was extended to a diverse range of other items, such as furniture, books, blankets, crockery, cigarette lighters and even radios [see Object 86]. Indeed, although clothes rationing only finally ended on 15 March 1949, post-war material shortages meant Utility production continued until 1952.

Items included in the Board of Trade's Utility scheme carried a distinguishing label or mark bearing an identifying 'CC41' logo. Designed by commercial artist Reginald Shipp, there is some debate about the logo and its meaning. A September 1941 Associated Press article suggested the 'two cheeses' or double 'CC's stood for 'Controlled Commodity', while others have suggested it represents the Civilian Clothing Order 1941. Another suggestion is that the supposed letters do not stand for anything and were just a simple, recognisable symbol designed by Shipp. Either way, it became a familiar symbol in the war and beyond. This pretty floral summer garment, bearing the CC41 label in its collar, met the requirements for Utility dresses, which were 'no more than two pockets, five buttons, six seams in the skirt, two inverted or box pleats or four knife pleats, and 160in (4m) of stitching. No superfluous decoration allowed. It should be simple, practical, agreeable-looking, inexpensive and made of good material.' While it might not be the most fashionable or glamorous, its label showed the wearer was doing her bit!

downs (whether they wanted to or not), bought second-hand clothing from friends or the black market. Women created the effect of stockings by drawing a line down the back of their legs with an eyeliner pencil to imitate seams. 'Liquid stockings', a temporary brown stain in a bottle, was also used, but not as widely as perceived today.

As a further aid, from 1942, the Board of Trade introduced Make Do and Mend: as the President of the Board of Trade, Oliver Lyttleton (1893–1972), explained to the nation: 'When you feel tired of your old clothes, remember that by making them do, you are contributing to some part of an aeroplane, a gun or a tank.' Advice was distributed in the form of leaflets and a popular booklet, giving tips on how to extend the life of clothing and even transform garments, such as making women's clothing from a man's suit

55: Ornamental Beer Tankard, 1941

In the First World War, teetotal Minister of Munitions David Lloyd George (1863–1945), declared war on Britain's brewing industry, stating: 'We are fighting Germany, Austria and drink; and as far as I can see, the greatest of these three deadly foes is drink.' The government closed breweries, cut pub opening hours to just five hours a day, reduced beer production and even made it illegal to buy or 'treat' a drink for a friend. However, come the Second World War, there was a governmental about-turn: realising social drinking was good for morale, not only did the government leave the brewing industry to 'carry on', but it never rationed beer.

The government did not restrict pub opening from pre-war hours. In theory, at least, pubs could open 11.30 am–3 pm, then 5.30 pm–10.30 pm. But the war still made its mark. Beer was often in short supply, with pubs running dry halfway through the night, resulting in a 'No beer' sign on the door. In 1941, some pubs tried to make their beer supplies last longer by only opening from 8 pm for a couple of hours, or even just on alternate nights. Similarly, although, officially, beer may not have been rationed, some landlords introduced their own restrictions to one pint per customer. Drinkers built up a thirst visiting all the pubs in their neighbourhood searching for just one pint. 'Outsiders' visiting a pub even received a cold shoulder from locals as they were viewed to be drinking 'their' beer supply!

Pubs were also not the relaxing sanctuary they used to be. Sitting in a draughty, dark, boarded-up pub was not unusual during the Blitz. Located on prominent corners or detached locations and with large windows, pubs were susceptible to bomb blast. A pub's entire supply of beer glasses and displayed bottles could be smashed by just one explosion, so drinkers often had to bring their own receptacles: it was not unusual to see the clientele drinking out of jam jars.

Though customers and staff were sometimes invited to shelter in beer cellars, the confined space of a pub resulted in several tragic incidents. One of the worst was on 12 December 1940, when the Marples Hotel, in Fitzalan Square, Sheffield, received a direct hit, killing seventy inside. By the end of 1941, 1,116 licensed premises had been destroyed by air raids, comprising 916 pubs and 200 off-licences.

Similarly, breweries, though well-built, were large, conspicuous buildings that looked like factories. Numerous breweries in the blitzed cities were damaged or even destroyed, such as Boddington's Strangeways Brewery, in Manchester, which was burned out by incendiary bombs on 22 December 1940. However, former

commercial rivalries were forgotten and many breweries helped each other out, brewing their competitor's beer and barrelling it, all for the common good.

Drunkenness disrupting war production was not such a concern as in the First World War, because although beer consumption rose by 25 per cent, it was diluted and the alcohol content lower. Due to the shortages, beer drinkers also slowly supped their pints to make them last longer. Beer prices, the perennial moan of drinkers today, also rose considerably in wartime. The Treasury realised there was money to be made for the war effort by taxing beer: in 1939, the excise duty on a barrel of beer was 24s [£67], by 1944, it was £7 [£300]. This had a knock-on effect for drinkers and the price of a pint rose from 6d [£1.50] in 1939 up to 1s 3d [£2.50] – although actually still quite cheap by today's prices.

Unlike today, where off-licences sell drink in bottles and cans, customers brought their own bottles and jugs to be filled, again due to the shortage of glass. Pubs also commonly sold similar take-outs to customers.

Spirits were even harder to come by, unless you wanted to spend a lot of money on the black market. The price of whisky had doubled to 25s 9d [£50] a bottle. During the war, only three short periods for distilling Scotch whisky were allowed and that was designated for export to bring in much-needed foreign revenue. Wine drinkers also had a tough war: the fall of France instantly ended wine imports and by 1943, if you could find a bottle of claret, some restaurants were charging £3 [£115] a bottle. Alternative supplies of wine were still imported from the Empire, but it was largely viewed as expensive and undrinkable.

The wartime shortage of beer glasses may have led to the production of these fancy decorative ceramic beer tankards, though a large percentage were probably for the export market. This example, made by the Wade Heath pottery, of Stoke-on-Trent, Staffordshire, around 1941, bears the appropriate wording 'Roll Out The Barrel', after the famous song, also known as *The Beer Barrel Polka*, composed in 1927 by the Czech musician, Jaromir Vejvoda (1902–88). Released in 1939, it was a wartime hit in many countries, from Germany to China, particularly as a beer-drinking song and was recorded by several artists, from the Andrews Sisters to the Glenn Miller Orchestra [see Object 89]. The tankard's handle is in the form of a uniformed Tommy, while other known examples, in blue and green glazes, feature Churchill instead. Though well-made, it is unlikely this tankard would have withstood the rigours of a pub, so it was probably for ornamental home usage.

56: Salvage Drive Leaflet, Autumn 1941

It may largely be forgotten now, but when door-to-door recycling schemes were widely introduced across Britain in the 1990s, there were many reactionary grumbles on letters' pages of local newspapers. Some moaned at the suggestion of having to put their waste into separate bins and said they would refuse. Rewind fifty years earlier and you'll find there were no such objections – Britons eagerly wanted to help the war effort with their salvage.

As the German blockade bit, the government initiated a campaign to reuse old materials. In a broadcast to the nation in July 1940, the first wartime Minister of Supply, Herbert Morrison, implored: 'I ask people to start now and save their paper, bones and scrap metal. In that way, we shall build up a great reserve of raw materials ready to be transformed into war materials.'

The public response was overwhelming: people of all ages turned up to hand over their aluminium pots and pans at salvage points in most towns and villages. From a largely pre-war generation who were used to slinging everything in the metal dustbin, it became second nature for households to divide their rubbish into separate salvage boxes for glass, paper, metal, rubber and rags. Although recycling technology was comparatively in its infancy, nearly everything that could be recycled was – and into a surprising variety of objects. Rubber could be reused to make tyres for army lorries, gas masks, escape dinghies and barrage balloons. Animal bones were reused to make glue for aircraft, glycerine for explosives and fertilisers for the field. Even a simple metal 9in saucepan could be remade into a bayonet.

YORKSHIRE COUNTY SALVAGE DRIVE: SEPT 6TH TO 20TH 1941

Mrs Smith is helping to win the war!

OLD METALS

WASTE PAPER

BONES

ASHES, BROKEN GLASS & CHINA, USELESS FOOD SCRAPS (See List) ONLY IN BIN

Every Yorkshire housewife can help to win the War by putting out for the Salvage Collector ALL Old Books, Magazines and Paper, ALL Old Metal Ornaments, Tools, Door Knockers, Etc., ALL Bones and ALL Rags—they're all needed for vital munitions and supplies. AND, all scraps of Food are wanted, too, to feed the Pigs and Poultry.

AND NOW, MAKE *Every* WEEK A SALVAGE WEEK!

Issued by the
LEEDS SALVAGE DEPARTMENT

Before the war, Britain had been largely dependent on overseas timber supplies, particularly from Canada.

When war came, although Britain's annual home timber production rose from 0.5 to 3.75 million tons, timber imports declined from 9.5 million tons to only 1.75 million tons in 1943 – an overall net drop of almost 50 per cent. Paper could be recycled for many uses, from maps to war manuals. It was even stated that 1 ton of paper made 300 mortar shell carriers or 110,000 washers for shells. Asides from collecting old newspapers and magazines for salvage, old books were also requested by the Ministry of Supply for repulping: in 1943, fifty-six million books were handed in, six million of which were considered too valuable to be destroyed and five million were sent to the troops as reading material.

When you see wartime photos today, you will notice there were very few items that could not be recycled: most clothes were of natural materials, not synthetic. Indeed, plastics, a huge cause of twenty-first-century pollution, did exist, but only in small quantities, in the form of Bakelite, usually used in larger, longer-life items, such as telephone sets or light switches, and certainly not in the quantity of the single-use disposable plastics of today. Instead, goods were either wrapped in paper, card or a metal can – all recyclable for the war effort. Indeed, later in the war, many food wrappings were banned altogether.

To encourage and help the salvage drive, from February 1942 part-time council Salvage Stewards were issued with a red plastic badge, those in shops and offices were given a blue badge and in factories, a green badge. The youth organisations, such as the Scouts and Guides, had helped collect salvage from the war's start, but children were also employed as junior salvage stewards, known as 'Cogs', under the direction of the WVS, and even had their own anthem: *There'll Always be a Dustbin*!

Over 6 million tons of salvage were collected during the war. These salvage campaigns not only had practical benefits towards the nation's war effort, but also contributed to galvanising the national spirit of 'we're all pulling together'.

Women – chiefly, housewives – were the main targets of the domestic household wartime salvage campaigns, mainly because they ran the household as the men were either away in the services or at the war factory [see Object 74]. In late 1941, there was a national scrap drive. This leaflet was templated across Britain, with a space, top and bottom, for the area and dates of the local scrap collections – although, ironically, this leaflet itself escaped the wartime salvage drive!

57: Bottle Of Concentrated Cod Liver Oil, 1942

While the War Office kept fathers fighting at the front or the Ministry of Supply kept them hard at work in the factory, the Ministry of Health helped the nation's mothers maintain another form of essential production!

In the middle of the biggest war in history, with food shortages, bombs raining down from the sky and an uncertain future, it may seem a strange time to bring a child into the world – yet, in 1939–45, 5.3 million babies were born in Britain. By the end of the conflict, there had even been a baby boom.

In 1939, despite a foreboding and bleak outlook, many couples decided to tie the knot and have a child. By the time the baby was born, the father could be away serving in the forces, possibly not to be seen again for another five years – if at all. Meanwhile, the mother would be fending for herself and her newborn on the Home Front, with all its shortages, dangers and difficulties.

The war's start was the worst time to have a baby. Many hospital wards were evacuated for the expected mass air raid casualties, so pregnant women in towns and cities were pressured to consider evacuation. In 1939, of 1.5 million evacuees sent to the country, 524,000 were mothers with children, while 13,000 were expectant mothers. Small county hospitals could not cope with the influx, so emergency evacuation maternity homes were opened, often in the fine surroundings of stately homes or converted grand hotels.

Unfortunately, once the baby was born, mothers were occasionally billeted with unfriendly hosts or in poor conditions, sometimes even with just a drawer as a cot. Thus, many mothers drifted back to the cities – just in time for the Blitz. The

stress and shock of an air raid could bring on a premature birth, stop milk production or even cause a miscarriage. It was not unusual for babies to be born in an air raid shelter: indeed, such was the regularity, ARP shelter marshals were instructed on how to deliver babies. However, with long working days, at night, crying babies were not popular among tired shelterers trying to get what sleep they could. The lowest birth rate of the war was in 1941.

At first, mothers received no extra help. There was no such thing as designer maternity wear or extra clothing coupons. The Board of Trade's advice was simply to adjust existing clothing. The lack of wood even led to a cot and pram shortage. Expensive utility cots cost the equivalent to two weeks' wages, while an ugly box-like pram cost three. Mothers soon grew tired of carrying their babies.

With compulsory call-up into war work for women from 1941, it was feared some were becoming pregnant to avoid long hours at the factory. Critics named pregnancy the 'prevalent disease'. Indeed, there was a rise in what was termed 'illegitimate births' 'out of wedlock': in 1939, there were 32,000 such births. This figure rose after the arrival of US forces, with 650,000 born in 1942–45. Many would never see their fathers again. Some mothers also discovered that their GI boyfriend had a wife at home. Although common now, in the 1940s, when many traditional values were standard, many viewed illegitimate births as a source of embarrassment and shame.

But the increased birth rate led the government to act. From June 1940, the National Milk Scheme made subsidised or free milk available to all pregnant women or nursing mothers. In 1942, the Vitamin Welfare Scheme was extended to allow expectant and nursing mothers, plus children under five, free or cheaper bottled orange juice, cod liver oil or vitamin A and D tablets. Also, the number of hospital maternity beds rose by 50 per cent during the war.

By 1942, infant mortality was below pre-war levels and in 1944, there was a peak of 880,000 births. Despite bombs, rationing and other pressures, 1939–45 saw the arrival of a whole new generation of 'war babies'.

Expectant mothers were issued with a special green ration book – and it sometimes allowed them to jump the queue outside shops. The Ministry of Food became the mother's ally, advising: 'Concentrated orange juice, rich in Vitamin C, gives vitality and good health,' while the extra pint of milk per day was 'the perfect food', providing Vitamins A and D, giving strong bones and teeth. So successful was the scheme, by 1944, expectant mothers were consuming more milk and eggs per person than before the war. In fact, it seems sometimes they may have had it too good: the ministry complained mothers diluted the official orange juice as a light cordial for children and gave them chocolate-covered vitamin tablets as sweets. One mum even admitted to feeding her cat the official cod liver oil!

58: Royal Observer Corps Battledress Blouse, 1942

In 1940, Britain had the most comprehensive radar coverage in the world, playing a key part in the defeat of the Luftwaffe during the Battle of Britain and providing warning of bombers approaching our shores in the Blitz. So, with this technological marvel, having thousands of observers spread across remote parts of the nation during a manpower shortage may seem an odd use of resources. However, despite its usefulness, radar had one big flaw – it only looked outwards across the sea: once enemy aircraft penetrated our coastline, radar was blind. It was at this point that basic but essential piece of equipment came to the fore: what Churchill is reputedly said to have called 'the Mk I Eyeball'.

Today, a stereotypical image of Britain's Observer Corps may picture a quintessentially English scene of wellington-booted, middle-aged men standing in distant fields, peering at the sky through binoculars or a strange, framework instrument, with one ear to a field telephone. Initially, at least, this would not be far wrong. However, as the war progressed, the corps became a uniformed, professional service, responsible for monitoring the skies over Britain.

But aircraft observers were not a Second World War invention. During the previous war, the Metropolitan Observation Service had monitored German bombers and Zeppelins over the South-east. A year after the Air Raid Precautions Committee was formed, an official Observer Corps was created on 29 October 1925.

Locally, volunteers were under the jurisdiction of their county police constabulary, but from 1929 the Air Ministry took overall control.

From the beginning, the Corps' uniform was minimalist. In 1929, a round, enamel lapel badge bearing the name 'Observer Corps' and its motto 'Forewarned is Forearmed' was issued for wear on civilian clothing. By 1939, the only other identifier was a simple blue-and-white-striped embroidered Special Constable's armlet, with additional wording, 'OC' or 'Observer Corps'.

During the Battle of Britain, the corps covered radar's blind spot, providing telephoned reports to RAF Fighter Command of the direction and number of enemy aircraft over land, and giving advanced notice to scramble fighters and sound air raid sirens, thereby saving thousands of lives. Following this sterling work, on 9 April 1941, King George VI conferred the OC's name with

the prefix 'Royal' – a fitting recognition of their essential service.

The year 1942 was a key one for the corps. Women were recruited, mainly at regional control centres, but also, in limited numbers, at observer posts. Also, in May, military-style battledress was introduced, replacing boiler suits and civilian dress.

In 1944, 796 ROC members temporarily left the mainland and enrolled in the Royal Navy as 'Seaborne' aircraft identifiers, to assist anti-aircraft gunners in the D-Day flotilla [see Object 85].

By the war's end, there were forty regional ROC report centres controlling over 1,560 observer posts, with around 33,000 personnel, providing truly comprehensive coverage over the British Isles.

The war years were a very important, but relatively short, part of the ROC's story, the vast majority of its operational service occurring fifty years afterwards in the Cold War nuclear age as part of the United Kingdom Warning and Monitoring Organisation. The ROC moved from surface observation posts to small, underground monitoring bunkers, its role to measure and report nuclear explosions. With the Cold War's end, the ROC was finally stood down on 31 December 1995.

Here is an ROC battledress tunic: its internal production label reveals the maker, Debenhams, and manufacture date of 1942. Handily, the owner has added his details: Leading Observer/Post Controller Bowerman, of Post Q3, Group 4, Kidlington, Oxfordshire. It was 'posh' compared to army battledress, with shiny, nickel-plated buttons at the front fastening, pockets and cuffs. Note the five red embroidered chevrons indicating Bowerman's five years' service, the embroidered ROC badge with the RAF eagle, plus printed leading observer rank arm badges.

Using a chest telephone, Mr P.C. Austin, former Tottenham Hotspur player, reports to the 17 (Watford) Corps Group Centre, as Mr E.C. Smith works the plotting instrument in ROC post C1, at Kings Langley, Hertfordshire. (*Public Domain*)

59: Ministry Of Food Cookery Book, 1942

Those today who consume a diet of ready meals and processed foods would have been hard-pressed to survive in wartime Britain. For a start, not only was there rationing, limiting what foods were available, but there were fewer pre-packaged and ready groceries anyway: this was the 'meat and two veg' generation, who made most of their meals from scratch.

During the First World War, Britain was relatively late in dealing with the food situation. The Ministry of Food was only created in 1916 and rationing introduced less than a year before the end of the conflict. In the interwar years, Britain imported 70 per cent of its food: the government knew that as an island, the nation was only too vulnerable to sea blockades, so made far greater preparations for food rationing and storage.

The Ministry of Food was resurrected the day after war was declared, with William Morrison (1893–1961) made Minister of Food (no relation to Minister of Home Security, Herbert Morrison). However, on 3 April 1940, Neville Chamberlain replaced Morrison with Frederick Marquis, Lord Woolton (1883–1964), who would hold the important post until December 1943, when he was transferred to the Ministry of Reconstruction [see Object 98].

Woolton realised that, apart from rationing, the population also needed educating in how to obtain the most nutritious diet. This was a technical and complicated task in wartime and for this he was advised by his chief scientific adviser, Jack Drummond (1891–1952). With a staff of 15,000 employees to implement the ministry's policies, there were nineteen regional food officers in Britain, 1,500 food control committees, plus 1,300 local food offices, which distributed ration books.

The Ministry of Food produced hundreds of thousands of leaflets with handy food tips and recipes, the most famous, the colourful twenty-four-part War Cookery Leaflet series, starting in 1943. The ministry also created recognisable cartoon characters to lighten the subject, including Potato Pete, Dr Carrot and his Walt Disney relatives, Pop Carrot, Carroty George and Clara Carrot!

Community cookery demonstrations, mostly by women such as ministry home economist Marguerite Patten (1915–2015), were held in large stores, such as Harrods or at a more local level, by Food Leaders in halls. From March 1942, over 200 informative short *Food Flash* newsreels were also shown at cinemas, each reaching an audience of around twenty million.

At the same time, measures were taken to safeguard the nation's food stocks. The ministry created railway buffer depots, often in remote places, miles away from bombing targets, where food was stockpiled in quantity, such as at Lauder, near Edinburgh, which held 6,000 tons of foodstuffs.

Also, in August 1940, it became illegal to waste food, such as feeding it to pets. Though cases were rare, public examples were made, such as in 1943, when a Bristol woman was fined £10 [£400] for feeding leftover bread to birds in her garden.

The Ministry of Food was amalgamated into the Ministry of Agriculture, Fisheries and Food after the end of food rationing in 1954. However, the ministry had served the nation well. It controlled the supply of food far better in the Second World War, with prices only rising by 20 per cent, compared to 130 per cent in the previous war. Also, its food information campaigns resulted in the British population emerging healthier than it had even been before rationing in peacetime.

The Ministry of Food also broadcast a popular early morning five-minute BBC radio programme called *Kitchen Front*, from studios in Oxford Street, London, hosted by Stuart Petre Brodie Mais (1885–1975), giving quick food tips and recipes. This booklet, published in 1942, contains some of the delicacies, including black pudding hot-pot, baked stuffed sheep's hearts (sic), roast calf's head and wartime canary pudding (don't worry, no canaries were involved – custard powder gave it its yellow colour). The publishers noted: 'Our thanks are also due to Fougasse [see Object 65] for designing the cover, but we warn our readers that this is not to be taken literally as a method of saving fuel!'

60: Dried Eggs Tin, 1942

Nowadays, we have a broad range of ready meals and alternative foods at our convenience. But in the war years, food technology was used for various reasons, from preservation of rare important dietary commodities to making alternatives of rationed treats. The results were not always the most appetising or convincing, but they were nutritional – and there was little other choice!

Britain's imported food supplies were reduced almost immediately, due to the German naval blockade. By January 1941, food tonnage had fallen by half. Although officially neutral, on 11 March 1941, American President Franklin D. Roosevelt (1882–1945) introduced the Lend-Lease programme, supplying essentials, such as food and oil, to Allied nations. Following the surprise Japanese air raid on the US naval base of Pearl Harbor, in Hawaii, America entered the war on 8 December 1941. From then on, US aid began to flow in increasing volume to Britain from what Roosevelt called the 'Arsenal of Democracy'.

Nonetheless, by the middle of the war, many basic food essentials were still drastically short. Plain white flour had been replaced in February 1941 by national flour, a type of wholemeal flour with 85 per cent extraction, used to make an unpopular and largely unpalatable national loaf, which replaced white loaves.

Milk, that wartime health essential, had been rationed in its bottled form from November 1941, to a maximum of three pints per person, per week, with more for pregnant women and children. In addition, the following month, the government also introduced imported US dried household milk. Each person was entitled to one can per month. When rehydrated, each

can was the equivalent to four pints of skimmed milk.

By 1942, eggs were rationed to one per person per week. However, in July that year, canned dried (or powdered) eggs were also introduced from America to supplement the ration. Each can held the equivalent to a dozen eggs. Powdered eggs could be used in baking or even, when rehydrated, to make omelettes or scrambled egg. Unfortunately, it was not very popular, many complaining about its taste and texture.

However, the advantage of both canned dried egg and milk was that it could be stored more easily, used less stowage space and did not need refrigeration, with a shelf life of up to ten years. Indeed, this was a time before the universal use of refrigerators: for many they were a luxury item that few could afford. Most food was stored in cupboards or a pantry, a small, cool room. Housewives also used other air-tight preservation techniques, such as manual canning machines and storing soft fruit in rubber-sealed glass Kilner jars. They also sealed eggs with lard or stored them in a bucket of isinglass (fish gelatine). Eggs were also pickled in jars, as were other vegetables.

Alternatively, instead of meat, vegetarians could claim an extra egg, cheese and milk. Veganism, a plant-based diet on the rise in the twenty-first century, which abstains from most of the above, was invented by pacifist AFS fireman Donald Watson (1910–2005), of Evesham Road, Leicester, in November 1944. However, three years earlier, the head chef at London's Savoy Hotel, Francois Latry (1889–1966), invented a ration-friendly, pure vegetable dish that he named after the Minister of Food himself, Woolton Pie. Unlike meat, vegetables were unrationed and the ministry recognised their nutritional value. The pie consisted of carrots, turnips, parsnips and potatoes in an oatmeal stock, topped with a pastry crust or mashed potato, and did not need to use up any milk, egg, cheese or meat ration.

61: Blended Chocolate Bar, 1942

One commodity was considered so vital to morale that the highest authorities, from the Prime Minister to government officials and business bosses, did their best to preserve its supply – sweets! Such was the value of these sugary comforts to blitzed Brits that government and industry managed to hold off sweet rationing for two and a half years after most essential food commodities had been put on the ration. However, it would be over a decade before confectionary supplies returned to normal …

Before the war, the government had made extensive plans for the stockpiling and rationing of basic foodstuffs. However, it was the initiative of the commercial industry that addressed the supply of luxury foods. Just days before war, Woolworth chairman William Stephenson (1880–1963) and his food buyer, Bill Lacey, persuaded the Ministry of Food not to ration ice cream, biscuits and chocolate. In return, the pair stated stocks would be reserved for the urban shops facing the worst air raids.

But, by Christmas 1939, stocks of confectionary were low, as many factories were going over to war work and the machinery used to wrap and pack sweets proved useful for the munitions industry. Factory output further diminished as attacks on merchant shipping limited the supply of imported sugar and cocoa. Nevertheless, Prime Minister Churchill tried to hold out from rationing sweets as he felt it would further damage morale while the war was not going well for Britain.

Yet, it wasn't the overseas cocoa or sugar shortages that made the first major impact on chocolate, but domestic milk production. In 1941, the government banned Cadbury's from using fresh milk in their products and replaced it with dried milk, compromising their Dairy Milk

RATION CHOCOLATE

This chocolate is an excellent food, and its recipe has been adopted to make the best possible use of ingredients under wartime conditions.

CADBURY BROS. LTD.
BOURNVILLE, ENGLAND.

bar, famous for its 'glass and a half of milk in every bar' slogan. Production was in such short supply that Cadbury placed advertisements in *Picture Post* magazine [see Object 45], requesting readers to save the chocolate for children, who needed its nutrition most.

However, despite these attempts to delay the inevitable, the rationing of sweets and chocolate began on 26 July 1942. The sugar ration, and therefore sweets, fluctuated during the war, ranging from 16oz (454g) a month, down to 8oz (227g), although children were allowed a few extra ounces at Christmas [see Object 71]. Then came the dilemma on what to do: you could blow your entire month's ration on an 8oz chocolate bar (dangerous, because you could eat it all in one go!) or you could impose your own ration of 2oz of loose sweets per week. Indeed, the sweet industry tried to maintain the variety available. Names still famous today, such as Mars, Kit-Kat, Rolos, Smarties, and Crunchie were all still available at your local sweetshop, albeit with utility ingredients and packaging, as were Quality Street, Cadbury's Milk Tray and Rowntree's Dairy Box, but in smaller boxes. Children's favourites, including lemon sherbets, barley sugar twists, liquorice, jelly babies, Fry's chocolate creams, pear drops, cola cubes, aniseed balls, gobstoppers, humbugs and occasionally

toffees were still displayed in large glass sweet jars for children to ogle.

But there were shortages and so the wartime spirit of ingenuity came into play: for 6d [£1.50], five chewy liquorice root sticks, known as Spanish Wood, could be bought from the chemist. Resourceful mothers would soothe a child's sweet tooth by sweetening cakes with parsnip or carrot, or rustling up toffee apples, coconut ice, carrot fudge and mock marzipan, with canned condensed milk and honey.

The sweet status quo would last for years. Initially, the government attempted to de-ration sweets in April 1949, but demand outstripped supply and they were re-rationed after just four months. It was only on 5 February 1953 that sweet rationing finally ended, with Minister of Food Gwilym Lloyd-George (1894–1967) finally de-rationing sugar in September that year, partly as a result of pressure from sweet manufacturers.

Despite retaining established brand names, wartime chocolate was darker, rougher and more powdery than its pre-war versions. At best, it would probably be the equivalent to today's stores' own-brand economy chocolate. The Cadburys Ration Chocolate bar was made with dried skimmed milk powder to replace the Dairy Milk bar range. Though, technically, this blended chocolate was inferior, it was still a treat for sweet-starved Britons. Similarly, the packaging was also an economy version: traditional tin foil wrapping was needed for other purposes, so the bar was sold in utility waxed paper. Incidentally, my great uncle, Edward Sidney Smith, a wartime London AFS fireman, recalled seeing melted chocolate 'bubbling like lava, running down the gutters' when he attended a Blitz fire at a warehouse in the docks – a tragic waste!

62: Sylvan Flakes Washing Powder, August 1942

There was one huge forgotten home army in Britain during the war, but they wore no uniform and received no medals. Nor is there any specific history book telling of their struggle on the Home Front. Orator J. B. Priestley, in one of his BBC radio Postscripts, said: 'It is ten times harder being a decent housewife and mother during a war than it is being a soldier. You have to make a far greater effort to keep going, for you have no training and discipline to armour you… [and] women folk have more and more responsibilities piled upon them.' Slightly patronising, yes, but the point stood: the housewife's lot was now more complicated and strenuous than ever.

Today, society has changed: for economic and social reasons, there are far fewer housewives than ever in British history. But in 1939, genders were firmly divided by domestic roles and duties. The husband went out to work and was the 'breadwinner', who earned the family's income. He did the more manual jobs around the house, such as gardening and general DIY. However, the rest of the housework – chiefly, all the 'c's: cooking, cleaning and childcare – was the duty of the housewife.

Come the Second World War, it was quickly realised the housewife's workload (and stress levels) would only rise. In November 1939, the Queen broadcast to the 'women of the Empire' this message of encouragement: 'I would say to all those who are feeling the strain: be assured that in carrying on your home duties and meeting all these worries cheerfully, you are giving real service to the country. You are taking your part in keeping the Home Front, which will have dangers of its own, stable and strong.'

The war's first impact was the evacuation of children: many a mother stood tearfully at steamy stations waving her children off into the distance, not knowing even if they'd ever see them again. Other mothers took on the responsibility of other people's children, as well as their own.

Feeding the family with a varied diet became even more challenging. Even though this was generally the 'meat and two veg' generation, finding these basic ingredients – and enough of them – entailed long queues and chasing around town to patch together meals. Housewives also had to learn new cooking techniques to make food go further. It was also not unknown for the housewife to sacrifice some of her own rations for the sustenance and health of her husband and children.

Cleaning was far more laborious than today. It was taken for granted that most housewives were 'house proud': publicly mopping the doorstep was a sign of domestic pride by working-class women. Hoover stopped producing vacuum cleaners during the war, so most housewives had to make do with the rather primitive pre-war models. But not all could afford them and many used carpet sweepers, a sort of pushed, boxed rotary brush that supposedly collected crumbs up from carpets. The greater usage of wooden furniture and fittings also required increased dusting and polishing.

Nor did housewives have the luxury of programmable electronic washing machines. Most working-class wives washed clothes in a 'dolly tub', agitating the clothes with a long wooden 'peg' – essentially, a basic manual washing machine. Dirtier clothes were rubbed up and down on a corrugated washboard, then manually turned through the wooden rollers of a mangle, to wring them out. Middle-class wives used a clothes boiler or 'copper', essentially, a gas-powered dolly tub. The closest thing to a washing machine, for those who could afford them, was an electric washer, with a top-loading lid.

Once the family had been fed their evening supper and the children put to bed, the housewife had some free time. Though she may have been exhausted, while sitting in the living room with her husband listening to the radio, she would unpick wool from worn clothes and knit it into new garments, such as jumpers, or darn clothes to make them last longer.

On top of all this, some housewives even volunteered for part-time work in the WVS [see Object 75] or ARP. Additionally, by 1943, 80 per cent of married women had been conscripted into war work. But, with the war's end, although they had shown their ability to do a variety of men's jobs, most had to leave these jobs for returning soldiers, though few begrudged a serviceman returning to the job he had been conscripted away from. In this way, the housewife also returned to her pre-war duties.

Clothes washing was tiresome. Soda crystals or solid blocks of soap led to worn hands. But gradually, more brands of washing powder – such as this wartime box of Sylvan Flakes, with its 'Do not destroy this carton, put it with other waste paper for the salvage collector' instruction – became available to help the housewife. There is an unusual story connected to this brand. Six days before the disastrous Allied landing at Dieppe, France, on 19 August 1942, when 1,524 Allied servicemen were killed, an advert for Sylvan Flakes appeared in newspapers with the heading 'BEACH COAT from DIEPPE'. An over-analysing agent at the Political Warfare Executive suggested that the six buttons on the coat pictured in the advert was code that the raid was in six days, while the word 'coat' was short for 'combined operations at'. Scotland Yard and MI5 investigated both the makers of Sylvan Flakes and the Graham and Gillies advertising agency. They deduced it was all an unfortunate coincidence.

63: Der Fuehrer's Face Song Sheet, 1942

Today, if you hear a tune you like, you can download it at the click of a button and it's yours to listen to, whenever and wherever you want. In the 1940s, it wasn't so easy. You could wait and hope to hear a tune on the radio or perhaps buy the record, which was still something of a novelty. Alternatively, you could do-it-yourself. For 6d [£1.50], you could purchase the song sheet, complete with the words and music score, as many homes, pubs, clubs, even air raid shelters, had a piano, which helped banish the blues away. Decades before karaoke, this DIY ethos was common to millions of Britons.

As with CDs and vinyl, artists and music publishers also relied on the income from song sheets but, unlike today, songwriters always received a credit on the cover. Also unlike today, the focus was often more on the song than the artist, so several singers performed the same tune. With colourful and jovial covers, often with witty lyrics, as war economy bit, song sheets became thinner and half the size. Interestingly however, their themes charted the course of the war and the popular mood: full of bravado, defiance, sentimentality, fun and romance, plus a big helping of humour – but all were written and designed to boost morale.

The war's start in 1939 saw some of the conflict's most memorable tunes. Pumped up and patriotic, their titles, such as *Somewhere in France With You* (performed by Joe Loss and His Orchestra), *Kiss Me Goodnight Sergeant-Major* (Renee Houston & Donald Stewart) and *The Washing On the Siegfried Line* (Billy Cotton and His Band) sounded straight from the First World War. The biggest hit though was *There'll Always Be an England* (Glyn Davies), which

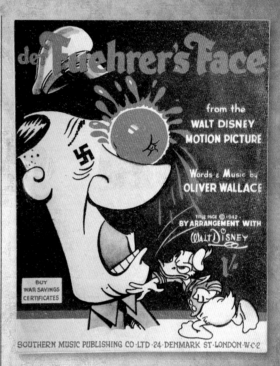

SOUTHERN MUSIC PUBLISHING CO·LTD·24·DENMARK ST·LONDON·W·C·2

sold 200,000 song sheets in two months. As the Phoney War continued in 1940, other favourites were *In the Quartermaster's Stores* (Al and Bob Harvey) and *Tiggerty-Boo! The Forces Thumbs-Up Song* (Joe Loss and His Band).

As the Blitz broke on Britain in 1940, songs such as *Meet Me in the Air Raid Shelter* (Bobby Telford), *London I Cannot Leave You* (by Tunney & Foley), and later in 1941, *London Pride* (by Noel Coward) plus *The King is Still in London* (Billy Cotton and His Band) [See Object 47] exuded Blitz Spirit.

War news was also covered in 1940, with singer Florence Desmond poking fun at dictator Mussolini after Italy's surprise defeats by Greece with *Oh! What a Surprise for the Du-Ce!* The year after, Bebe Daniels praised American Lend-Lease policy with *Thanks, Mr Roosevelt!* But in

1942, when the war was not going so well for Britain, de Lange and Stept reminded the nation *This is Worth Fighting For*. Although Churchill liked Noel Coward's 1943 dry humour hit *Don't Let's Be Beastly to the Germans*, the irony was lost on many listeners, with the song initially banned by the BBC following complaints. On the other hand, 1944 hit *Lilli Marlene* was the war's only song popular in both Britain and Germany, despite its creation by the latter.

The arrival of the Americans had a big influence of British pop culture, as reflected in songs such as *G.I. Jive* (Johnny Mercer) in 1943 or *Got Any Gum Chum?* (Billy Cotton and His Band) in 1944. The already popular swing and early rock'n'roll sounds performed by big bands reached a peak with bandleaders such as Tommy Dorsey, Artie Shaw and Woody Herman, but it was Major Glenn Miller who led the pack [see Object 89].

Since 1941, several songs had alluded to the war's end, such as *When They Sound the Last All Clear* (Dorothy Ward), *There's a Land of Begin Again* (Jack Payne & His Orchestra), 1943's *I'm Going to Get Lit-Up* (Caroll Gibbons) and 1944's *When We're All Together Again* (Doris Hare), but ironically, when the war ended, there were very few songs extolling victory.

Britain's most prolific singer was East Londoner Dame Vera Lynn (1917–), whose hits spanned the course of the war, including *We'll Meet Again* (1939), *A Nightingale Sang in Berkeley Square* and *It's a Lovely Day Tomorrow* (1940), *(There'll be Blue Birds Over) the White Cliffs of Dover* (1941), *When the Lights Go on Again (All Over the World)* (1942), *Be Like the Kettle And Sing* (1943) and *I'll Be Seeing You* (1944), while in the latter years she toured the Far East performing her songs as the 'Forces Sweetheart'.

Incidentally, classical music saw a resurgence, though not necessarily mainstream, with sheet music by all the main composers selling well. New compositions, such as Richard Addinsell's 1942 *Theme From the Warsaw Concerto* and author A. P. Herbert's 1940 *Song of Liberty* to music by Elgar, also proved popular.

The unsubtle cover for the 1942 hit *Der Fuehrer's Face*, by Oliver Wallace, reflects the song's craziness, which was hugely popular on both sides of the Atlantic, recorded by comedian Tommy Trinder (1908–89) in Britain and bandleader Spike Jones (1911–65) in America. The lyrics, sung in a mock German accent, were interspersed with raspberries blown during the chorus: '*Ven der Fuehrer says 'Ve iss der Master Race', ve Heil! Heil! Right in der Fuehrer's face. Not to luff der Fuehrer iss a great disgrace, so ve Heil! Heil! Right in der Fuehrer's face.*' Not the most sophisticated of satires, but it was a satisfying thumb to the nose at 'Der Fuehrer'.

64: The Home Front Children's Book, 1942

Innocence and a lack of worldly experience may be a hindrance as an adult, but as a child in wartime it was a partial blessing. For children, the war was a bewildering mixture of excitement, fun and frights. And, even more bizarrely, despite all the hardships, many who were wartime children later testified that the war years were the greatest time of their lives, with a sense of togetherness, adventure and exhilaration.

With no television or computer games to burn up the hours, children had to find their own amusements. Despite a shortage of toys, books and games, there was still, surprisingly, plenty to see and do. For a start, whereas before the war, aeroplanes had largely been a novelty on the cinema screen, now, there was a seemingly myriad amount of different types in the skies over Britain – thankfully, most of them 'ours'. Plane-spotting became an obsession of boys. Similarly, with the demands of war production, the nation's railways were busier than ever, becoming a magnet for young trainspotters. A convoy of tanks or soldiers on manoeuvres also always attracted a group of youthful onlookers, as often witnessed in the background of wartime photos and films.

Bombsites became adventure playgrounds for children, who would often complete the damage caused by Hitler's bombs. Indeed, shrapnel collecting and souvenir swapping practically became a currency of the young, rather like football stickers did for later generations.

There was also a chance to make new friends, or, initially at least, some foes. Small village schools suddenly became packed with evacuees, so much so, some teaching days were split in half, with local children having lessons in the morning and the evacuees in the afternoon. These newcomers, with their different accents and upbringings, often seemed like outsiders impinging on local life, sometimes resulting in friction. However, after a few months of fraternisation, generally, all got along, occasionally leading to lifelong friendships. Many teachers were called up into the forces and were often replaced by their predecessors

called out of retirement, who proved to be either a pushover in class or Victorian, strict and only too keen to wield the cane.

There were also far more youth organisations than today. By far the largest were the Boy Scouts, who eagerly embraced the war effort. More than 60,000 Scouts over the age of fourteen were awarded the Scout National Service badge. Scout civil defence and war service badges were also introduced. In 1939, there were 530,000 Girl Guides in Britain and they too contributed towards the war effort, from knitting comforts to collecting salvage. Other specifically wartime services, such as, from 1941, the Girls Training Corps, prepared teenagers for life in the services. Also, from summer 1940, counties set up their own Youth Service squads, who also aided the Home Front.

Incidentally, it shouldn't be forgotten that there wasn't really any such thing as 'teenagers' before the 1960s. Children were dressed as little adults in suits, albeit sometimes with shorts, or smart dresses: T-shirts and jeans were mainly imported into British post-war culture from America.

Children generally left school at fourteen years old to go straight into the world of work to become apprentices or fill the vacancies left empty by those who had joined the forces. They also served in the ARP as messengers, facing the same dangers as the adults. By 1945, nearly 80 per cent of boys and 70 per cent of girls aged fourteen to seventeen worked full-time in jobs ranging from agriculture and retail, to office and industry. From 1941, all boys and girls aged sixteen to eighteen had to register for national service, even if they had a full-time job. At eighteen, boys had to join the armed services and girls the auxiliary services or other essential work. Then, their youthful innocence ended as they became adults – and experienced the actualities of war.

Just how do you explain a world war and its effects to a young child? In a spirited manner, twenty-seven-year-old *Daily Express* war reporter Hilde Marchant told children how the adults were keeping the home fires burning (or not) in her 1942 book *The Home Front*, published by popular wartime publishers, Raphael Tuck & Sons Ltd [see Object 68]. Marchant described the civilian services and the air raids, but, interestingly, did not mention deaths. Her book proved so successful, it was published in two editions, a larger with colour illustrations and a smaller with photos. She concluded her book:

Though the raids subsided after many months, the firm and steady anger of the women of Britain did not. They planned their future revenge by their hard-working hands. Now they support the Home Front, while the expanding army takes away the men of the cities and villages. They have been left in charge of the civil life of Britain. Week by week, they rise to take their place in factories, civil defence … This is total war, you say, Hitler? The men and women of Britain will give their total effort to defeat you.

Marchant was a hard-working journalist, described by her former editor Arthur Christiansen as 'the best woman reporter who ever worked in Fleet Street'. Yet, today, she is largely forgotten, having died destitute after collapsing under a railway arch.

65: Comic Art, 1942

At first glance, the concept might seem quite simple: how can just a few lines and squiggles drawn on a page be influential? But cartoons proved immensely popular in print and film during the war. Their eye-catching allure was used on the Home Front to attract observers of all ages and inform, entertain, amuse, and even change public perception. In the battle for message and morale, the artist's pen was mightier than the sword.

American colour cartoon films, made by Walt Disney (1901–66), such as *Pinocchio* and *Fantasia* (1940), *Dumbo* (1941) and *Bambi* (1942) were escapist works that diverted the minds of children and adults from the war. Other cartoon characters, such as Bugs Bunny, Donald Duck and Daffy Duck, were all deliberately recruited to aid the war effort [see Object 63].

Britain's national newspapers carried a daily cartoon, usually a political satire, which often said as much as a full article of words. Artists included the *Daily Express* cartoonists Carl Giles (1916–95) and Sidney Strube (1892–1956). The war's most powerful and controversial cartoon was drawn in 1942 by the *Daily Mirror*'s Philip Zec (1909–83), showing a torpedoed sailor adrift, captioned: 'The price of petrol has been increased by one penny. Official.' It was meant to be an anti-waste message, but the government thought it was accusing the petrol companies of profiteering. Churchill had MI5 investigate Zec and the *Daily Mirror* was almost closed. However, Zec later produced the war's most famous newspaper cartoon on VE Day, showing an injured soldier holding a peace garland, saying 'Here you are! Don't lose it again.'

Cartoon characters, such as Firebomb Fritz and the Squander Bug [see Object 76], were

effectively used in propaganda. Fougasse, pen name of Cyril Kenneth Bird (1887–1965), produced numerous wartime posters, most notably his eight *Careless Talk Costs Lives* designs, all with a humorous cartoon featuring Hitler. These were also published in his book *… And the Gatepost* (1940). His cartoon observations of the Home Front featured in *Running Commentary* and *The Little Less* (1941), *Sorry No Rubber* (1942), *Just a Few Lines* (1943) *and Family Group* (1944). Other British propagandist and *Punch* cartoonist David Langdon (1914–2011), famous for his *Mr Brown of London Town* cartoon posters, advised passengers of blackout precautions on the London Underground, while his Half Trained Harry character appeared on Fire Guard training posters. Langdon also published books of his funnies, including *Home Front Lines* (1941), *Meet Me Inside* (1941), *It's a Piece of Cake* (1943) and *According to Plan* (1945).

Less famous, Dr S. Evelyn Thomas, better known for his ARP instruction manuals [see Object 36], also showed he had a not so serious, humorous side, publishing a series of cartoon compilation *Laughs With ...* booklets, featuring titles with *ARP, Home Guard, Home Front, RAF, Navy, the Forces, the Land, Workers* and *the Line.*

Of course, children have always been fascinated by cartoons. Asides from those shown on Saturday mornings at the cinema, cartoon characters were the cornerstone of comics. The humour was anarchic and the gloves were truly off for 'baddies' such as Hitler and Mussolini. Each comic had its lead characters, some whose names will prove familiar, others who have now been lost to time. *Beano* featured Eggo the Ostrich and Musso the Wop ('He's A Big-A-Da Flop'); *Comic Cuts* featured Plum and Duff; *Dandy* featured cow pie-eating cowboy Desperate Dan and Korky the Cat; *Illustrated Chips* featured Casey Court, Weary Willie and Tired Tim; *Knock-Out* featured Our Ernie, The Gremlins, Our Happy Vaccies (evacuees), plus Home Guard heroes Sandy and Muddy; *The*

Magic featured Vicky the Vacky and Koko the Pup; *Radio Fun* featured stars Tommy Handley and Arthur Askey; *Rover* featured Nosey Parker; *The Magnet* featured ever-hungry Billy Bunter; *Tiger Tim's Weekly* featured the Bruin Boys and *Tiny Tots* featured the Comical Kittens.

There were even comic books for grown-ups, featuring, shall we say, more adult-orientated humour, such as *A Basinful of Fun, Men Only* and *Razzle. Jane,* a cartoon strip in the *Daily Mirror*, was based on model Chrystabel Leighton-Porter (1903–2000), whose clothes kept falling off, but brought cheer in wartime – Churchill even calling her 'Britain's secret weapon'.

A lesser-known but interesting regional cartoonist was Arthur Joseph Keene (1900–86), pen name 'Van Art'. Coventry-born Keene was a fine artist who decorated Riley Cars in the city. However, he became best known locally for his humorous cartoons depicting life on the Home Front. His illustrations reached peak fame in 1942, when his work was to be brought to a wider audience via 20,000 copies of a booklet called *Going to It!*, mimicking the stresses of life in war factories. However, wartime paper restrictions resulted in only a fraction printed, making it a rare book now. Nonetheless, Keene's art brought many smiles to war-weary Midlanders and examples of his work now reside in London's Imperial War Museum. Incidentally, art runs in the family: both his son, also Arthur, and now his grandson, Los Angeles-based Tobias, are renowned artists.

66: Royal Ordnance Factory Shell Gauge, 1942

The interwar drive for peace meant that when another world war came along in 1939, Britain was woefully unprepared to fight it. Short of adequate arms and ammunition, the government instituted a programme of building Royal Ordnance Factories (ROF), quadrupling their number during the war years. It was left to thousands of civilian workers to fuel the guns on the front line. However, despite strict safety measures, it was still one of the most dangerous jobs on the Home Front.

Before the British Army's defeat at Dunkirk, there were only eleven ROFs in Britain producing armaments. With the country now facing a German invasion, Britain had to boost its arsenal and in the space of three months, the armaments industry became leading employers, taking on 80,000 new employees, most of them women. Over the next five years, over thirty new munitions factories were built across Britain, largely, for safety reasons, in remote parts of the country, such as Wales or northern England, further away from the risk of air raids.

There were three main types of ROF: engineering works, explosives manufacturing, and shell-filling. As the war developed and Britain moved on to the offensive, the demand for arms and ammunition grew. The engineering works manufactured different and larger types of guns, the explosives establishments also produced content for RAF Bomber Command's increasing campaign and the shell-filling factories produced millions of shells for the coming invasion of Europe.

To meet this demand, by 1942, forty ROFs employed around 300,000 workers, up to 80 per cent of who were women, working up to fifty-eight hours a week on shifts. There were ten shell-filling factories, nine explosives plants and twenty-four engineering works. The work was tough, exacting and dangerous: although many of the ROFs had their own railway stations, their remote locations sometimes meant early starts and late arrivals home. ROF sites were huge: for example, ROF Filling Factory No. 1, at Chorley, Lancashire, employed 28,000 workers in 1,500 buildings over a 928-acre site, which had a 9-mile perimeter fence, complete with its own military defences.

Although this work was well-paid, an element of it was danger money. However, safety precautions were extensive. To avoid sparks, workers changed into clothes with no metal buttons but were tied instead. Workers had to empty their pockets of any coins, remove watches and rings. But even following procedure, accidents did happen, with 134 workers killed and many

more maimed. Some seventy-four awards were made for gallantry to ROF workers, with thirty of them at ROF Kirkby alone. On 15 September 1944, an explosion occurred during the packing of cluster bombs, killing fourteen workers at the shell-filling factory on Merseyside. Consequently, twenty-four bravery awards were made to the workers, including a George Medal to Richard Bywater (1913–2005), the only civilian to be awarded both the George Cross and George Medal.

By 1943, ROF production was so copious, Britain ran out of underground storage, so shells and ammunition were kept under tarpaulins or roadside Nissen huts in country lanes. However, even the supposedly safe official underground storage ammunition depots were not without accident. The worst incident occurred at 11.11 am on 27 November 1944 at the RAF Fauld underground storage facility near Burton-on-Trent, Staffordshire. A careless accident sparked an enormous explosion, detonating 4,000 tons of bombs. A farm completely disappeared into a half-mile wide crater and seventy-eight workers and 200 cattle were killed, in the largest explosion in British history. The crater remains today.

A lesser-known aspect is chemical weapons production. Although all the major powers had signed the 1925 Geneva Protocol that forbade the use of poison gas, the treaty did not prevent its manufacture. The Allies and the Axis both secretly mass-produced huge stockpiles. The two main British production plants were ICI factories at Runcorn, Cheshire, and Rhydymwyn,

Women working in the Royal Ordnance Factory at Fazakerley, near Liverpool, during 1943, assembling breech blocks for Sten sub machine-guns. (*Public Domain*)

North Wales. Here, mustard gas was produced and stored in large quantities. Civilian workers had to wear full protective suits and gas masks in case of leaks, which did occur, fortunately, with few casualties.

The engraved writing on the back of this 14in-long ROF gauge tool reveals that it was made in October 1940 for measuring the depth of the cavity in shells and bombs. This was to ensure that the shell had been cast correctly and there were no internal faults. With a sliding measure in inches, as a safety feature it is made of bronze to be spark-proof. I wonder how many shells its user inspected during their wartime ROF service?

67: Polished 'V' Coal, 1942

Coal: we now understand that this fossil fuel has a detrimental carbon emission effect on the planet. But back in wartime, the number one priority was to win the war and as coal was the nation's chief source of power, it was an essential war-winning commodity. Coal fed the power stations. Coal fed the steel mills. Coal made the gas that supplied the cookers, which fed the war workers. Britain would not have been able to win the war without coal – and the men who mined it.

Before the war, the nation's mining industry was so large, Britain exported surplus coal to the Continent. However, the industry's success was not all it seemed and trouble was brewing. The mines had an ageing labour force, as younger men were not coming into the industry. Before 1939, 25 per cent of miners were aged twenty-

five to thirty-five. By 1945, this had dropped to 18 per cent, even with the conscription of younger miners. The government also made an error in the early years of the war, directing younger miners into the armed forces. There were 766,000 miners in 1939, but this fell to 709,000 in 1942. These factors, coupled with the greater demand for coal to feed the expanding war effort, piled pressure on to an already stretched mining workforce, with coal production dropping from 231 million tons in 1939 to 206 million tons in 1941.

In December 1943, the Minister of Labour and National Service, Labour politician Ernest Bevin, a former trade union official, tried to circumvent the decline by introducing the 'Bevin Boy' scheme. Some 10 per cent of young men, aged eighteen to twenty-five, waiting to be

conscripted into the armed forces were diverted into the mines. A small proportion, such as conscientious objectors, also volunteered as an alternative to military service. This random ballot also meant those who were not necessarily cut out for life underground also joined the mining workforce. They were not always welcomed by the miners or mining communities. In total, nearly 48,000 Bevin Boys served in the collieries. They were not released from service until March 1948 and received no recognition or medal, until retrospectively, on 25 March 2008, the sixtieth anniversary of the end of their service, a Bevin Boy veterans' lapel badge was awarded to veterans.

As they had been for centuries, the mine owners were private companies. Miners' pay was twenty-third in the table of British workers and it was alleged that the mine owners had made minimal investment in mechanical coal cutting, meaning mining was still largely laborious and by hand. On 2 January 1942, all 4,000 miners came out on strike at Betteshanger Colliery, in Kent, even though it was illegal to do so under Defence Regulation 58AA. A token handful were imprisoned. Similarly, two years later, when the government did not immediately recognise a tribunal's recommendation for a pay rise, over 250,000 miners went on strike. Neither side really budged and coal production continued to dwindle to the war's end.

Conditions underground were not the only dangers miners faced. The Luftwaffe also deliberately targeted collieries. Indeed, pits were sites of such importance that most had their own Home Guard units, comprised of the miners themselves.

Again, Churchill believed that compulsion would be bad for morale, so coal was never rationed during the war. Instead, a *Save Fuel for Battle* poster campaign chided Britons for coal-draining faux pas, in their homes for having more than 5in of water in the bath or using too much coal on the fire, and in the factory for leaving machines running or being 'fuel-ish', leaving too many lights on. From January 1943, Fuel Watchers were appointed in factories, offices and other commercial establishments to encourage fuel economy in the workplace. The campaign worked and by 1944 British homes were using 11 million tons or three-quarters less coal than in 1938. However, houses were much colder and less homely during the war.

In 1942, author Charles Graves stated in a national magazine: 'Coal is the life-blood of Britain's war industries.' This 5in by 3in polished lump of 300 million-year-old anthracite coal has the letter 'V' (for victory), with its Morse code symbol above [see Object 52], together with the date '1942' engraved on its smooth face. In this case, the exact significance of the date, if there is any, is unknown, as is its source, possibly made by an off-duty miner. However, this poignant shiny ebony souvenir reminds us that not all the important battles of the Second World War were fought above ground on the traditional battlefield. Men also battled in grim and dangerous conditions underground – with, shockingly, on average, around 900 miners a year dying in mining accidents – to feed the war effort and ensure victory.

68: Our Railways In War-Time Book, 1942

For around a century, up until the Beeching cuts of the 1960s, plus the mass expansion of car ownership and road haulage, Britain's railways were the nation's transport arteries, enabling the movement of passengers and goods to every corner of the country. In 1940, the nation's rail network composed of 50,555 miles of track, with a route mileage of 19,131 (around double that of today), plus 6,698 passenger stations, 6,908 goods stations and 581,401 staff. Unlike today, it was cheap, affordable and reliable. But, the Second World War would prove to be this vital network's greatest test.

The railways were instantly put on a war footing. Control of the network was passed to the Railway Executive Committee from the 'big four' rail companies, the London, Midland and Scottish Railway (LMS), London and North Eastern Railway (LNER), Great Western Railway (GWR) and Southern Railway (SR), plus the numerous small local branch line companies.

In the first year of the war, the demand was the movement of people: in one weekend in September 1939, over 1.3 million children were evacuated from the cities to the countryside in 3,000 special trains. Nine months later, 600 special trains moved around 319,000 Allied troops that had been evacuated from Dunkirk to camps and hospitals across Britain.

Soon after, station names were painted out to confuse invaders (and it didn't help travellers, either), plus blackouts were introduced on trains and in stations as an ARP measure. The Luftwaffe deliberately targeted track, trains and stations, destroying 482 locomotives and damaging 13,314 passenger carriages and 16,132 freight trucks. However, both track and stations were repaired quite quickly by the many labourers employed on the network. Indeed, many railwaymen were excluded from military service because railway work was a reserved occupation essential to the war effort, although many joined up nonetheless.

Their jobs were filled by women recruits, whose number reached a peak of 105,703 in 1943. Women did pretty much every manual job, from porter and station announcers to oilers and greasers, except drive the train.

Demand on the railways increased as Britain's industrial output grew and the nation moved on to the offensive, with the number of locomotives in service peaking at 19,625 in 1942, though many were repaired stock. The number of freight trains more than doubled, from 20,888 in 1940 to 45,583 in 1943, as the railways transported everything from troops and industrial workers, to new tanks and aircraft, to scrap metal and fresh vegetables. They also helped power the nation, moving at least 3 million gallons of oil and petrol per day and 4 million tons of coal per week. All this additional freight impacted on domestic passenger services, which were reduced and often delayed. As a result, travel for leisure was heavily discouraged during the war [see Object 80].

The railways were essential in the supply and success of the Allies' D-Day invasion in 1944 [see Object 85]. In the two months prior, the railways ran 24,459 special trains, conveying troops, stores and ammunition, reaching a peak in the preceding three weeks – one of which saw the record total of 3,636 trains.

Word must be made of the courage of the locomotive footplate crew, namely the drivers and firemen. As well as facing air attack, at night they operated almost blind, with no radios or electronic warnings, not knowing if the track ahead had been bombed: a single crater could cause the train to be suddenly derailed with resultant fatalities. It was on 2 June 1944 that an ammunition train exploded in Soham, Cambridgeshire, after a spark from the locomotive ignited bombs. Greater disaster was averted as the crew separated the burning carriage, but engine fireman James Nightall and signalman Frank Bridges were both killed in the explosion. The driver, Benjamin Gimbert, and Nightall were awarded the George Cross for preventing a greater explosion. In total, 395 railway staff were killed and over 2,400 injured on duty.

When peace came, it was not just railway staff who were exhausted: the overused track and rolling stock were worn out. They had seen more service than at any time in history. In an attempt to get the nation's network back on track, the railways were nationalised on 1 January 1948.

Numerous books were published during the war recognising the importance of Britain's railways. Once again, Raphael Tuck & Sons Ltd, 'Publishers to Their Majesties the King and Queen and Queen Mary', stepped up to the mark, producing in 1942 probably the most impressive, if not the most colourful, picture book on the subject, *Our Railways in War-time*, written by Cecil J. Allen and illustrated by Roland Davies. Allen wrote: 'When the record of this greatest of all wars comes to be written, and it is possible to tell the full story, it will be realised that British railways have played a magnificent part in bringing the war to a successful conclusion.' So successful was the book, a smaller, thinner, economy version, *My Train Book*, was also published.

Incidentally, the publishers also had a tough war. Started in 1866 by German Raphael Tuck, their heyday was in Victorian times, when they made their fortune publishing postcards and greetings cards. However, on the night of the 'Second Great Fire of London', 29 December 1940, their headquarters, Raphael House, off Tenter Street, Aldgate, was burned out, destroying seventy-four years of records, including over 40,000 original illustrations and photographs. The company never fully recovered and merged in 1959.

69: Postcard From A British Prisoner Of War, 1942

Churchill later ruminated: 'Before Alamein we never had a victory. After Alamein, we never had a defeat.' It is true that, for Britain, the Egyptian Battle of El Alamein, in November 1942, was the famous turning point of the war. It is also true that before this crux, Britain and her Commonwealth forces suffered several big losses: in 1940, Norway, France and Belgium; in 1941, in Greece and the Mediterranean and in 1942, in the Far East, hundreds of thousands of British troops were captured by the Japanese and became prisoners of war. For both the captured and their relatives, it would be the start of several long years of limbo, separation and worry.

Over 170,000 British and Commonwealth serviceman became PoWs in German-controlled territory. However, as Germany and Italy were signatories to the 1929 Geneva Convention, British PoWs were treated relatively well, especially when compared with their Russian counterparts. British officers sent to Oflag camps were not required to work, were treated with greater respect and were allowed some extra privileges. Other army ranks were sent to Stalag camps. RAF airmen were sent to Stalag Luft camps, Royal Navy personnel to Marlag camps and Merchant Navy prisoners to Milag camps. As a neutral intermediary, based in Geneva, Switzerland, the International Red Cross was allowed access to deliver mail and food parcels to PoWs.

PoW camps were remote and strictly guarded. Contrary to the movies, only around 1,200 prisoners – less than 1 per cent – managed to escape back to Britain. Although there were

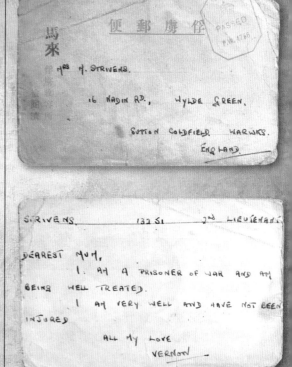

exceptions, escapers, especially if caught in civilian clothing, could be summarily shot. However, brave Europeans risked their lives to help run escape lines to try and smuggle Allied PoWs home.

On the other hand, those 190,000 British and Commonwealth troops captured by the Japanese in the Far East would receive a very different PoW experience. Japanese military philosophy held that anyone surrendering was beneath contempt and, as Japan did not sign the Geneva Convention, their troops felt no obligation to treat their prisoners humanely. Similarly, the International Red Cross had very little access to the camps and the Japanese withheld aid parcels and post. Many Japanese PoW camps had no fences, because as they were located so deep in the jungle, escape was virtually impossible. Besides, Allied PoWs were so malnourished, ill and worked to exhaustion, they were in no fit state to make an escape. During the construction of the infamous 258-mile Burma railway, 61,000 Allied prisoners were used as slave labour to build a Japanese military railway between Ban Pong in Thailand and Thanbyuzayat in Burma. Over 12,000 PoWs died in its construction and were buried in the Far East.

News of the outside world was withheld from the PoWs: for all they knew, Britain may have been invaded or their relatives killed in an air raid. But, it worked both ways: the first PoWs knew of the Japanese capitulation in 1945 was when British forces suddenly arrived at the gates of their camp and the Japanese guards laid down their arms. However, 24.8 per cent of British PoWs would not be going home – they had died due to their harsh captivity (compared to 3.5 per cent under German captivity). Those that did return were shockingly skeletal in their appearance. In time, they would recover in hospital: however, the mental scars and nightmares would remain for the rest of their lives.

Meanwhile, at home, relatives could support regimental or county PoW funds, which would organise, collect and send comforts to those in camps. In return, these groups would try to use their connections to acquire any extra news about the PoWs. Being a relative of a PoW was also very stressful, not knowing of their health, welfare or future. It must have constantly played on their mind. In March 1942, the British Prisoners of War Relatives Association was formed to provide some support for the families of PoWs, organising activities such as children's Christmas parties or sending cigarettes to PoWs.

When the war ended in 1945, there was much relief and many happy reunions. One woman recognised her husband's footsteps walking down the drive, even after several years of separation.

This meagre, worn and undated postcard was received by Mrs M. Strivens, of Sutton Coldfield, Warwickshire, from her son, 13251 2nd Lieutenant Vernon Strivens, on his capture, via the International Red Cross. The wording was deliberately sparse, so there was less for the Japanese censors to translate. How well the prisoners were being treated was debateable and there is the thought they could hardly write the opposite. Strivens' nephew recalled:

It was a subject he very rarely spoke about. After finishing his schooling in England, Vernon decided to follow in his father's footsteps and went to Malaya to become a rubber planter. As I understand, when war broke out, I think he joined the Free Malay army and was captured by the Japanese, where he was sent to work on the Burma Railway. I do know he suffered terrible illnesses in captivity, including Beri, Malaria and Dysentery, plus general humiliation and ill health. However, he survived the war and returned to Malaya after the war to continue his career.

70: The Beveridge Report, December 1942

As a young man, William Beveridge (1879–1963) had worked as a researcher in London's East End, where he witnessed first-hand the poverty and unemployment. Between the wars, Beveridge was the director of the London School of Economics. In June 1941, he was appointed as chairman of the government's Social Insurance Committee. Beveridge used his position to address what he identified as the five 'Giant Evils' in society: squalor, ignorance, want, idleness, and disease.

Beveridge knew that to overcome inequality and poverty, he had a huge challenge on his hands. His proposals would not be a free handout, but paid for by individuals' contributions to social insurance. In turn, the state would provide a minimum standard of living if the individual's ability to earn was interrupted by illness, old age or unemployment.

To ensure governmental infrastructure could implement his ideas, Beveridge proposed an overhaul and rationalisation of the old benefits system. But it was the new tenets of his report that were the most radical and popular with the public. He recommended a new state allowance for the welfare of children, a national health service 'available to all members of the community ... without a charge on treatment at any point', plus 'full' use of the state's powers to maintain employment and tackle unemployment. Essentially, the state would look after its citizens from the cradle (maternity grants) to the grave (funeral grants).

The government, however, wanted Beveridge's report published after the war, but he insisted that his findings were a war aim, saying 'the purpose of victory is to live in a better world than the old world', and, nudging the government,

said: 'each individual citizen is more likely to concentrate upon his war effort if he feels that his government will be ready with plans for that better world'. So, on 1 December 1942, Beveridge's report was published. It was an instant hit. The BBC broadcast extracts in twenty-two languages and the national press covered it in detail. Mass Observation found that 88 per cent of the population approved and thought that the government should implement it.

Although the Beveridge Report was popular with the public, many MPs were hesitant. Officially, Churchill and the Conservatives approved of it, though quietly, many thought it

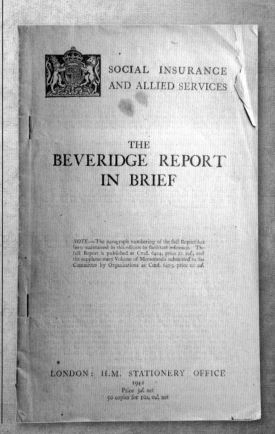

unaffordable Utopia or even a sort of communism by the backdoor. Surprisingly, Labour, well-known campaigners for social justice, were also lukewarm about the report, believing it would steal the unions' thunder. Only Home Secretary Herbert Morrison showed any enthusiasm: when challenged 'Can we afford to do this?' he replied, 'Can we afford not to do it?'

Eventually, the government accepted sixteen of Beveridge's twenty-three recommendations 'in principle'. But it started the ball rolling for social reform in Britain. By 1944, the government had produced a series of white papers to enact the Beveridge Report. Not only that, but also in that year a new Education Act was passed. It was, in the words of Beveridge, going to be 'a people's war for a people's peace'. Writing of the Second World War, historian A. J. P. Taylor stated that it was 'a brief period in which the English

people felt they belonged to a truly democratic community'.

This may look like another of the thousands of rather dull, yellowed official government tracts that were printed on thin economy paper during the war years, but its significance was anything but bland. The night before its publication, long queues formed outside the headquarters of His Majesty's Stationery Office, in Kingsway, London, to buy a copy of the 300-page report. Together with this sixty-three-page resumé of the report, over 635,000 copies were purchased by war-weary citizens all over Britain. Why? Because it was a symbol of hope, of better things to come and a decent quality of life – for all Britons. It was the foundation of what became known as the Welfare State and its significance was so resounding that over seventy-five years later we all still benefit from its implementation.

William Beveridge (1879–1963), author of the Social Insurance and Allied Services report, pictured in 1943.

71: Christmas Carol Songbook, December 1942

Christmas has always been a traditional celebration of light among the darkness and in wartime it gained extra importance – though, despite its holy significance, it too, could not escape the impact of war. Families were still faced with the shortages, losses and separations, just as any other day of the year. But extra effort went into making it a special family occasion, come what may.

There was little difference between pre-war Christmases and that of Britain's first wartime one in 1939. With the Phoney War in full swing and no fighting at the front, most menfolk were still based in Britain and were given forty-eight hours' leave to spend Christmas with their loved ones. It was also still a month before rationing would be introduced, so turkeys and other food luxuries were still in good supply. Many of the toy factories had not been fully turned over to war production, so gifts for children were still widely available in the shops, usually with a military theme, from model barrage balloons and wooden aircraft to tin soldiers. The only real fly in the ointment was one of the worst blizzards in memory, with drifts 6ft deep, that lasted into the new year. However, 1939 would be the last plentiful Christmas of the war.

Christmases became bleaker as wartime hardships took their toll. The iconic ten-minute propaganda newsreel *Christmas Under Fire*, by the Ministry of Information's Crown Film Unit, showed plucky Britons cheerfully celebrating while sheltering in the London Underground. Narrated by famous American journalist Quentin Reynolds (1902–65), it was made mainly for his home audience, but captured the

spirit of Christmas 1940. For four days at least, the Nazis observed the unwritten Christmas truce [see Object 40].

During the remainder of the war years, Christmas largely stayed the same. People still exchanged Christmas cards, although the distances they were sent were greater and, with paper restrictions, the cards were smaller.

The traditional midnight mass was held during the day to avoid blackout accidents, but there was no traditional carol service at Westminster Abbey at all as all the choirboys had been evacuated to the country. Carol singers'

lanterns were obscured for the blackout and their hand bells were forbidden, as this was now the all-clear signal after a gas attack!

Long hours of war work resulted in greater wages, but there were now few gifts in the shops to buy. Anguished parents did their best to find gifts for their children, but it wasn't easy: Father Christmas's wish lists largely stayed wishful thinking: it was difficult enough to obtain the stocking, let alone the gifts that went in it – the traditional orange was almost as mythical as Santa himself! Board games had a distinctly utilitarian feel: Monopoly only had a small box for the pieces, which were made of card instead of metal, plus a card spinner instead of wooden dice. Off-duty fire staff made wooden toys for children. Christmas decorations were now handmade: paper chains were crafted from old newspaper and only coloured if there was paint available.

By the middle of the war, the Christmas meal proved a distinct challenge. Despite efforts to increase supplies, turkeys became a real luxury: in Christmas 1943, the government announced only one in ten families would get a turkey or goose, so chicken often had to make do – if you could get one. There was an extra sugar ration, but Christmas puddings were difficult to make due to a shortage of fruit. Alcohol was in particularly short supply. Many who did not want to buy on the black market or could not afford the spivs' prices made their own drinks.

On Christmas Eve 1944, Hitler sent over his own 'gifts' to Britain: Heinkel He 111 bombers air-launched fifty V1 flying bombs over the North Sea, bound for Manchester. The worst incident was at Oldham, Lancashire, where thirty-two people were killed and forty-nine injured. There was a lull on Christmas Day, but the V-weapon onslaught resumed on Boxing Day, with a V2 rocket killing sixty-eight celebrants in a packed pub in Islington, north London.

The main aspect of Christmas, family togetherness, was the one thing that could not be recreated. Children were often evacuated or spouses served far away in North Africa or the Far East, unable to get leave or, worse still, were imprisoned in a PoW camp. The loneliest were those whose loved ones had been killed in action – there was one space at the Christmas table that could not be filled.

Nonetheless, it became imperative more than ever, almost as a national patriotic duty, to try and enjoy Christmas. Just being with friends, having a dance or sing-song, temporarily at least, idled away wartime worries. This fifteen-page songbook, packed with words and music of traditional Christmas carols, tried to bring a bit of yuletide colour to the proceedings – its well-thumbed condition and various food and drink stains showed it probably succeeded!

72: US Army Tunic, 1942

For over two years, together with Commonwealth and exiled allies, Britain fought on against the might of the Axis, who occupied most of Continental Europe. However, even with these allies, Churchill knew that Britain could not win the war on its own and needed the industrial strength and hitting power of the world's richest country – America. From the moment he became prime minster, Churchill had done everything in his power to try and draw America into the war on the side of the Allies. But after the horrors of the First World War, America became isolationist and its people wanted nothing to do with a European conflict on the other side of the Atlantic. Even President Roosevelt's policy of Lend-Lease to Britain was pushing the boundaries of American neutrality. However, following the bombing of Pearl Harbor and Hitler's ensuing declaration of war against America, this 'Arsenal of Democracy' entered the conflict. Churchill knew that once the might of the US was behind Britain, victory would no longer be 'if' but 'when'.

Although Japan was the most immediate threat to America, Churchill persuaded Roosevelt that Germany was the greater threat to the free nations and world economy and that the Nazis should be defeated first. Just over a month after entering the war, 37,000 American troops crossed the Atlantic bound for Britain, arriving in Northern Ireland on 25 January 1942. They would be the first wave of thousands more US troops to arrive in Britain, under Operation Bolero.

The American troops – or 'GIs', as they became known, after the official US army term 'Government Issue' – made a big impression on the war-weary British, particularly among many women and children. With their smart uniforms, Hollywood accents, good wages and seductive gifts of stockings and cigarettes – unrationed in the US – American servicemen whisked local women off their feet: in all, around 70,000 became 'GI brides'. While British hosts welcomed the American guests with civility, the new arrivals were not altogether popular: their brash, extravert personalities and a penchant for flashing their money around in pubs or hogging

partners at dances did not endear them to local men. The resentment was particularly felt among British troops, as the Americans were on better pay – £3 8s 9d [£145] a week compared to the Tommy's measly 14s [£30] – and they had better rations and properly tailored uniforms: fights became quite common.

The 'Yanks' were popular among sweet-rationed children, who followed them down the street asking 'Got any gum, chum?' or cadging coins off the Americans, who, initially, were unused to Britain's convoluted currency of pounds, shillings and pence. Some children conned the Americans out of money by offering to arrange a date with an older sister, only to never be seen again. That said, many good friendships were kindled between American troops and British families, the guests always bringing unrationed gifts when invited to 'tea'.

Britain seemed very small to our American guests: after all, it was only a third of the size of the US state of Texas. In the build-up to D-Day, the American presence became huge, with 1.5 million troops stationed in Britain. In East Anglia, the bomber and fighter airfields of the US 8th and 9th Air Forces transformed this quiet rural idyll. In Suffolk, every sixth person was a GI. In south-west England, US troops trained for the forthcoming invasion along the coasts of Devon and Dorset. In the Midlands, American paratroopers of the 82nd Airborne practised parachute drops over Leicestershire and Rutland – just four years after locals had been told to watch for German paratroopers descending from the skies.

Thanks to their sheer number, the huge supplies of equipment and the bravery of these young American men, the tide of the war was turning in the Allies' favour …

Just from its cut and style of insignia, this US 'Ike' pattern jacket is unmistakably American: it is easy to see how it both instantly impressed and embittered war-weary Britons. The number and name 'F3625 Freeman' is penned inside the jacket. Carson Mosser Freeman, born 1919, of Lehigh, Pennsylvania, USA, enlisted on 11 April 1944. The internal pocket label reveals that his 'Jacket, Field, Wool', was made by the Jersey Coat Co. on 30 May 1944 (a week before D-Day) and was issued by the Philadelphia Quartermaster Depot. The rank stripes indicate Freeman was a sergeant. On one shoulder is the rare red/white/blue British-made embroidered insignia of LBC (London Base Command). LBC was formed in October 1942 and was a major element responsible for overseeing materiel supplies and personnel in Greater London/south-eastern England before and after D-Day. The standard US Army Air Force (USAAF) collar dog badges and the 8th Air Force insignia on the other shoulder suggest Freeman originally served with the 8th, but was reassigned to LBC. The communications specialist badge on the left cuff suggests he was a ground-based radio operator/telegraphist. On the other cuff are three gold bars, indicating Freeman's one and a half years' service overseas. We know a little of Freeman's movements: in one pocket, was half a third-class Great Western Railway monthly return from Oxford to London Paddington ticket, dated December 1945, plus two half cinema tickets to the famous Cinephone cinema, on the Champs Elysees, Paris, indicates he and a friend were able to enjoy some of the fruits of victory in the months after the war. Freeman died on 5 March 2015, aged ninety-five, and was buried at Kansas Veterans Cemetery, Fort Riley, Riley County, Kansas, USA.

73: A Short Guide To Great Britain Booklet, 1943

I n 1942, playwright George Bernard Shaw wryly observed: 'England and America are two countries separated by the same language' – he was not wrong! Though the two great nations share a common ancestry, in the intervening 166 years since American independence many customs and words had changed: as befuddled Brits and their baffled brethren soon found out, living with distant visiting relatives is not always easy.

It worked both ways. Many British youngsters, fed on a diet of Saturday morning movies or comics, believed the Americans would arrive talking like cowboys or acting like Chicago gangsters. Even the highbrow *Times* newspaper had to explain to its readers in 1942 that GIs were 'friendly and simple' rather than 'Hollywood stars or two-gun Texans with five-gallon hats'.

On the other hand, British life could be bamboozling to Yanks. On arrival, many Americans expected 'Old London Town' to be full of historic palaces and lords and ladies: after more than two years of war, the reality was an anticlimax. Britain looked drab, dull and bomb-damaged. Britons walked the streets in dowdy or even raggedy clothes. Adjusting to simple things, such as which side of the road to drive on, could cause accidents. Then, also take into account that road signs had been removed as an anti-invasion measure, so many Americans got lost. Food could also prove challenging: rationed portions seemed minuscule compared to the plentiful diner meals the visitors were accustomed to at home. And, as for beer, which most American bars served chilled, the unrefrigerated ale British pubs served was distinctly lukewarm, even unpalatable!

Although social mores were more relaxed in wartime Britain, American mannerisms were comparatively liberated. The most common observation of American troops was that they were 'oversexed, overpaid and over here'. The Yanks countered that the British 'Limeys' were 'underfed, underpaid, undersexed and under Eisenhower', referring to General Dwight D. Eisenhower (1890–1969), the American Supreme Allied Commander of the Allied Expeditionary Force.

Yet, the Americans did bring with them something that was not rationed, but often lacking in reserved Britain – fun. American culture soaked into British society. The visitors brought with them pinball machines, jukeboxes, jitterbug dancing,

baseball, Coca-Cola, donuts and ice cream. Although American music was already popular via records and song sheets, regular dances held at US bases gave Britons the chance to hear big band music, swing, blues and jazz live, by the nation that invented it [see Object 89].

However, despite being the 'Arsenal of Democracy', America was still deeply divided on race issues – and the military brought this with them. Black American troops were given more menial duties, such as driving lorries or moving stores: they were banned from the Marines and bomber squadrons. Around 100,000 black US troops arrived in Britain, but not only were they segregated from white troops in different bases, black troops were banned from certain pubs or even whole areas. Unfortunately, these troubles occasionally flared into violence, gunfights and even deaths.

It should be remembered that although the Americans seemed very glamorous and enchanting to their British hosts, many had never left the city or town they grew up in, so crossing several thousand miles to a country they would only have read about in school books or magazines was a whole new experience. To help these transatlantic strangers in a strange land,

American soldiers, some of the first to arrive in the UK, pictured at No.10 Downing Street on 28 February 1942. (*Historic Military Press*)

in 1943, the US War and Navy Departments produced the small booklet, *A Short Guide to Great Britain*. It was packed full of slightly admonishing, but worthwhile advice to help avoid any misunderstanding:

The British will welcome you as friends and allies. But remember that crossing the ocean doesn't automatically make you a hero. There are housewives in aprons and youngsters in knee-pants who have lived through more high-explosives and air raids than many soldiers saw in first class barrages in the last war. Don't comment on politics. Don't try to tell the British that America won the last war. NEVER criticise the King or Queen. Don't criticise food, beer or cigarettes.

Other words of wisdom included: 'Saying 'I look like a bum' is offensive. For the British, this means you look like your own backside'!

74: 'Waralarm' Clock, 1943

Almost exactly a century after the peak of the Industrial Revolution, Britain's workers turned their hands to their biggest challenge yet – not only saving the country from invasion, but producing the weapons and equipment to defeat the greatest foe this nation has ever faced. And without their efforts and long hours at the lathe or desk, Britain's armed forces would have been unable to win the war. But this huge industrial achievement was far from easy.

In peacetime, workers could pretty much pick and choose where they worked. On 22 May 1940, under Regulation 58A of the Emergency Powers (Defence) Act, Minister of Labour Ernest Bevin was able to 'direct any person in the UK to perform any such services as he might specify'. This was further compounded on 5 March 1941 by an Essential Work Order, which made important industries, such as engineering, aircraft production, shipbuilding,

mining and building, top priority: managers could not dismiss workers without the decision of a National Service officer, while workers could not leave their job without permission – and could end up in court for persistent lateness or absenteeism.

The growth in war industry required new labour. However, people were not just thrown into war work. Most towns and cities had a Government Training Centre, where unskilled labourers were taught basic factory skills for work in industry.

Despite the social changes brought about by the First World War, when the manpower situation was much the same, little had really changed in the domestic role of women. Before the war, around five million single women worked, but most would be expected to leave as soon as they married or had children. A married woman's role was still defined as a housewife at home, while men went out to work as the wage earner. It was also accepted that single women who worked were paid less than men.

However, with the conscription of men into the armed forces, the government once

WARALARM

A ONE DAY ALARM CLOCK

Model No. 84   Black Finish

Made in La Salle, Illinois, U. S. A.

again mobilised women to fill these industrial vacancies. Under the Essential Work Order 1941, every woman in Britain aged eighteen to sixty had to be registered for work. In December 1941, for the first time in British history, the National Service Act (No. 2) made the conscription of single women aged nineteen to thirty liable to call up into the armed forces. About a third chose to go into industry instead and by mid-1943, almost 90 per cent of single women and 80 per cent of married women were employed in some type of war work.

In this way, despite various pressures, Britain was able to fulfil its industrial and military requirements. For a besieged island, it was impressive. In 1939–44, British shipyards produced over 700 major warships, over 5,000 smaller craft and 4.5 million tons of merchant shipping. The nation's aircraft output was equally prodigious. In 1938, Britain produced 8,000 warplanes, but by 1944, it had reached an annual peak of 26,461, with 1.7 million workers employed by the Ministry of Aircraft Production. Not only that, each year bombers became bigger and fighters became faster. But to get this far not all was as it seemed. For example, Britain's famous Spitfire fighter was not just made at the parent factory of Vickers Supermarine, in Castle Bromwich, West Midlands, but three-quarters of the aircraft's components were sub-contracted out for production, often by much smaller factories and workshops across the country. Indeed, the Spitfire's famous Merlin engine was made by Roll-Royce Ltd, who used 300 sub-contractors. In this way, Britain produced 120,000 war planes, more through a national pooled effort, than by individual companies. Britain's aircraft industry, and later others, were also helped by a pre-war Shadow Scheme started in March 1936, which involved using the motor industry's expertise to help production.

At the heart of this effort were the nation's workforce: men, women and children, some as young as fourteen, working long hours, five days a week, often far from home, requiring stays in remote work hostels and lengthy separations from loved ones. Industrial life was monotonous, tiring and unending – but it brought victory closer with each rivet or ball-bearing produced.

One strange shortage of the war was that essential assistant of the worker, the humble alarm clock. Something most people take for granted to wake them in the morning, before the war most of Britain's supplies came from America, France, Switzerland, Italy, even Germany. However, by the middle of the war, when supplies had long dried up, thousands of hours of war production were being lost due to exhausted workers oversleeping. The production of clockwork mechanisms had also largely been turned over to the production of bomb and shell fuses. As historian Norman Longmate noted, to overcome this shortage, 'an ugly, clock in a black economy pressed-wood fibre case', a Westclox 'Waralarm', was imported from America, from mid-1943. The shortage remained so extreme that from February 1944 it was announced alarm clocks would only be sold to workers with permits issued by employers and trade union branches, to those who regularly needed to get up between midnight and 5 am: the shortage was so severe, it was impossible to raise the qualifying time to 6 am. By June 1944, the Board of Trade stated that they had issued more than half a million permits, but within a month, MPs were complaining that many of these cheap Waralarms had already broken – needless to say, this example does not work either! Production of Waralarms ceased in May 1944. By October, however, the shortage was so severe, one MP suggested an alarm clock was needed to wake up the minister responsible!

75: WVS Hat, 1943

On the face of it, their work may have seemed relatively menial: washing thousands of tea cups in canteens, sorting donated clothing at depots or organising salvage collections – but this was only a fraction of the many tasks the hard-working ladies in green of the Women's Voluntary Service (WVS) performed in wartime. Indeed, the WVS were the oil that kept the cogs of the Home Front turning.

The roots of the WVS lie in the ARP organisation. Civilian precautions against air attack had been publicised since the mid-1930s. However, the Home Office realised much of this publicity, with posters such as *ARP: Here's a Man's Job!*, excluded the other half of the population – women.

Home Secretary Sir Samuel Hoare (1880–1959) approached the Marchioness of Reading, Stella Isaacs (1894–1971) to form a women's organisation for the promotion of ARP. On 18 June 1938, the Women's Voluntary Services for ARP was launched, with much publicity. By February 1939, the WVS's role had expanded, so its name was changed to WVS for Civil Defence.

In theory, in keeping with the marchioness' wishes, there was no rank system in the WVS. Instead, there was a system of appointments or titles. Similarly, her intention was that the WVS was to be egalitarian and classless, appealing to women of all backgrounds. However, WVS uniform was not free: in 1940, a full uniform suit, coat, hat and scarf cost £9 4s 7d [£475] – around two weeks' wages, which not all women could afford. Thus, it often tended to be the higher-status and wealthier women who were uniformed and held higher positions. For the others, a simple green or grey WVS armlet sufficed.

Many women, such as mothers, could not devote much time to the WVS, but still wanted to help. From 1940, a part-time WVS Housewives Service was introduced, renamed in 1942 the Housewives Section and often assisting directly on a woman's street. It proved popular, with 264,899 members in 1943.

Indeed, by 1943, WVS numbers had rocketed to 966,425 members – over ten times the total strength of its sister Home Front organisation, the WLA [see Object 81]. The WVS's role had also greatly expanded from purely ARP work: they staffed communal British restaurants and mobile canteens, served school meals, organised rural workers' food schemes, helped billet evacuees, ran nurseries for war workers' children, administered clothing stores, information bureaux, post-raid incident enquiry points, forces' canteens at home and abroad, fed the Home Guard, provided help in hospitals, undertook salvage drives, collected for National Savings funds, staffed volunteer car pools, as well as working in general clerical roles. The WVS helped win the war on the Home Front.

But the WVS did not disband with the war's end. Come the new threat of the Cold War, once again the WVS stood shoulder to shoulder with Britain's resurrected civil defence force. In recognition of their good work for the nation, in 1966 the word 'Royal' was added to the organisation's title, becoming WRVS. This was not the only change to their name: in 2013, the gender prefix was dropped, to become Royal Voluntary Service. Over eighty years after its formation, the organisation's volunteers still provide welfare support, to the elderly and from hospital outlets. The RVS also retain a civil defence role, staffing rest centres and emergency feeding stations after major incidents.

For practical reasons and esprit de corps, in June 1939, a new WVS uniform was announced.

Similar to the Women's Land Army, the WVS would not only have a variety of clothing, but it would be well designed, by London couturier Digby Morton (1906–83). The colour green was chosen as it was one not used by any of the other Home Front services. A smart WVS jacket and skirt uniform, made of thick, grey-green tweed supplied by Harrods, was sold for 57s 6d [£160]. An eye-catching maroon blouse, in artificial silk, was also available and for winter 1939, a woollen scarf in the red-grey-green WVS colours, plus a warm overcoat, in matching tweed, for Britain's tough weather. To top the look off, there was this green felt hat, with a red band bearing the WVS metal badge, for 6s 6d [£20].

A mobile laundry, staffed by members of the Women's Voluntary Service, in action in the East End of London in early May 1941. (*Historic Military Press*)

76: Pre-Decimal Money, 1943

Although most things seemed to be in short supply during the war, ironically, one important commodity was surprisingly plentiful – money. For much of the population in the cities and countryside, the 1930s had been a long decade of severe economic hardship. This was due to worldwide repercussions of the 1929 American stock market crash and ensuing Great Depression, resulting in widespread unemployment and poor

wages for those who had jobs. So, the onset of a world war that would cost the British economy £10 million [£550 million] per day would hardly seem to benefit hard-pressed Britons – but, strangely, it did.

Almost immediately, the need for war production created a huge demand for manpower. Within months, unemployment rates were the lowest they had been in decades – and that was not the only change. Previously,

in peacetime, there had usually been only one breadwinner, the husband, per household, with the wife as full-time housewife and child carer. But, with war industries offering women good rates for factory work and later conscription into war work, family incomes were almost doubled.

This war production-based economy also reversed traditional male incomes. White collar office incomes had been greater in the 1930s, but fell behind those of blue collar manual workers who worked longer shifts. Indeed, ironically, British soldiers risking their lives on the frontline were quite poorly paid in comparison.

Although from 1938–44 the cost of living rose by 50 per cent, weekly earnings rose by just over 80 per cent. However, there was little in the shops to spend these increased wages on and monetary values were turned upside down. The petrol shortage meant cars could be bought for £3 [£150], yet a bottle of spirit could set you back £5 [£250] – enough to sober even the most drunken.

Leading British economist John Maynard Keynes (1883–1946) said that tax needed to rise to pay for the war and the government was quick to capitalise on surplus public money. A new Excess Profits Tax of 60 per cent was levied on war industries and a Purchase Tax was introduced on shop goods to slow public spending. In June 1943, the government also introduced Pay As You Earn (PAYE) income tax, which exists today.

But all these economic measures still only raised 55 per cent of the income needed to fund the nation's war effort, so the government 'borrowed' the rest from the public in the form of the National Savings war contributions [see Object 77], whereby workers loaned or invested in the nation for a small amount of interest to be repaid post-war.

In this way, the National Savings movement helped to balance the economy, removing spare cash, preventing overspending and retail price inflation. To drive home the message, in 1943, National Savings introduced their own publicity anti-hero character, the Squander Bug, whose aim was to browbeat careless spenders. This devilish little imp, bedecked with swastikas, was created by National Savings employee, artist Phillip Boydell (1896–1984), while in bed with influenza. Boydell's Squander Bug appeared on graphic posters and even home-made 'cuddly' toy versions were made. With each invested penny a bullet, Britain successfully weaponised money as the financial ammunition that won the war.

Today, we have decimal currency, meaning money is divisible in tens. However, from the eighth century until 15 February 1971, Britain's currency was divided into a system of pounds (£), shillings (s) and pence (d). Each pound was divided into twenty shillings. Each shilling (also known as a bob) was worth twelve pennies. So, there were 240 pennies in a pound. There were also four farthings in a penny. A guinea was twenty-one shillings. Two shillings made one florin. Two shillings and six pence were known as half a crown. Five shillings were a crown. A ten-shilling note was nicknamed half a bar. Got all that? Funnily enough, although, it was more complicated and proved something of a financial nightmare for Allies based in Britain, its daily use helped Britons learn division and multiplication. Indeed, many people who used this pre-decimal system said they preferred it to today's currency. There was also a wider range of coinage than there is today: below the £1 and ten shilling note are, top row, from left: 1943 half penny, 1940 farthing, 1940 half crown, 1941 two shillings (florin). Bottom row, from left: 1940 sixpence, 1939 silver three pence, 1942 one shilling, 1936 one penny and a 1942 brass three pence.

77: Wings For Victory War Savings Plaque, May 1943

Britain's military effort in the First World War was not only funded by taxes, but also voluntary public donations, under the auspices of the new National Savings movement. But it was during the Second World War that the organisation really made a difference, raising considerable amounts of money that helped achieve victory.

The massive National Savings movement began in March 1916. It continued throughout the interwar years, but, again, was mobilised for war in 1939, under its president, former banker Lord Robert Kindersley (1871–1954). The movement's key strength was that not only did it have central government backing, but also 1,200 grassroots volunteer committees throughout Britain, which oversaw savings groups in every district, neighbourhood, workplace and school. Add to that the assistance given by local councils and businesses, plus the general support of the public, then it is easy to see why the movement was such a success.

However, National Savings' publicity started off very formal and staid, with First World War-style phraseology, 'Lend to Defend the Right to be Free', and a design of St George battling the dragon. From March 1940, the King granted permission for the royal crown to be used, to boost the movement's image.

The National Savings committee were quick to learn from the success of the Spitfire Funds [see Object 24], starting a parallel campaign in September 1940, called War Weapons Week, which ran for over a year. This was focused on rebuilding Britain's armed forces. Almost as soon as it ended, its successor, Warship Weeks, began in October 1941, ending in March 1942, this time focusing on the Royal Navy. During Warship Week each community raised a sum to 'adopt' an individual vessel. Starting in May 1943, the Wings for Victory campaign funded RAF aircraft. Spring 1944 saw the Salute the Soldier campaign. Rather than individual weapons, the target was usually a large sum towards the British Army. Of course, all these campaigns didn't 'buy' a bomber or 'adopt' a warship, but filled government coffers to fund the war effort.

National Savings produced a huge amount of printed promotional material, probably the greatest of any government department. Around 500 different-sized posters, in many colourful designs, with eye-catching and evocative slogans, were issued. Similarly, the movement produced around 200 different leaflets.

Thanksgiving Week was the final wartime campaign, in the latter half of 1945. Largely forgotten now, it also almost was at the time, such was the jubilation of victory. Instead of raising funds for weapons, its focus was on rebuilding Britain. But, after six years of donating, the public had developed charity fatigue and the sums raised were considerably lower.

The National Savings movement, its employees, volunteers and donators, had mobilised the nation's personal wealth as a weapon of war and played an important part in funding victory, raising £2,777 million [£100 billion].

Some of the most impressive National Savings objects are the presentation plaques.

Starting with the 1941 Warship Weeks campaign, a thick brass plaque was gifted from the adopted ship to the sponsor area, usually for mounting in the town hall. However, with the 1943 Wings for Victory campaign came standardised plaques. Instead of scarce metal, economy, ivory-coloured urea formaldehyde plastic was used. Made by De La Rue Plastics, of Walthamstow, they measure 23in by 14in. Bearing the RAF's *Per Ardua ad Astra* ('Through adversity to the stars') motto, plus the RAF winged badge, the main relief, in a classical design realised by sculptor William McMillan (1887–1977), refers to the biblical book of Revelations, showing the archangel Michael fighting Lucifer, represented by a three-headed hydra. St Michael is also the guardian of the souls of man, so metaphorically, the RAF is shown battling the Nazi enemy for the common good. Plastic plaques were repeated for the following 1944 Salute the Soldier campaign.

Avro Lancaster B Mark I, 'O for Orange' (L7580 'EM-O') of 207 Squadron in Trafalgar Square for the 'Wings for Victory' week in March 1943. (*Historic Military Press*)

78: RAF Bomber Command Crew Photos, May 1943

By 1943, if you heard aircraft in the sky, chances are you would not have had to take cover: now, the awe-inspiring fleets of bombers with deadly payloads were not the invading Luftwaffe but, by day, the B-17 Flying Fortresses and B-24 Liberators of the US 8th Air Force and, by night, the Avro Lancasters and Handley Page Halifaxes of RAF Bomber Command. The boot was now on the other foot: as Churchill had stated in his famous 'Do your worst, we'll do our best' speech of 14 July 1941, Britain was now meting 'out to the Germans, the measure, and more than the measure, that they have meted out to us'.

Although RAF Bomber Command had made a noble effort to disrupt German invasion preparations in 1940, its attempts against German industry had been less successful, ironically, largely for the same reason as the Luftwaffe: an inadequate medium bomber force of twin-engine aircraft. There was also a fear that heavier bombing would bring tit-for-tat reprisals.

Yet, throughout 1941, bombing was seen as the only front on which Britain could hit back against Germany and bolster morale at home. However, the Butt Report of August 1941 made disturbing reading for the RAF: of those aircraft recorded as attacking their target, only a third got within 5 miles of their target. The RAF did not have the equipment to carry out a heavy or accurate enough bombing campaign.

All this was to change on 22 February 1942, with the appointment of pugnacious Air Chief Marshal Sir Arthur Harris (1892–1984) as Air Officer Commanding-in-Chief of Bomber Command. His speech was uncompromising: 'The Nazis entered this war under the rather childish delusion that they were going to bomb everyone else, and nobody was going to bomb them. At Rotterdam, London, Warsaw, and half a hundred other places, they put their rather naive theory into operation. They sowed the wind, and now they are going to reap the whirlwind.'

Harris copied the Luftwaffe's technique of using incendiary bombs to mark and ignite the target. He was also ordered to implement the Area Bombing Directive and the strategy of 'de-housing', devised by government adviser Professor Frederick Lindemann (1886–1957) to target German industrial areas and the 'morale of industrial workers'.

Soon, Germany was experiencing a 'round the clock' bombardment, with night bombing from 101 RAF Bomber Command airfields, forty-nine of which were in the 'Bomber County' of Lincolnshire, plus day bombing from forty-two airfields of the US 8th Air Force in Norfolk and Suffolk and the sixteen airfields of the 9th US Air Force in Essex.

The campaign came with a terrible cost to all concerned. Up to 600,000 civilians were killed in Germany, over ten times the amount killed by German attacks on Britain. RAF Bomber Command crews also suffered a high casualty rate: 55,573 were killed, 44.4 per cent of their 125,000 aircrew. A further 8,403 men were wounded and 9,838 became PoWs. The US 8th Air Force lost 26,000 killed, 7.4 per cent of their 350,000 aircrew, while 23,000 became PoWs.

It has been estimated that the Allies' bombing campaign tied up around a million Germans on anti-aircraft and home defence duties who could have been fighting and possibly turning the tide on other fronts. German industry was also battered, increasing costs.

The controversy of their bombing campaign resulted in Bomber Command being largely deliberately forgotten about at the war's end. However, with hindsight and perspective, on 27 August 2006, a memorial stone was unveiled at Lincoln Cathedral. Similarly, on 28 June 2012, a large memorial building was unveiled by Queen Elizabeth II in Green Park, London, and on 2 October 2015, a memorial spire and named walls of remembrance were unveiled at the new International Bomber Command Centre, Lincoln.

By chance, I spotted and rescued these two poignant photographs among a stack of papers waiting to be binned. The airmen's faces seemed so engaging, young and full of life. Written on the back was a name and little else. A little research revealed the story behind these young airmen.

On 12–13 May 1943, a Vickers Wellington Mk. X bomber, HE157 OW-N, of 426 Squadron, Royal Canadian Air Force, took off from RAF Dishforth, North Yorkshire, at 2349hrs. It was one of 572 bombers targeting the city of Duisburg, Germany's largest inland port, which suffered severe damage including the sinking of thirty-four vessels. A total of 273 people were killed.

Thirty-four aircraft were lost – including HE157, which was shot down at 0328hrs, returning from the city, by Feldwebel Karl Leopold of 1./NJG 1, piloting a Messerschmitt Bf 110 night fighter from nearby Gilze-Rijen airfield, Holland. The Wellington crashed at Noordschans, near Breda, Holland. All its crew, believed pictured here standing outside the mess at RAF Dishforth, were killed. They were, from left, tail gunner Flying Officer Howard Ralph Drake, aged twenty-three, of Winnipeg, Manitoba; navigator Flying Officer George McMillan; pilot Warrant Officer II Kenneth Franklin Fighter, twenty-eight, of Esquimalt, British Columbia; bomb aimer Flight Sergeant David Chester Maxwell – and, standing front, wireless operator/air gunner Sergeant 1219830 Eric 'Jock' William Betts, twenty-one, of Leicester, the only Englishman in the Canadian crew.

This was to be Feldwebel Leopold's only aerial victory: just six days later, he was also killed, in a mid-air collision with another German night fighter over his airfield. Eric and his comrades are buried in the Canadian section of Bergen op Zoom war cemetery, Holland. The epitaph on Eric's war grave reads: 'The fragrance of a good life abideth forever.'

79: Jack Warner Wings For Victory Programme, May 1943

Laughter, as the old adage goes, is the best medicine – and during the Second World War, Britain's entertainers mobilised the nation's sense of humour as a munition of war, keeping the Home Front smiling. Modern stand-up comedy is big today, but it's often forgotten that its roots lay in early twentieth-century music hall routines, where multi-talented variety artists not only told jokes on stage, but also sang, played musical instruments and even performed magic tricks.

These front-line soldiers of mirth and merriment employed all their skills in the battle for morale to keep their audiences smiling. There were many entertainers, but several big name stars stood out among the crowd, becoming household names. Despite his buffoonish behaviour, behind his beaming smile, George Formby (1904–61) was a skilled entertainer who giggled his way through suggestive lyrics while strumming his ukulele. The Wigan-born comic, who was managed by his wife Beryl Ingham (1901–60), also saw success with a series of cinema films. In his signature eye-catching flowery suit, stand-up comedian Max Miller (1894–1963), known as 'The Cheeky Chappie', was even less subtle. Heavy on innuendo, his risqué humour bordering on 'blue' was quite radical for the time. South Londoner Tommy Trinder, with his trilby, wide grin, prominent chin and cry of 'You lucky people!' was, indeed, a people's comedian, often ad-libbing to the audience. Singing duo Bud Flanagan (1896–1968) and Chesney Allen (1894–1982) were the most successful comedians of comedy troupe The Crazy Gang, a favourite of the royals, which

also included Jimmy Nervo (1898–1975), Teddy Knox (1896–1974), Charlie Naughton (1886–1976) and Jimmy Gold (1886–1967).

All the above comedians toured the country to military bases, factories, theatres and even went overseas to perform their routines. Many performed as part of ENSA (Entertainments National Service Association), set up in 1939 by theatre impresario Basil Dean (1888–1978) and comedy actor Leslie Henson (1891–1957) to provide touring shows to boost morale. But quality varied and, unfortunately, ENSA

was sometimes said to stand for 'Every Night Something Awful'!

However, the main medium for comedy was the radio [see Object 86], where many of the big entertainers had their own programmes. From the beginning of the war, *Band Waggon*, made 'Big-Hearted' Arthur Askey (1900–82) a star overnight, with his catchphrases 'Hello playmates!', 'I thang you' and 'Before your very eyes', accompanied by his pal, Richard 'Stinker' Murdoch (1907–90). The show was prime-time Saturday night programming, with one-third of adults – eleven million – tuning in. However, the show only lasted three months, with Murdoch joining the RAF and Askey pursuing a solo career.

In its place, *Band Waggon's* competitor, *ITMA* (It's That Man Again – an oblique reference to Hitler), flourished. Presented by Tommy Handley (1892–1949), it was scripted by Ted Kavanagh (1892–1958), who packed 100 gags into every thirty-minute show. Thus, each programme was filled with numerous fictitious comic characters who became as much household names as the players behind them. Each had their own memorable catchphrases: there was Funf, the mysterious German spy ('This is Funf speaking …'), Ali Oop the pedlar ('I go, I come back'), the Diver ('Don't forget the diver'), Claude and Cecil ('After you, Claude', 'No, after you, Cecil'), Colonel Chinstrap ('I don't mind if I do') and Mrs Mopp the Corporation Cleaner (with a rather ribald 'Can I do yer now,

sir?'). *ITMA* regularly drew audiences of sixteen million listeners – a figure only matched by the BBC news – and its catchphrases became common parlance in everyday conversations.

Other popular variety shows were *Hi Gang!* featuring Vic Oliver (1898–1964) plus American couple Bebe Daniels (1901–71) and Ben Lyon (1901–79) and *Happidrome*, with Harry Korris (1891–1971) as music hall manager Mr Lovejoy, 'aided' by his dim-witted assistants, Ramsbottom and Enoch.

Initially, *Band Waggon* was replaced by *Garrison Theatre*, a music hall series that made a star of Cockney comedy actor Jack Warner (1895–1981), who also used several catchphrases, including 'Mind my bike!', 'blue-pencil' and 'my bruvver Syd'. Warner developed his acting career with his first film in 1943, *The Dummy Talks*, but became most famous, post-war, as a policeman in TV series *Dixon of Dock Green*. This rare autographed programme, for a 1943 Wings for Victory fundraiser [see Object 77] at The Hippodrome Theatre, in Coventry, is signed by Warner, bottom left, with the greeting 'Good luck little un'! Warner appeared as one of the 'guest artistes', including actress Dorothy Summers (1883–1964), who played *ITMA's* Mrs Mopp. Warner also auctioned off two sovereigns, a bottle of whisky, six pairs of stockings and two bananas to raise money for the fund. The programme is also signed by beauty queen winner 'Coventry's First Lady of the Wings', Mary P. Flynn, plus some of her Maids of Honour.

80: Holidays At Home Programme, July 1943

Going anywhere nice for your holidays this year? What's your plan to get away from it all – fly somewhere hot in the Med or maybe Airbnb on the other side of the world for a fortnight? How does a week off sitting in your local park or lazing on the lawn in your back garden sound? Probably not that appealing, but by the middle of the war, this was the only real choice millions of Britons had for a brief respite.

In the 1930s, holidays were quite different to those taken today. International commercial air travel was largely the preserve of the rich, so trips abroad were only really possible by ship, which took far longer to reach their destination. So, most Britons spent their holidays visiting the more famous picturesque and popular coastal resorts around Britain, often travelling by train and staying in a guesthouse. Come 1939, all this was about to change and it would be six years before holidays returned to normal.

Many Britons were still on holiday when war was declared: their immediate thought was to rush home, but if you lived in a city, it was safer away on holiday! During the Phoney War, a certain privileged few remained out of the way at their holiday hotels, which were derided in the press as 'funk holes'. For many children, evacuation was almost like a holiday to somewhere new and unexplored.

Though it may have been sunny, summer 1940 was not conducive to a relaxing holiday. With the Nazi invasion threat, bathing beaches were filled with land mines and barbed wire, their approaches obstructed with anti-tank blocks and pillboxes. Seafront guesthouses were requisitioned as billets for troops or closed and boarded up 'for the duration'. Even the traditional seaside pier had its central section removed to prevent it being used as a landing point for the invasion armada! Anyway, few holidaymakers would have been able to even reach the seaside, as a 20-mile-deep restricted zone was introduced, only allowing locals with a pass to enter. Not only that, traditional seaside holiday camps were used, initially, to house 'aliens' [see Object 14] and resorts, such as Blackpool and Skegness, were taken over by the RAF as training towns.

By the middle of the war, 'pleasure motoring' had been banned to save rationed petrol. The railways were largely turned over to the transportation of troops and supplies, so that train travel entailed spending hours standing on

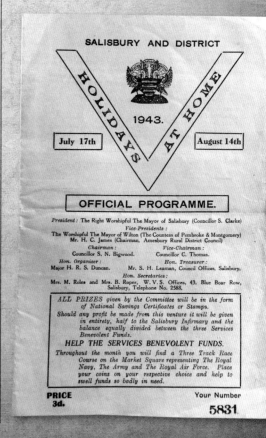

a packed and delayed journey to your destination – hardly the way to start a much-needed break. Indeed, it would have been better to stay at home – which is what the government wanted Britons to do, with guilt-inducing posters at stations asking 'Is Your Journey Really Necessary?'

From 1941, the government started promoting 'Holidays at Home'. Responsibility was placed on local councils to organise numerous large-scale events to keep people entertained in their home towns and cities. Summer concerts and open-air dances were held in local parks, as were fetes and fairs. The nearest thing to the seaside, outdoor lidos drew the crowds, often hosting swimming galas and beauty pageants.

There was one way to get a free holiday in the countryside – and that was to Lend a Hand on the Land at a Harvest Camp. Many working class families went hop-picking before the war, so this was not so unusual. Although it may have been tiring working on the land, it still allowed a chance to get away from it all – and help the nation at the same time.

As the war situation improved, from summer 1944, the coastal anti-invasion defences were gradually removed and sections of beach opened for bathers. However, the resorts were run down and dilapidated after four years of stasis. Summer 1945 saw the return of peace and holidays returned to normal.

It's not the most attractive and impressive looking of holiday brochures – but this is all there was! Despite being just 40 miles from the coastal resort of Bournemouth, in July and August 1943, the Wiltshire town of Salisbury did everything to persuade its inhabitants to Holiday at Home. His Worship the Mayor, Councillor Sydney Clarke, stated in this official programme: 'My Committee cannot give you the sea, but we have tried to give you all the other amusements of the seaside,' adding rather wistfully, 'Remember, short Holidays At Home this year may mean long holidays at the sea next.' The events, mostly held on Victoria Park, the Market Square and the Guildhall, included dancing, concert parties, treasure hunts, open-air whist drives, boxing, ATS netball, health and beauty displays, polo, American baseball, cinema programmes, fancy dress processions, a dog and rabbit show, local singing contests, baby shows, sheep dog trials and a pram-pushing competition – now, where could you get all that abroad?

81: WLA Service Armlet, 1943

They were the largely forgotten army of Home Front heroes, who, without cover from the weather or Hitler's bullets, shells, bombs and V-weapons, helped feed the nation at home and fighting forces abroad. Although they wore uniform, this army was not equipped with rifles, but pitchforks and instead of tanks, tractors – and it was entirely female: they were the Women's Land Army.

The WLA was a First World War creation, formed towards the end of the conflict in March 1917. It only had a tenth of its Second World War strength and continued for just six months after the Armistice, ending in May 1919. Nonetheless, it carried out good work and sowed the seeds for its larger and more successful successor twenty years later.

The WLA was re-formed on 1 June 1939, three months before the outbreak of war. It was through the strident determination of Lady Gertrude Denman (1884–1954), Director of the WLA, that, despite a comparatively small budget, the organisation was so successful. Her tenacity to get the job done was positively bulldog in spirit.

However, that is not to say the WLA was ever really very large. Despite the perceived image of fields full of WLA personnel, in reality, there was often just one or two working on a farm. At its peak in 1943, the organisation had 87,000 members, a fraction of other Home Front services, such as more than two million personnel in the Home Guard.

Members were issued with a distinctive uniform of brown felt hat, cream Aertex short-sleeved shirt, brown corduroy jodhpur-style breeches, brown leather belt, green pullover, brown woollen long socks, an imitation-silk green tie and brown leather shoes. For farm work, land girls sometimes wore buff cotton dungarees, officially called 'bib and braces', or a brown cotton drill coat, called a 'milking jacket'. However, although WLA clothing was smart and quite well-designed, it was not great for winter work. Land girls often had to borrow waterproofs from farmers.

Indeed, bright, colourful WLA recruitment posters showed glamorous, smiling young women in a sunny field of golden corn or cuddling a cute calf: there was no mention of the rain, cold or mud ahead. The work was long and tough: forty-eight hours a week in the winter, fifty to fifty-four hours a week in the summer and the women's pay was 20 per cent less than the low-paid male labourers they replaced.

Land girls, as they were known, often either lived on farms or in one of 700 new WLA hostels. It is interesting to note that only a third

of the members came from the cities: the other two-thirds came from the countryside, so the life was not necessarily as alien as TV dramas like to portray. Similarly, despite the regular screen portrayal of land girls as pasty, skinny and svelte, archive photos reveal that with several years' service, good food and hard work on the land in all weathers, many were actually quite buxom, tanned, stocky and tough! Indeed, from 1942, the forestry wing of the WLA, the Timber Corps, were felling trees and producing timber for everything from pit props to rifle butts. By the war's end, the Timber Corps was 6,000-strong.

Although the war ended in 1945, the battle for food did not. Land girls continued helping stock the nation's post-war larder for another five years, until the WLA was disbanded on 30 November 1950.

At the war's end, the WLA were not entitled to the Defence Medal [see Object 96], despite the dangers and importance of their job. Only in 2008 did land girls receive recognition, although not in the form of a medal: around 45,000 surviving members received a pin badge and certificate signed by then-Prime Minister Gordon Brown. It's a pity they had to wait sixty years for an official token of recognition, with many, if not most, land girls having already passed on, but most veterans are stoic and proud of their service.

The most conspicuous item of uniform was the woollen button-backed WLA armlets, which not only acted as an identity symbol, but also indicated a length of service. Initially, a simple, reissued First World War pattern of a red crown on a green armlet, they became more elaborate over the years. The next type was also green, but with red 'WLA' initialling added. A similar armlet, but with red edging and two diamonds, indicated two years' service. A red armlet with four diamonds indicated four years' service; a yellow armlet, with six diamonds and black edging, indicated six years' service and finally, a most impressive yellow and green armlet, with eight red diamonds, indicated eight years' service – the whole war period.

Members of the Women's Land Army at work on the land. (*Historic Military Press*)

82: Dig For Victory Advice Book, 1943

Small or large, immaculately tended or overgrown and forgotten, British gardens took on a whole new significance during the war. Their purpose changed rapidly from ornamental to nutritional. Out went the colourful flowers, replaced by rows of vegetables. The garden shed became the gardeners' armoury and in this battle for food, spades and forks were the weapons.

As part of their pre-war planning, aside from agricultural land, the government realised that there were millions of acres of fertile land adjoining homes in both the city and country. Just two days after the outbreak of war, the largest and most successful public information campaign of the conflict was launched – Dig for Victory. The campaign was led by Ministry of Food agricultural economist Professor John Raeburn (1912–2006). The aim was to replace imported food, freeing shipping space for more valuable war materials. As Lord Woolton, Minister of Food, said in 1941: 'This is a food war. Every extra row of vegetables in allotments saves shipping … the battle on the kitchen front cannot be won without help from the kitchen garden.'

Soon, other short and catchy encouraging slogans appeared on posters: *Grow Your Own*, *Food is a Munition of War* and *Dig on for Victory*. The authorities also provided written help, such as a series of twenty-six free *Dig for Victory* leaflets from February 1941 until the early post-war years, plus larger *Growmore* bulletins, issued by the Ministry of Agriculture and Fisheries from their requisitioned Berri Court hotel headquarters in Lytham St Annes, Lancashire. In 1942 alone, the ministry issued ten million leaflets.

While vegetables were unrationed, they soon became scarce in the shops: it was not unknown for a single onion to be auctioned or given as a prize. As for imported fruits, such as oranges or bananas, these largely disappeared overnight. In their place, both ministries suggested alternatives, such as carrots. In 1941, there was a bumper harvest of the orange root crop, so a new cartoon character, Dr Carrot, heavily promoted their nutritional benefits. It was said that RAF night fighter pilots regularly ate carrots as they improved their vision. Carrots contain Vitamin A and beta carotene, which are good for eyes, but the publicity was actually partial cover for the introduction of airborne radar. Nonetheless, the natural sweet taste of carrots was used as a

replacement for rationed sugar and sweet fruits, via recipes for carrot cake, carrot marmalade, even carrot cookies.

Any available land was used to grow food: from parks and school playing fields to rooftops and bombsites – even the 15in of protective earth covering Anderson shelters was used to grow marrows and cabbages. Waste ground was also requisitioned by the Ministry of Food and allotments proliferated: by 1943, there were 1.4 million in Britain.

Incidentally, another, more unusual bird began to appear in back gardens – the chicken. In 1940, millions of commercially farmed hens were slaughtered as there was a shortage of foodstuffs to feed them. This led to an egg shortage and rationing. Residents began to keep hens, plus ducks and geese, in home-made coups. The catch was, they had to forfeit their egg ration, but instead received grain to feed their poultry. By 1943, over one million householders were feeding hens with their kitchen waste and eventually produced a quarter of the nation's egg supply. Rabbits were also kept for their meat and fur – though dinnertime often ended with tears at the table when children discovered that Fluffy had quietly disappeared and was the main course.

Pig clubs were also started, with neighbourhoods depositing edible garden and kitchen waste into street pig bins for a share of the meat: enough scraps were collected each month to feed 210,000 pigs.

Overall, the campaign was a massive success: by 1942, it was estimated that there were five million allotments and 'Victory Gardens', as they became known, which by the following year, were producing over 1 million tons of produce. By 1945, around 75 per cent of food consumed was produced in Britain. As rationing did not end until the 1950s, allotments and vegetable gardening continued until then and beyond.

There was no shortage of advice to help even the most clean-fingered of gardeners – and not all of it official. Perhaps the unofficial commanding officer in this Dig for Victory battle was Cecil Henry Middleton (1886–1945), known simply as 'Mr Middleton', the first of the BBC's 'celebrity' gardeners, who broadcast regularly on radio and wrote four books on wartime gardening. However, several other gardeners also put down their spades and turned to print, writing commercial booklets – and most of the advice still stands good today. This *Victory Library* edition of the *Spring Wartime Gardening Guide*, by P. Dyer, was published by Burke Publishing in 1943. Its introduction, by Roy Hay, of BBC Radio *Allotment*, notes:

At this stage of the war, a great deal of the suitable land conveniently situated for cultivation as allotments has already been dug … During the next few winters, the man or woman who can draw a steady supply of food from a garden or allotment may well be envied by less enterprising neighbours. We must make every endeavour to utilise our land to the best advantage. Like the farmers, we hold our gardens and allotments in trust during wartime. We must not fail to see that they yield their utmost at the time of our greatest need.

By the mud stains and threadbare condition of this book, its owner did make 'every endeavour'!

83: CD Warden's Uniform Tunic, February 1944

In September 1941, the term 'ARP' was renamed 'Civil Defence', officially, at least, 'to emphasise the growth and increased importance of what were known originally as the ARP General Services and their essential unity with other branches of civil defence'. In truth, however, the Luftwaffe had outmoded the term ARP by proving there were only a limited amount of precautions that could be taken against their air raids.

However, at the same time, Hitler provided the new CD services with a certain amount of respite by turning his attention 180 degrees in the opposite direction, towards Russia. This lull, in turn, allowed the Home Office to reform and improve the CD services. Subjects such as incident control and rescue techniques were improved and the organisation refined. However, with the reduced raiding, fewer personnel were needed and numbers were cut by 103,000 to 1.68 million in 1942. As a result of these cuts, in 1943, CD first aid parties became Light Rescue parties and original Rescue parties renamed Heavy Rescue. With the resumption of bombing, CD personnel figures later rose to 1.85 million in 1944.

Although the Luftwaffe's forces had largely been diverted eastwards and were never able to repeat the heavy, daily Blitz of 1940–41, that is not to say that they did not stop making their presence felt. Between April and July 1942, in the so-called

Baedeker Raids, Britain's historic cities of York, Norwich, Canterbury, Exeter and Bath were targeted, killing 1,637 civilians in a knee-jerk response to RAF Bomber Command's growing strength over Germany. In August 1942, the Luftwaffe experimented with a few specially adapted aircraft to carry out very high-level bombing from 40,000ft and hitting a handful of targets in southern England, notably Bristol.

Operating at the other extreme, since the end of the Blitz in summer 1941, the Luftwaffe had been launching low-level single-seat fighter incursions as far inland as London. From March 1942 to June 1943, these daytime attacks, known as Tip-and-Run raids, were focused on towns

along the south and east coasts. On 13–14 June 1943, the Luftwaffe launched a particularly vicious attack against the east coast towns of Grimsby and Cleethorpes, dropping around 3,000 2kg 'Butterfly' SD2 anti-personnel bombs, killing 114. Also, throughout 1943–45 the Luftwaffe targeted both US and British bomber bases in East Anglia with night intruder raids.

All these types of terror attacks achieved very little for Germany: they killed civilians, but failed to impede Britain's growing industrial and military might. Indeed, they also diverted (and destroyed) valuable Luftwaffe air power needed on the long Eastern Front. But this was all the token effort Hitler's once-powerful air force could muster against Britain.

The Luftwaffe's main swansong raids came in January–May 1944. Known variously as the Steinbock, Baby, Little or Last Blitz, fast-flying nocturnal 'scalded cat' bombers attempted to ignite firestorms in London and the South-east. However, their younger, less experienced crews, coupled with better radar, anti-aircraft and night fighter defences took their toll on the attackers. The raids killed 1,556 Britons, but statistically, for every five Britons killed the Luftwaffe lost one bomber and four airmen. Essentially, the Luftwaffe was inflicting as much damage on itself.

The Steinbock raids also marked the peak performance of the CD services. Now fully uniformed, better trained, equipped and organised, the men, women and children of the fully integrated various civilian organisations were able to blunt the damage done, preventing the much-feared firestorms. By this time, for example, the Fire Guard were extinguishing more incendiary bombs than the fire service, relieving pressure and allowing brigades to tackle larger fires. However, the day of the manned German bomber may have passed, but within a month of the Steinbock Blitz's cessation a whole new revolutionary concept in modern aerial bombardment would begin …

With the new CD organisation of late 1941 came a whole new uniform and insignia. Experience of the Blitz had proved that the ARP denim bluette uniforms [see Object 35] were not up to the job. In their place came warmer and more durable military-style woollen battledress tunic (coded ARP 57), trousers (ARP 58) and beret (ARP 68) for men and a smart jacket (ARP 71), skirt (ARP 72) or slacks (ARP 73) and trilby-style hat (ARP 44) for women. This uniform bore smart badging, with embroidered (printed from 1943) 'CD' motif, area and shoulder titles of the specific branch in 'old gold'. The internal manufacturer's label in this ARP 71 women's CD tunic reveals it was made by Laurence Marshall Ltd in 1942. It was issued to a 'Mrs Gibbon', as written on the label, who was a CD warden in the Bedfordshire county area. The jacket has printed 'Warden' shoulder titles, plus three printed service chevrons on her right cuff, indicating she had served three years (and was thus entitled to the Defence Medal [see Object 96]). The yellow lanyard holds a warning whistle in her top pocket.

84: Merchant Navy Uniform, February 1944

The battle for Britain's food and raw materials did not just occur in the nation's fields and Dig for Victory gardens. Hundreds, indeed, thousands of miles away, the sailors of the Merchant Navy were struggling and dying to maintain Britain's supply lifelines. Without their efforts, the nation faced starvation and its war production may well have ground to a halt. And that's no empty statement: in 1939, Britain was importing 55 million tons of supplies, including 70 per cent of its food, far more than many, both then and now, realised was essential for the survival of an island nation.

Britain's merchant fleet was independently operated by commercial shipping companies. However, on the outbreak of war, the Ministry of Shipping, later part of the Ministry of War Transport, took control of this fleet. Britain's merchant fleet was the world's largest, employing 144,000 men and women, aged fourteen to seventy. A large number were Indian, Chinese and West African sailors.

But, as in the First World War, this largely unarmed merchant fleet was highly vulnerable to German air, sea and submersible attack. Losses in 1940 and 1941 were acute, with 779 merchant ships sunk and 16,654 seamen killed or missing – 49 per cent of all crews. To make matters worse, until May 1941, merchant seamen received no pay from the moment their ship sank.

Long-range Luftwaffe aircraft, Kriegsmarine warships and mines posed a threat to merchant shipping, but it was the U-boat (submarine) that was the greatest danger: indeed, Winston Churchill later confessed: 'The only thing that ever really frightened me during the war was the U-boat peril.' Lurking and shadowing along merchant shipping lanes, U-boats took a

heavy toll of Allied merchant vessels. Applying strength in numbers, a merchant convoy system was quickly introduced, providing Royal Navy and RAF escorts as a deterrent against U-boat attack.

The Merchant Navy served on all the world's seas and oceans, including the hazardous Arctic convoys, delivering supplies to Russia. However, the most significant routes became known as

relied on them. Their war required immense courage. In the open elements, hundreds of miles from land, the merchant seaman's chances of survival were poor. They faced death by bombing, drowning, hypothermia, or being burned alive in oil tankers. The Japanese Navy were also known to machine-gun survivors in the water. There was little chance of rescue, as others ships were not allowed to stop in case they became targets themselves.

Tragically, 54 per cent of Britain's merchant fleet was sunk, with 36,749 seamen, including around fifty women, killed by enemy action, plus 4,707 wounded and 5,720 seamen taken prisoner, totalling 47,176 casualties. The Merchant Navy's gallantry in keeping Britain supplied was recognised with 8,449 awards, including five George Crosses.

This smart 1944-dated Merchant Navy uniform, made by naval outfitters Monnery's, was worn by Second Engineer 7353 Geoffrey Leach pictured left, who was born in West Ham, London, in 1921. At 3.30 pm, on 29 February 1944, while en route from Liverpool to Calcutta, in India, via Cape Town, Colombo and Madras, carrying a general cargo of 700 tons, Leach's ship, the 5,419-ton Royal Mail Lines vessel MV *Palma*, was struck by two torpedoes fired by German submarine U-183, 400 miles south of Ceylon (now Sri Lanka). Seven of *Palma*'s crew were killed and forty-six rescued by HMS *Balta* and HMS *Semla*. Ironically, on 23 April 1945, while patrolling the Java Sea, U-183 was sunk with fifty-four of her crew, including commander Kapitänleutnant Fritz Schneewind, by another submarine, the American USS *Besugo*, leaving only one survivor. Incidentally, there are white specks of paint on the cap from when Leach used it to cover his hair while painting ceilings after the war! Leach died in Bristol in 1994.

the Battle of the Atlantic. This, the war's longest campaign, was costly to both sides. Some 3,500 Allied merchant ships and 175 warships were sunk attempting to bring supplies to Britain. However, the battle's crux came in May 1943, when improved radar, air cover and Enigma decryptions of coded German naval messages revealed U-boat patrol courses. The U-boats became the hunted. By the war's end, 783 U-boats and forty-seven German surface warships had been sunk in the Atlantic. Also, to counter this war of attrition, Allied shipyards rushed to replace those ships that were sunk, with eighteen American shipyards building 2,710 Liberty ships, the largest number of ships ever produced to a single design.

The Merchant Navy are the largely unsung and forgotten heroes of the Second World War. Apart from when they docked in port towns, they were mostly unseen – yet nearly every Briton

85: D-Day Newspaper, June 1944

It started with a distant, growing rumble, but within a minute had developed into a roar overhead, as the summer's lighter night sky was filled with dark shadows of aircraft passing over. But no air raid sirens sounded and no one ran for cover: quite the opposite, woken from sleep, they leaned out of windows or stood in the street, eyes to the sky, slack-jawed in amazement at the aerial armada passing above. It was the early hours of Tuesday, 6 June 1944 and history was being made. Two years in the planning, Operation Overlord had begun, with swarms of paratrooper-carrying aircraft and bombers towing gliders over southern and eastern England, bound for Normandy, France. On this day rested the future of the war, the freedom of Europe – and the lives of thousands of men, women and children: D-Day had arrived.

Despite being prepared in great secrecy, many Britons – and Germans – knew the invasion was imminent – they just didn't know when. Since 1942, Britain had increasingly become a vast military camp, holding troops of all Allied nationalities, particularly American [see Object 72].

From March 1944, efforts were made to hide these tented troop marshalling camps based in woods and in the grounds of stately homes, between Sussex and Dorset. Camouflage nets were hung between trees and over roads, while barbed wire fences and signs stating 'Do not talk to the troops' surrounded the camps. By May 1944, there were 2.9 million Allied troops ready for the invasion.

The coming attack required wide-scale manoeuvres and these made an impact on local communities. The village of Tyneham, Dorset, was requisitioned by the War Office, while 750 families were compulsorily evacuated from their homes in South Hams, Devon, so that the area could become a training ground for US troops.

The growing military build-up could not be missed by even the most myopic locals. Roads became clogged with mile-long convoys of lorries and armour, rumbling through quaint southern villages. Railway trains comprised seemingly endless flatbed trucks carrying tanks and tarpaulin-covered crates. Some sights were more eye-catching: around Beaulieu and Chichester Harbour, unusual new DUKW amphibious vehicles parked. In Conwy, North Wales; Clyde, Scotland; Portsmouth, Southampton and London's Surrey Docks, mysterious giant concrete and metal constructions appeared: few knew they were sections of the Mulberry Harbours, built by 45,000 workers, that would prove so crucial to the landing's success.

But some of the military build-up was made deliberately visible to civilians and, hopefully, Luftwaffe spy aircraft. The Allies wanted the Germans to think the landings would be at Calais, rather than Normandy, so embarked on a giant deception plan called Operation Fortitude. As part of this, under Operation Quicksilver, conspicuous dummy vehicles, such as inflatable tanks, were planted across south-east England, with dummy landing craft in the ports of Dover, Folkestone and Great Yarmouth, plus in the rivers Deben, Stour and Orwell.

Under Operation Neptune, the invasion armada readied on 5 June 1944 at the embarkation ports of Southampton, Portsmouth, Newhaven, Shoreham, Weymouth, Portland, Torquay, Brixham, Dartmouth, Plymouth, Falmouth, Tilbury and Felixstowe.

Following overnight Allied paratrooper landings, at 6.30 am, on 6 June 1944 the first American troops landed at their codenamed beaches of Utah and Omaha, followed an hour later by the British at Sword and Gold beaches and the Canadians at Juno beach.

The first official confirmation Britons heard was at 9.32 am, when the calm, authoritative voice of BBC newsreader John Snagge [see Object 86] announced the exciting news: 'D-Day has come. Early this morning, the Allies began the assault on the north-western face of Hitler's European fortress.' By the end of the day, 152,715 Allied troops had set foot on French soil advancing along a 30-mile front – in doing so, around 10,500 made the ultimate sacrifice for the liberation of Europe.

Unlike the state-run Nazi press, which regularly lied to its audience as part of its propaganda policy, the British press did not lie *per se*, but had to be selective about what truths it could tell readers. Articles were often directed by the Ministry of Information and cleared by the Press and Censorship Bureau. The government could also implement 'D' (Defence) Notices, pressuring editors not to publish an article. This was not gratuitous heavy-handed officialdom, but censorship to stop careless printed words revealing secrets to the enemy, losing battles and costing Allied lives. Interestingly, on D-Day, both the BBC and some of the press initially relied on broadcasted German information until the Ministry of Information released greater detail a couple of hours later. Newspaper sellers were besieged by those wanting to read about D-Day's progress, with Londoners queueing fifteen minutes to buy the midday edition of the *Evening Standard*. Vendors soon sold out and penny [£1] newspapers were resold for half a crown [£5]. The *Standard's* rival, *The Evening News* (1881–1980), once London's biggest-selling daily newspaper with the world's largest evening net sales, filled all the columns in its four war-rationed broadsheet pages with small print about the invasion. The front page quoted Supreme Commander of the Allied Expeditionary Force, General Eisenhower: 'Our home fronts have given us an overwhelming superiority in weapons and munitions of war, and placed at our disposal great reserves of trained fighting men. The tide has turned. The free men of the world are marching to victory.'

86: Utility Radio, June 1944

Britain's first regular television broadcasts had started in 1936, but were taken off air in 1939 for fear German bombers would use their VHF transmissions as a homing beacon to bomb London. Even so, televisions were not hugely missed as it was only the privileged few who could afford them. On the other hand, radio, or 'the wireless', as it was called, was in most homes and became the TV of the 1940s, with families gathered to hear the news, important broadcasts by Churchill or comedy and entertainment programmes to relax after a long day.

In 1939, nine million 10s [£25] radio licences were issued, enabling Britons to have a full year's news and entertainment. Most radios throughout the war years were actually 1930s pre-war models, as production had been turned over to the war effort. Although most radios were actually quite simple in construction, their valves and spare parts were scarce. However, once tuned, their glass valves and wooden cases gave a clear, rich, warm sound.

The national public broadcaster, the BBC (British Broadcasting Corporation), founded in 1922, was responsible for the transmission of radio programmes. Like the nation, the BBC, under four directors, General Frederick Ogilvie (1893–1949), Cecil Graves (1892–1957), Robert Foot (1889–1973) and Sir William Haley (1901–87), had a tough war, with various demands from government and politicians, attempting to direct its output. Its Broadcasting House base, in Portland Place, Marylebone, London, was bombed twice, with seven staff killed.

The BBC's most important role as trusted broadcaster of news, both nationally and internationally, became more challenging than in peacetime. Its journalists reported from all the front lines, at home and abroad, often under fire. On the Home Service channel, for the first time, its newsreaders, including John Snagge (1904–96), Alvar Lidell (1908–81), Bruce Belfrage (1900–74), Stuart Hibberd (1893–1983), Frank Phillips (1901–80) and Wilfred Pickles (1904–78), introduced themselves by name to foil potential Nazi radio imposters. Also, as a counter to the negativity of Lord Haw-Haw [see Object 10], in 1940, the BBC started broadcasting weekly *Postscript* talks by novelist J. B. Priestley. His positive social commentary, delivered in a homely Yorkshire accent, drew huge audiences. However, his perceived socialist slant led to his broadcasts being cancelled the following

year. The BBC's most popular broadcaster was Prime Minister Winston Churchill [see Object 16], who delivered thirty-three major wartime speeches. His epic oration inspired millions, at home and abroad.

Under the terms of the BBC's broadcasting contract, it also produced a wide range of radio programmes for all tastes and options. For highbrow philosophical discussions, *The Brains Trust* panel of experts answered listeners' questions. *The Radio Doctor*, Dr Charles Hill (1904–89), offered daily health advice. A *Forces Programme* played light, relaxing music for the nation's troops, while lively tunes were broadcast on *Music While You Work* and *Workers' Playtime*, to cheer industrial listeners. *Children's Hour*, which had run since the corporation's inception, adapted, explaining the war in a way young minds could understand. To top it all, the BBC also boosted morale with various light comedy and variety shows [see Object 79]. Despite paper rationing, the *Radio Times* still managed to list all the above programmes every week.

Although its 'Nation shall speak peace unto Nation' motto may have been somewhat compromised, despite the difficulties faced the BBC still succeeded in its main objective: providing quality public service broadcasting.

Radios of the interwar years were stylish, elegant art deco furniture, the eye-catching centrepiece of every living room – but not so the War-time Civilian Receiver, or, Utility Radio! As radio production had been turned over to the war effort, spare parts for domestic sets were scarce. The government directed Britain's forty-two radio manufacturers to produce sets to a simple standard design with as few components as possible. Designed by Dr G. D. Reynolds of Murphy Radio Ltd, the Utility Radio was essentially a three-sided wooden box with a pressed-card rear panel, containing three receiving valves, plus a Westector detector and thermionic power rectifier. It had two knobs, one for volume, the other for tuning, although it could only tune into medium wave, between the 200–550 bands. On top, it bears a gold transfer label, stating 'War-time Civilian Receiver – produced by the radio industry under government direction', while to the rear was the notice, 'In the interests of wartime economy, switch off the set when not in use.' As it was made to a pooled design, the manufacturer's name was not readily displayed, but was identified by a coded letter 'U' and number – in this case, U7, Murphy Radio, of Welwyn Garden City, Hertfordshire. Despite its utility, it was not cheap at £12 3s 4d [£475] per set. However, around 175,000 sets were sold after its release in June 1944, just in time to follow the historic developments of D-Day, the Battle for Normandy and the final year of the war.

87: V1 Attack On London Logbook, June 1944

Exactly a week after D-Day, on 13 June 1944, Londoners looked to the night sky and cheered. A long flame and sudden crash led them to believe they had just witnessed a German bomber being shot down. They had not. They had just witnessed the world's first cruise missile, the V1, making its devastating arrival in the capital, killing eight of their fellow Britons.

Within weeks, this new weapon had gained several new names: doodlebug, buzz bomb or simply, flying bomb. In Civil Defence reports it was labelled 'fly'. Flying bomb was technically accurate, as the weapon was the first aerial unmanned weapon to attack Britain. Hitler also approved of its unofficial name, *Vergeltungswaffe Eins* ('Vengeance Weapon 1/V1).

In 1937, German engineer Fritz Gosslau (1898–1965) proposed the development of a remote-controlled aircraft with a 1-tonne warhead. Two years later, he added a pulse-jet to his design. Development accelerated when the project was overseen at the Peenemünde Army Research Centre. In 1942, together with other scientists, Gosslau worked on the Fieseler Fi 103, its first flight coming that December.

The 27ft-long missile was catapulted at 250mph from a launching ramp. After three minutes, at a cruise speed of 400mph and height of 3,000ft, a directional gyroscope took control. At a pre-programmed distance, measured by a wind-driven impeller in the nose, the Argus pulse-jet cut out and the missile fell on its target.

D-Day had brought forward the missile's intended launch date. Although British intelligence knew of the weapon's development, its deployment came as a surprise to most Britons.

At its peak, more than 100 V1s a day were fired at southern England. Londoners learned to 'keep an ear open' for the V1's distant throaty grumble, like the strains of an old motorcycle. When the engine cut out, those under its flightpath dived for cover and waited ten seconds for the explosion. The V1 was essentially random, with an 'accuracy' radius of 7 miles, at best.

Nonetheless, it proved devastating. Its blast, equivalent to a large parachute mine, levelled rows of houses. One of the worst incidents occurred on Sunday, 18 June 1944, when a V1 hit the Guards' Chapel, on Birdcage Walk, London, during a service, killing 121 soldiers and civilians. Earlier that day, an NFS fireman manning a rooftop observation post on Dulwich fire station, south London – directly below the

V1 flightpath to the capital's centre – hurriedly scribbled pencilled notes of their journey and deadly impact in this rare logbook. In one hour, from the start of his shift at 4.50 am, the fireman noted eight V1s passing over. Interestingly, in his record of this early V-weapon 'Attack on London', he calls the missiles 'Aerial torpedoes', but over the next few days, starts to refer to them as 'P. Planes' (Pilotless) and 'robots'. The fireman's shaky scrawl must have been at least partly caused by his exposed position in the high observation post with V1s passing by and exploding around him. The log only lasts seven days, possibly indicating he was a relief fireman brought in from outside London, but records later that day a V1 was 'chased by two Spitfires', while the following day, notes a V1 was 'shot down by Bofors [AA gun] at Dulwich'.

However, intercepting V1s over the capital often downed missiles that could have flown past, resulting in avoidable casualties. Around this date, under *Operation Diver*, Churchill ordered the redeployment of London's AA defences to Kent and Sussex. The following month, these defences were moved further south, creating a coastal band of over 500 AA guns and 2,000 barrage balloons. This allowed RAF fighters, including the new Gloster Meteor jet, to intercept their unmanned prey over the open countryside, where there was less chance of the missiles causing damage. These combined ground and air defences accounted for 4,261 V1s, saving thousands of lives.

However, 1,176 V1s were also air-launched from Heinkel 111 bombers over the North Sea, extending the weapon's range into northern England.

The only true way of defeating the V1 menace was the destruction of their Continental launch sites by Allied heavy bombers or capture by ground troops. The last V1 to hit Britain landed at Datchworth, in Hertfordshire, on 29 March 1945, without casualties, just over a month from VE Day.

In total, over 10,000 V1s were launched against England. Some 2,419 reached London, causing 6,184 fatalities. But this was only the first of the new generation of Nazi terror weapons to arrive.

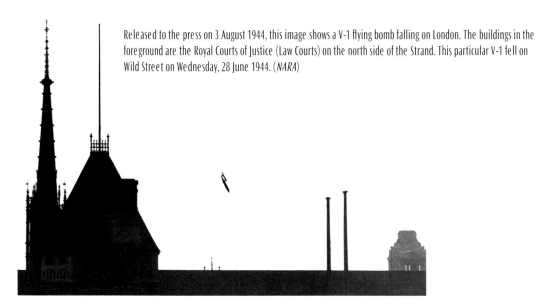

Released to the press on 3 August 1944, this image shows a V-1 flying bomb falling on London. The buildings in the foreground are the Royal Courts of Justice (Law Courts) on the north side of the Strand. This particular V-1 fell on Wild Street on Wednesday, 28 June 1944. (*NARA*)

88: Axis PoW Pecking Hens Toy, Summer 1944

Tens of thousands of enemy soldiers did set foot in Britain – not, however, as victorious invaders, but defeated prisoners of war. An island far from the battlefront and their homeland, Britain became the ultimate moated PoW camp.

In 1939, there were just two PoW camps in Britain. Due to the Phoney War and the lack of land battles on the Continent, the first few German PoWs to be captured were usually downed Luftwaffe airmen or Kriegsmarine sailors. Indeed, PoWs were something of a novelty: the first German officer PoWs were held at Grizedale Hall, in the Lake District, prompting an MP to ask sarcastically 'would it not be cheaper to hold them at the Ritz Hotel in London?'

But with the Battle of Britain in 1940, 925 German aircrew were shot down. Then, from July 1941, thousands of Italian prisoners were captured in North Africa: this became the first major influx of PoWs into Britain. However, the biggest arrival of German PoWs occurred after D-Day in summer 1944. They were sorted at transit camps, usually racecourses, before being sent to PoW camps in Britain or even America and Canada.

After capture, more important prisoners, such as officers were sent for interrogation. The rest were divided into three categories. Those judged to be non-political or passive were graded 'white'. Prisoners who possibly posed a threat were graded 'grey'. But it was the committed Nazis and SS PoWs who were categorised as 'black'.

They were imprisoned in the more remote PoW camps, where they often informally 'ran' the camps through bullying and mob justice, even lynchings.

There were both individual escapes, such as by Luftwaffe fighter ace Franz von Werra (1914–41), who made four attempts in late 1940, and group attempts, such as at Island Farm PoW camp at Bridgend, South Wales, in March 1945, when seventy PoWs tunnelled to freedom. However, all were caught and no PoW managed to escape Britain's shores directly to Germany. In reality, most PoWs were just relieved to be away from the fighting and were quite happy to sit out the war.

Perhaps surprisingly, PoWs were fed the same amount of food as British troops. This was more than British civilians received, so, in effect, the PoWs enjoyed better rations than the general populace. But the privileges ended there. Most PoWs lived in draughty prefabricated or Nissen huts, constantly fighting boredom. By the war's end, there were over 600 PoW camps in Britain.

Both German and Italian PoWs could be hired by farmers to help on the land, usually escorted by armed soldiers. Following the surrender of Italy in September 1943, thousands of former Italian PoWs volunteered to work as 'co-operators', with a greater degree of liberty. By 1945, there were 155,000 Italian co-operators in Britain.

At the war's end, Britain became a stop-off point for returning prisoners from America and Canada and the peak number of German PoWs reached 402,200 in September 1946. They were put to work helping rebuild Britain, with 22,000 in the building trade and 169,000 in agriculture.

However, not all PoWs wanted to return home. Germany was in ruins, with little employment and half of their home nation was now occupied by the Russians. From Christmas 1946, German PoWs had been freely allowed to visit British homes and developed friendships. Some 24,000 decided to stay in Britain, sometimes even marrying local women, although they were not always welcomed by neighbours and returning British servicemen. The last PoW was repatriated back to Germany in November 1948.

With time on their hands, just as their Napoleonic PoW predecessors had done over a century earlier, many prisoners made novelty items from scraps. Old wood, tin cans, even chicken bones, were used to make toys, trinkets, engraved jewellery boxes and the like: basically, any item that could be sold, bartered or gifted to enable a slightly better quality of life in captivity. This pecking hen children's toy was made by an Axis PoW in Yorkshire: it has been fabricated from wood offcuts and a packing case. A red hot wire has been used to engrave patterns. A wooden counter-balance block suspended below causes the four hens' heads to peck up and down when the handle is moved. It must have offered children sheer seconds of fun!

89: Glenn Miller Snapshot, July 1944

If you could pick a theme tune to Britain's Home Front that reflected fun-fuelled disregard for bombs, bullets and the Nazis, it would have to be a song written by the legendary Major Glenn Miller. Such was the American big band leader's success and array of memorable top tunes, choosing just one would be a harder task.

Alton Glenn Miller was born in Clarinda, Iowa, USA, on 1 March 1904. Although he began playing a mandolin, by the age of just eleven Miller had made enough money milking cows to afford his first trombone and joined the town orchestra in Grant City, Missouri. By the age of sixteen, he had moved to Colorado and became fascinated by dance band music, forming an ensemble with classmates. In 1923, Miller entered the University of Colorado, although he dropped out after failing classes due to absenteeism, practising and playing gigs instead.

However, the determination to follow his heart soon paid off. In 1928, he moved to New York, playing in Broadway bands and as a guest trombonist on records. He also arranged music and other musicians' bands. Miller first recorded his own band for Columbia Records on 25 April 1935, but did not arrange an orchestra under his own name until March 1937. But success was not instant: the band failed to make an impact as there were so many big bands at the time.

Although downhearted, it proved the spur he needed. Miller developed a unique sound that stood out from his competitors. It was noticed

and in September 1938 his band was signed to the Bluebird record label. The legend was born and in 1939–43, he became the world's best-selling recording artist with twenty-three number one hits, more than the Beatles and Elvis did in their longer careers. Hits included *In the Mood*, *Moonlight Serenade*, *Pennsylvania 6-5000*, *Chattanooga Choo Choo*, *A String of Pearls*, *(I've Got a Girl in) Kalamazoo*, *American Patrol*, *Tuxedo Junction*, *Elmer's Tune* and *Little Brown Jug*.

After America entered the war, although at thirty-eight Miller was over the age for conscription, he still wanted to use his talents to help the Allied war effort. He applied to the US Army and in September 1942 became an officer in the US Army Air Forces. He initially served in the US, at Maxwell Field, Alabama, broadcasting his own radio show. Miller then formed a fifteen-piece Army Air Force band and took it to England in June 1944, where he recorded songs for EMI at London's Abbey Road Studios.

Miller chiefly wanted to perform for Allied troops. However, after D-Day those troops moved to the Continent, so at the end of the year he planned to move his band to France. At 1.55 pm, on 15 December 1944, Miller took off from RAF Twinwood, Bedfordshire, bound for Paris. Somewhere over the English Channel, the single-engine UC-64A Norseman aircraft disappeared, along with its pilot, Flight Officer John Morgan, and passengers Lieutenant Colonel Norman Baessell and Major Miller. Various suggestions have been made for the mysterious disappearance, from alleged eyewitness claims to downright salacious and ridiculous conspiracies. However, the most plausible theory remains that put forward by the original 1945 US air force inquiry: a build-up of ice during the flight caused the aircraft to crash.

Aged just forty, Miller left behind a wife, Helen (1902–66) and two adopted children, Steven and Joannie. Miller was posthumously awarded the Bronze Star for 'meritorious service in connection with military operations as Commander of the Army Air Force Band (Special), 9 July 1944–15 December 1944'.

Major Glenn Miller disappeared without trace in 1944, yet his wonderful legacy of lively tunes acts not only as his own impressive epitaph, but as a joyful and emotive soundtrack that defied six long years of darkness – and, timelessly, still brings pleasure today. If you've not heard his music, it's worth discovering the magic of Miller.

In the five months during which Major Miller's US Air Force band toured England from 14 July 1944 they played at least seventy-one concerts, mainly to US personnel at thirty-five air bases. Due to his popularity and star status, many photographs were taken of Miller and his orchestra playing in England – however, here is one I believe has never been published before. This 3in by 2in snapshot, printed on Velox paper, is uncaptioned. However, careful comparisons with photos in the book *Glenn Miller in Britain Then and Now* suggests this was taken in front of Hangar 3, at US 8th Air Force Base 582 Warton, near Blackpool, Lancashire, between 4 and 5 pm, on 14 August 1944, before 10,000 US servicemen. Miller can clearly be seen playing his trombone, centre left, surrounded by his band, with the service caps of troops in the foreground and the partially opened hangar doors in the background. Miller's guest singer was Dorothy Carless (1916–2012). The following day, the band left for their next venue in two B-24 bombers. Just nine days later, a crashing B-24 from Warton base caused the Freckleton disaster [see Object 90].

90: Freckleton Air Accident Parish Magazine, August 1944

Some have small stone memorials in distant corners of the British Isles that few people see or even know about. Others have no memorial at all and few realise this was the site where their young lives ended abruptly: the airmen who died in flying accidents are the largely forgotten casualties of the Second World War.

Little has been written about the Allied air crews who came to grief over their home base. Indeed, the exact number of these unfortunate casualties remains unknown. For a variety of

reasons, thousands died, crashing into mountains or the sea. RAF Bomber Command lost around 8,000 aircrew in training accidents, while the US 8th Air Force register 1,084 aircraft 'destroyed through non-operational causes'. In total, Historic England estimates over 10,000 Allied aircraft crashed in Britain during the war years.

Fortunately, today, air accidents are comparatively uncommon, standing out in news headlines due to their rarity. So, it must seem unusual that there were so many air crashes during wartime. But, for one, aircraft technology is far better today. Long missions of up to eight hours, in extremes of temperature, were not uncommon, putting stress and wear on airframes, engines – and crews – alike. Also, especially by the later war years, few serving airmen were pre-war aviators: most were either conscripted or volunteers with little experience. Similarly, many pilots were young, mostly in their early twenties: it was not unusual for them to be flying a four-engine bomber to Berlin and back yet be unable to drive a car.

However, it's the more high-profile air accidents that are remembered today. On 25 August 1942, thirty-nine-year-old Prince George, the Duke of Kent, set off aboard a Short Sunderland flying boat, bound for Iceland on official business. The aircraft flew into a mountain called Eagle's Rock, Caithness, in the Scottish Highlands, killing fourteen of the fifteen aboard. It was the first time in more than 450 years that a member of the Royal family died on active service. An RAF Board of Inquiry determined the crash was the result of 'controlled flight into terrain'. As with the deaths of other famous

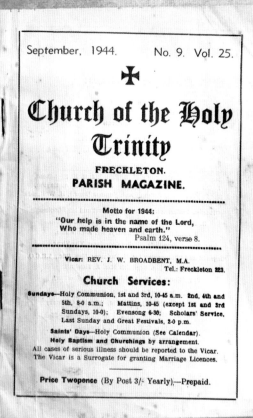

September, 1944.   No. 9. Vol. 25.

✠

Church of the Holy Trinity

FRECKLETON.
PARISH MAGAZINE.

Motto for 1944:
"Our help is in the name of the Lord,
Who made heaven and earth."
Psalm 124, verse 8.

Vicar: REV. J. W. BROADBENT, M.A.
Tel.: Freckleton 223.

Church Services:

Sundays—Holy Communion, 1st and 3rd, 10-45 a.m. 2nd, 4th and 5th, 8-0 a.m.;   Mattins, 10-45 (except 1st and 3rd Sundays, 10-0);   Evensong 6-30;   Scholars' Service, Last Sunday and Great Festivals, 2-0 p.m.

Saints' Days—Holy Communion (See Calendar).
Holy Baptism and Churchings by arrangement.
All cases of serious illness should be reported to the Vicar.
The Vicar is a Surrogate for granting Marriage Licences.

Price Twopence (By Post 3/- Yearly).—Prepaid.

people, the crash spawned various conspiracy theories.

Britain's worst military air accident occurred at 10.47 am on 23 August 1944, when, during a storm, a US B-24 Liberator on a test flight crashed into the centre of the village of Freckleton, Lancashire. The bomber demolished Holy Trinity School, three houses and a servicemen's snack bar, killing sixty-one, including thirty-eight children. This rare edition of the Freckleton monthly parish magazine, published just a week after the accident, contains a forward by the vicar of Holy Trinity Church, the Rev. J. W. Broadbent, who had just presided over the funeral service and interment in a communal grave of the victims, the vast majority of whom had attended his Sunday School. The vicar noted:

I still find it difficult to write or say what I feel after the experience of last week … Nothing like the catastrophe which descended on our village has been seen here before. Those who witnessed it cannot possibly ever forget it. With a suddenness unimaginable … something had struck and brought down the roof of the Infants' School, and immediately fire broke out trapping the little children where they were. We have not forgotten the poor pilot and other members of the crew. Our hearts go out to the members of their families and friends.

A memorial garden, new school and village hall now mark the site of the tragedy.

These are only two of the most infamous air accidents: the vast majority involved the loss of the 'unknowns', those known only to their loved ones. Even today, on remote, windswept uplands, twisted, weathered aluminium wreckage lies among the rocks – the last corroded testimony to these unfortunate aviators.

91: Next Of Kin Letter, 1944

We live in an era of instant communication. We can talk to nearly everyone we know (and even those we don't) via social media, emails, mobile phones and texts. In the 1940s, letter writing was commonplace and for most folk the main form of long-distance communication: telephones were a luxury to which working-class families could only aspire. The red telephone box was the nearest thing to a mobile phone. In 1940s Britain, there were two main companies responsible for the nation's communications: the Royal Mail, which delivered letters, and the General Post Office (GPO), which received mail and was also responsible for most of Britain's telephone network.

The GPO is largely forgotten now, but it was huge: indeed, it was Britain's single largest employer. During the war it ran 24,000 post offices and handled twenty million letters and postcards per day. It also operated 5,800 telephone exchanges, serving nearly four million telephones. Both military and civil defence services also relied on telephone communications. Such was the importance of these telecommunications, Home Guard battalions were formed from GPO staff to guard their own sites.

Both the Royal Mail and GPO had a tough enough job on their hands sorting and delivering post in peacetime, but in wartime it became even more complicated. People were bombed out, moved districts on war work or were evacuated, resulting in sixty million changes of address. Post offices and their inflammable paper contents were burned out. Yet, due to the importance of postal communications, this service was maintained as a priority – and all for the price of a stamp.

Letter writing was widespread. It was a morale-booster for those at the front and at home. Some couples wrote to each other every day: this might seem excessive, but it was just the equivalent of a daily email today. However, even the war impacted on letter writing: eventually, envelopes had to be reused, with economy labels to reseal them. Postcards were also very popular, particularly the comic type by companies such as Bamforth with the artwork of Donald McGill (1875–1962), which were cheeky, but not as risqué as in post-war years.

Two other novel ways of communication from the front line to those at home came to the fore. The Airgraph, invented in the 1930s by the American Eastman Kodak Company, with Imperial Airways (now British Airways) and Pan-American Airways, was a clever way of reducing the amount of post carried overseas. The letter was written on an Airgraph form, photographed, reduced and sent on rolls of microfilm. At the destination, the images were enlarged, printed and delivered as Airgraphs. The GPO claimed that 1,600 Airgraphs on a microfilm weighed just 5oz, whereas 1,600 hardcopy letters weighed 50lb. In total, 330

million Airgraphs were sent. Also, in the closing years of the war, the NAAFI organised the recording of messages from servicemen in the Far East on small discs called *Voices of the Forces Around the World*. This allowed those at home to hear their loved one's voice – but the delicate discs could only be played a few times before becoming unlistenable.

Not all post brought good news. It must have been devastating for those serving at the front to receive a 'Dear John' letter from a lover thousands of miles away at home. But even worse correspondence was received. Official telegrams from the military could bring the news that a son, husband or fiancé was 'Missing', which gave some hope, or 'missing, presumed killed', which gave little hope and left the recipient in limbo. The ultimate blow was 'Deeply regret to inform you that … has been killed on war service.' All were short, somewhat blunt and delivered in an envelope marked 'Priority', by a telegram boy, often no more than fourteen years old. Their unfortunate arrival bearing such bad news led them to be nicknamed 'angels of death'.

This was only one of a series of communications that would be sent to the bereaved. A typed letter of confirmation could also come from the serviceman's unit and a small printed standard letter of condolence from King George VI was specially delivered. But the most poignant letter would be sent from the deceased's commanding officer – just one of many he would have to write in the course of his duties. The contents were usually some words of comfort to reassure the recipient that the deceased's death had been quick or painless. This moving follow-up letter was sent to Mrs Frances Pearson, of Golcar, Huddersfield, on 4 November 1944, by Captain Robert Elliston-Walker, of the 2nd Battalion, the King's Royal Rifle Corps, following the death of her son, Rifleman Irvin Pearson, aged twenty-four, on 1 September 1944, who is now buried at Airaines Cemetery, Northern France. After writing: 'I am very glad that I was at least able to set your mind at rest,' decades on, Captain Elliston-Walker's poignant penultimate sentence still strikes home today: 'The War has caused a lot of sorrow & hardship, and if we manage to achieve a lasting Peace, I hope that future generations won't forget the terrible price that was paid for it.'

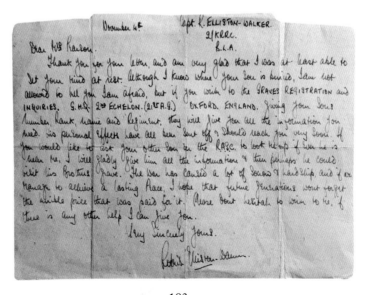

92: Home Guard Service Certificate, December 1944

By 1942, the Home Guard were a fully trained and equipped home army, trusted with the responsibility for the defence of Britain. Though the Nazi invasion threat may have dwindled, the Home Guard's growing strength meant that the regular army could move on to the offensive and take the war to the enemy.

Although it was only two years prior, long gone were the days of armbands and shared rifles. By the end of 1940, the Home Guard had been issued with regular army battledress uniforms. Indeed, whereas the force may have started as a separate entity developing on its own, by now it had been reined in and moulded as an adjunct of the regular army, with the same training and battle drills.

In many cases, older Home Guards were quietly retired and the initial volunteer spirit was diluted when, on 16 February 1942, conscription of men aged eighteen to fifty-one into the force was introduced under the terms of the National Service (No. 2) Act. Compulsion boosted numbers to a peak of 1,850,757 Home Guards at the end of the year. However, by this stage of the war, for many, especially conscripts, Home Guard service was becoming a chore on top of their long hours of war work. But, as group photos taken in the latter years reveal, the influx of new Home Guards in their late teens waiting for call up into the regular forces also brought the force greater agility.

Nevertheless, the Home Guard was a better-equipped and professional fighting force, now capable of engaging and causing serious damage to any invaders. For a start, each Home Guard now had a personal weapon – and better guns were arriving: the 9mm Sten sub machine gun was available in numbers, as were a wide range of grenades. Most importantly, the force now had a reasonable anti-tank capability: the Northover Projector drainpipe weapon of mid-1941 had been superseded later that year by the 29mm Blacker Bombard spigot mortar, and this from summer 1942 by the 3in Smith gun sub-artillery. Neither were first-choice weapons of the regular army, but they were sufficient to ambush and disrupt a column of invaders.

Not only that, but to help ease manpower shortages, 141,676 Home Guards were made responsible for the partial manning of light and

In the years when our Country
was in mortal danger

F. BURTON

who served 14.5.1940 to 31.12.1944
gave generously of his time and
powers to make himself ready
for her defence by force of arms
and with his life if need be.

George R.I.

THE HOME GUARD

heavy AA sites (downing several aircraft), with 7,000 in coastal artillery and a similar number in auxiliary bomb disposal sections.

Although, officially, forbidden to fire weapons, women had been involved with the Home Guard from the beginning as helpers or WVS. However, from June 1943, they were officially invited to join as 'Nominated Women' and, from June 1944, as 'Home Guard Auxiliaries', with 32,000 serving in medical, signalling and administrative roles.

The Home Guard were put on alert in summer 1944, in case of German counterattacks to D-Day, but with the growing success of the Allied invasion, the force looked increasingly redundant through wider events. This led to growing frustration among Home Guards as the government offered no future plans.

On 3 December 1944, the Home Guard was stood down, with ceremonies across Britain and a large national ninety-minute parade of 7,000 representative Home Guards marching through central London, saluting the force's Colonel-in-Chief, King George VI. It was a grey, rainy day and so ended the largest recorded home defence force in history.

Most Home Guards were presented with this service certificate, designed by war artist Abram Games (1914–96), bearing a facsimile signature of the King. In this case, Volunteer F. Burton served the full duration of the LDV and Home Guard, in 1940–44. Many Home Guards were also entitled to the Defence Medal [see Object 96]. Since the war, the popular BBC sitcom *Dad's Army* (1968–77) has become synonymous with the Home Guard. While the series captures the determination and comradeship of the force, the comedy has largely clouded the serious reality: had the Nazis invaded, it would have been no laughing matter. Many thousands of Home Guards would have been killed doing their duty – as this certificate ('… with his life if need be') poignantly notes – a point often forgotten today. As it was, officially at least, 1,206 Home Guards died in training accidents and air raids (however, this figure is conservative: for example, the Commonwealth War Graves Commission lists six Home Guards as having died in Leicestershire – I have traced another thirteen service fatalities).

Behind the uniforms and ceremony, the Home Guard were created to slow and wear down a ruthless and powerful enemy, giving time for the regular army to arrive. Each second gained would have probably cost the life of a Home Guard, but would have given greater chance for Britain's survival.

93: V2 Rocket Section, January 1945

If there was anything grotesquely merciful about the V2, at best those killed knew nothing about it: one second they may be sitting relaxing in their home, the next second, instant oblivion. For, unlike its predecessor, there was no warning of the V2's arrival: in a vicious irony, the rocket descended so fast its explosion occurred before the roar of its descent was heard.

The V2 was a truly monstrous weapon – it was also a contradiction: it was humanity's most advanced technological achievement in avionics – yet it was also designed to destroy humans: what Churchill had called four years earlier, 'the lights of perverted science'.

The existence of the V2 was due to the unbridled ambition of German scientist Wernher von Braun (1912–77). Studying rocketry since the 1920s, von Braun flourished at Berlin Technical University. When the Nazis came to power, German artillery captain Walter Dornberger (1895–1980) encouraged his research. By 1943, von Braun had developed a working version of his giant A4 rocket – a far cry from his pre-war efforts.

Despite being enveloped in secrecy, the A4 had not gone unnoticed by the Allies: on 17 August 1943, 596 RAF heavy bombers were sent to attack the German army research centre at Peenemünde, on the Baltic, delaying development by seven weeks. A4 production was moved underground to the Mittelwerk mountain factory in central Germany, harnessing slave labour from the Mittelbau-Dora concentration camp.

As with the V1, the D-Day landings hastened the A4's deployment. At 6.43 pm, on 8 September 1944, the first rocket struck Staveley Road, Chiswick, London, killing sixty-three-year-old Ada Harrison, three-year-old Rosemary Clarke and twenty-eight-year-old Sapper Bernard Browning on leave from the Royal Engineers, injuring twenty-two. It would be the first of 1,358 V2s to fall on the capital.

To lessen this terror weapon's effect, the government initially blamed the explosions on 'faulty gas mains': few were fooled and the new rockets were satirically dubbed 'flying gas mains'. Two months later, the Germans officially announced the weapon as *Vergeltungswaffe Zwei* (V2).

The 46ft-tall, 12-ton rocket was fuelled by liquid oxygen and alcohol, reaching 50 miles into space, from where it would descend on its target 200 miles away at a staggering 3,545mph, detonating its 1-ton warhead which levelled whole streets. Britain's worst V2 incident was at New Cross, on 25 November 1944, when 168 Londoners were killed by a single rocket.

Due to its speed, there was no viable anti-aircraft defence against the V2: as with its predecessor, only bombing or the capture of its Dutch launch sites could lessen the assault, which finally ended on 27 March 1945, at Orpington, Kent, the V2's final fatality being thirty-four-year-old Ivy Millichamp.

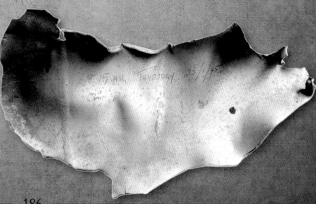

The aftermath of a V2 strike on 15 March 1945. Beyond the crater caused by the blast is Tottenham Grammar School. Two boys were killed, several more injured. (*Historic Military Press*)

The V2 was the last desperate and spiteful gasp of the dying Nazi beast. Some 1,402 V2s struck Britain, killing 2,754 – less than two persons per rocket. Despite its advanced technology, the V2 was a costly and uneconomic drain on German resources, compared to the cheaper and more lethal V1.

As for von Braun, after the war he faced no war crimes trial. In the post-war scrabble for scientific talent, the Americans got their man. He helped develop nuclear missiles and upscaled the V2 into the Saturn V space rocket, which took man to the moon on 20 July 1969. Von Braun's legacy and the V2's dichotomy remain today: humans now have the ability to travel into space – but also the ability to end all human life on Earth.

At 16in wide, this piece of aluminium V2 fuel tank wreckage is unusually large: aside from the combustion chamber, normally only small pieces of crumpled metal survived the fearsome explosion. It is part of the 601st V2 to arrive in Britain, over the Dudden Hill estate, Willesden, west London, at 8.19 am on 25 January 1945, as the pencilled writing on it testifies. A weld mark is visible on the left. Due to the extreme pressures of re-entry, it exploded in the air before impact, fortunately only injuring two civilians.

94: VE Day Bunting, May 1945

Throughout early 1945, Britons tuned their radios daily to listen for developments as the Allies made the final push against the German homeland. The war in Europe dragged out, as the Germans put up stiff resistance, but the end of the Third Reich was now clearly in sight.

The Russians entered the suburbs of Berlin on 21 April 1945. Four days later, American and Russian forces met at the Elbe River, in eastern Germany. On 30 April 1945, Adolf Hitler, the war criminal whose nationalist rabble-rousing fervour led to the deaths of millions, chose to avoid justice via a single 7.65mm bullet, hiding in his Berlin bunker. On 7 May 1945, temporary German leader Grand Admiral Karl Dönitz (1891–1980) travelled to Allied HQ in France, and senior officers signed the document of unconditional surrender. The war in Europe was finally over.

In Britain, rumours had circulated for days that hostilities were almost over. People listened intently to their radios for updates. Suddenly, the Nazi surrender was announced. The following day, 8 May 1945, would be celebrated as VE (Victory in Europe) Day. Many didn't wait until then and started celebrating immediately, continuing on throughout the night.

On VE Day, crowds gathered in cities, towns and villages. Tables were set up in streets, brimming with sandwiches, cakes and drinks, all saved, despite the rationing, for this historic day. Flags and bunting were hung from houses and children wore fancy dress. Adults dressed in red, white and blue clothing and drink flowed freely. Gramophones and pianos were rolled out into the street, providing music for dancing and singsongs. Traditional British reserve was temporarily cast aside as strangers randomly kissed each other. It was the biggest and greatest party Britain has ever known.

At 3 pm, in front of massed crowds, Churchill appeared on the balcony of the Ministry of Health, in Whitehall, London. Broadcasting live to the nation, he said:

This is your victory! It is the victory of the cause of freedom in every land. In all our long history, we have never seen a greater day than this. Everyone, man or woman, has done their best. Everyone has tried. Neither the long years, nor the dangers, nor the fierce attacks of the enemy have in any way weakened the deep resolve of the British nation. God bless you all … Advance Britannia!

Huge crowds also gathered outside Buckingham Palace, chanting 'We want the King!' The Royal Family appeared on their balcony no fewer than eight times that day. At 6 pm, the King broadcast to the nation. That night, the princesses were allowed to leave the palace and secretly mingled with the jubilant crowds.

During the evening, every spare piece of flammable material was gathered and huge bonfires were made in streets across Britain.

Japan) Day on 15 August 1945: at last, the Second World War was over.

In Britain, VJ Day celebrations were quieter than they had been on VE Day. Though famous buildings in London were floodlit, the crowds were smaller and less euphoric. Reflection had replaced jubilation and the nation paused to think. The bloodiest war in human history had ended. It was time to look forward and build a positive future.

This 7ft-long length of victory bunting is made of rough cotton, with nine printed colour flags of victorious Allied nations, including, clockwise from top left, Holland, Belgium, Great Britain, Norway, Nationalist China, Greece, Poland, the USA and USSR. There are rusty pin holes in each end of the tape, suggesting this bunting may have stayed up for some time in celebration, possibly outside on the front of a house. These national flags sit side-by-side in unity of victory. However, this unity would soon fragment, as the flags would become divided by the East versus West politics of the new Cold War (1947–91).

Effigies of Hitler were publicly hanged and then thrown on to the fires. Across the land, pubs were drunk dry.

But, for those who had lost loved ones or had relatives still fighting in the Far East, celebrations were muted. In his speech, Churchill reminded the nation that 'Japan remains unsubdued'. Bitter fighting continued until early August 1945, when the US dropped two atomic bombs on Hiroshima and Nagasaki, effectively knocking Japan out of the war. The world celebrated VJ (Victory over

A group of soldiers and civilians celebrate Victory in Europe by posing on a Bren Gun carrier in the high street of a Scottish town or village, 8 May 1945. (*Historic Military Press*)

95: Thanks For The Victory Banner, May 1945

The Second World War took a horrendous toll in human lives: it is estimated that up to eighty million people died on all fronts, including up to fifty million civilians. On the British Home Front, 60,595 civilians were killed by enemy action, with at least 86,182 injured. Of these, 2,379 ARP/CD, police and fire service personnel were killed, with at least 4,459 seriously injured.

The Commander-in-Chief of the Luftwaffe, Hermann Göring and his führer, Adolf Hitler, who ordered these raids, both cheated the justice of a war crimes trial. Amongst numerous other serious charges, Göring was indicted for launching air war against civilians at the Nuremberg war trials. On 15 March 1946, he openly testified: 'Birmingham and Coventry were targets of most decisive importance for me. I decided on Coventry because there the most targets could be hit within the smallest area. I prepared that attack myself with both air fleets … I ordered the attack and gave directions for it to be carried out as long and as repeatedly as was necessary to achieve decisive effects on the British aircraft industry there.' Exactly seven months later to the day, Göring, like his führer, chose not to face the hangman and committed suicide, with a hidden cyanide capsule.

For the first time in almost 300 years, since the plague pits of 1666, Britons had been buried

in mass communal graves. Whole families were wiped out in the bombing. Some victims were never found, the remains of others were collected and fitted in small pouches. Scanning lists of British civilian war dead, the ages of children in single figure years, or even months, seem particularly pitiful. They had their futures snatched away by an aggressive politics and a conflict they could not even comprehend. Other victims were left with life-changing injuries: my grandmother knew a woman who, fifty years on, still intermittently 'bled' glass after being caught behind a blast-shattered window. The psychological effect of the bombing also made a lasting impact. Wartime local newspapers reported of directly related suicides caused by the stress of air raids 'whilst the balance of their mind was disturbed'. My aunt worked in a London psychiatric hospital in the 1970s and revealed that many of the permanent patients had been there since the war as the result of deep-seated trauma caused by the air raids. They are the forgotten, long-term victims of the Blitz. If all this makes grim reading, that's because it is.

However, ironic as it may seem, there is much reason to see good shine through the darkness of the Blitz's legacy. While Britain's AA defences may have been unable to stop the bombers getting through, it's clear that the nation's ARP and Civil Defence services achieved a level of success that can be viewed positively. Many thousands of people owed their continued existence to the selfless, altruistic and brave deeds of the CD organisation and, technically, many more to the careful planning and contingencies taken by both local and central ARP authorities.

When people talk of Second World War heroes, they commonly focus on the more obvious daring fighter pilots or machine-gun-brandishing special forces. But, although their bravery is undoubted, elite soldiers faced the enemy armed with weapons – the CD services faced the enemy's bombs, bullets and flames with little more than their training and sense of duty. When I think of Second World War heroes, I think of ARP wardens braving bombs to report and summon help to incidents; I think of the rescue parties risking their lives under tons of rubble to recover the trapped; I think of the first aid parties giving immediate assistance to the wounded; I think of the nurses caring for an influx of casualties and surgeons saving broken bodies on the operating table. I also think of AFS and NFS crews battling fires as bombs and flames threatened to engulf them. The unarmed men of the bomb disposal squads fought a war of nerves and possible instant oblivion, too. In a war that typified humans' ability for inhumanity, these heroes of the Home Front proved that humanity was the ultimate victor.

This rare 35in by 25in colour printed cloth banner was made for the VE celebrations by the appropriately named New Era Company, of Wembley, north London. Little is known of the company, although it made several such banners in 1945 featuring the victorious Allied war leaders, Field-Marshal Montgomery and even one headed 'Lest We Forget', showing a bearded Russian soldier with the flag of the USSR. Though their efforts and sacrifices may have largely faded from public memory today, clearly, the company thought the CD organisation and NFS also deserved a banner: firemen are shown below their NFS emblem battling flames before London's St Paul's Cathedral, while a rescue party is shown recovering a bombing victim below their CD symbol. Simply, the banner states: *Thanks for the Victory*.

96: The Defence Medal, May 1945

Those who served the 'red, white and blue' on the Home Front, both in a civil and military capacity, were entitled to a campaign medal with a ribbon of green, black and orange, recognising their war service. However, the 1939–1945 Defence Medal is often overlooked now and viewed as less important than the campaign star medals that were issued for service on other fronts. This should not be the case: its recipients also served, fought and died on this Home Front.

Those eligible for the Defence Medal had to have served in Britain during the period of the war in Europe in a civil or military capacity for 1,080 days (three years' service) or, because of their life expectancy and the danger of the job, ninety days (three months' service) in a Royal Navy mine or Army/RAF bomb disposal

unit. Those serving on Home Fronts in British colonies were also eligible.

The Defence Medal is 36mm in diameter and is made of cupro-nickel. The front was designed by Thomas Humphrey Paget (1893–1974). It shows the profile of King George VI, with the wording: 'GEORGIVS VI D : G : BR : OMN : REX F : D : IND : IMP', which is a Latin abbreviation of 'George VI, by the grace of God, King of the Britons, Defender of the Faith, Emperor of India.' The rear was designed by sculptor Harold Parker (1873–1962) and shows the royal crown resting on an oak sapling, flanked by a lion and lioness, above waves. The dates '1939' and '1945' and wording 'The Defence Medal' identify the award.

Above the medal is a straight bar and suspension mounting that allows the addition of a 32mm-wide coloured ribbon. This ribbon was designed by King George VI and comprises three colours: a central flame-coloured orange band representing the fires of the Blitz, two thin black bands representing the blackout and a green background, representing Britain's 'green and pleasant land'.

The medal was issued to ARP and CD personnel, Home Guard, the fire services, WVS, police, nurses, Royal Observer Corps, coast guard, lighthouse keepers and members of the armed forces who were based in Britain. Unfortunately, one notable service not included in the list were the Women's Land Army [see Object 81]. Metal shortages meant many did not receive their medal for another two years. Issue was also patchy: some who were entitled to the medal never received one. Others did not bother applying: they were moving on and thinking of the future in the post-war world. However, next of kin can still apply today to the MoD for the Defence Medal, providing they have proof of their relative's service. The medal was sent through the post in a small cardboard box, with a small certificate of issue and list of other campaign stars. Unlike medals of the First World War, Parliament decreed that medals would not be individually named. However, some recipients had their names added by commercial engravers.

Other higher medals for service were awarded to those who served on the Home Front, including 5,672 MBEs (Member of the Order of the British Empire), 3,127 OBEs (Officer of OBE) and 1,166 CBEs (Commander of the OBE), 18 DBEs (Dame Commander of the OBE), 122 KBEs (Knight Commander of the OBE), 3 DGBEs (Dame Grand Cross of the OBE) and 29 GBEs (Knight Grand Cross of the OBE).

Gallantry awards were also made for brave service on the Home Front. On 24 September 1940, King George VI inaugurated the George Cross and George Medal to mark outstanding acts of bravery by the military and ARP services, of which twenty-one GCs and 705 GMs were awarded. Some 6,276 BEM (British Empire Medals) were also awarded, as were 2,696 King's Commendations for Brave Conduct. It should also not be forgotten that the PDSA instituted the Dickin Medal in 1943, recognising gallant acts by animals, of which eleven were awarded to animals that served on the Home Front, such as CD rescue sniffer dogs.

Of course, there were many daily acts of bravery and good service that were never recognised by any medal. These actions were just taken for granted as part of the job. However, the apparently humble Defence Medal, which can commonly be found at collectors' fairs for as little as £10–£15, should today be viewed from a reappraised perspective as *the* campaign and service medal of the Second World War Home Front.

97: Soldier's Welcome Home Banner, 1945

That the horrors of the war on the Continent didn't come to Britain, we can – and do – give thanks every year on 11 November in Remembrance services across the nation. But the cost was colossal. The Commonwealth War Graves Commission estimates 580,497 British, Colonial and Commonwealth troops died for the luxury of the freedom we enjoy today, 264,443 of those from Britain alone. Fatal casualties of the individual British services were reckoned in 1945 to be British Army 144,079, Royal Air Force 69,606 and Royal Navy 50,758, with 284,049 service personnel of Britain and Crown Colonies wounded. It is a debt successive generations will never be able to repay, but only remember these sacrifices.

For the servicemen and women who survived the war, the relief and adulation of returning home must have been overwhelming. But it was not so straightforward. The process of releasing hundreds of thousands of personnel was delayed: Britain's huge war machine could not be deconstructed overnight. Those who had entered the forces at the war's start were demobilised first in 1945, while those who entered later were not 'demobbed' for up to another two years, as late as 1947. The former Axis countries were broken and British servicemen were needed to help instil law and order and rebuild them as new democracies. They were not the only ones still in uniform: teenagers who thought they were going to be free from conscription in this new world of peace, from 1949 until 1963 found themselves called up for eighteen months' National Service.

Just as after the First World War, ex-servicemen – with their new government-issue demob suit and choice of flat cap or trilby hat –

did not find themselves in a 'land fit for heroes'. Britain looked tired and worn, with vast swathes of war-damaged areas: often the landmarks and familiar places returning troops knew had been bombed out of existence years earlier.

There were many joyful reunions for loved ones after years of separation, but not all. People change, and grew apart over six years of war. Some even found new partners. Perhaps most heart-breaking of all, as they had been babies when their father had left for war, some children no longer recognised him and shunned this stranger in their home. Relationships had to be rebuilt.

The experiences and sights the men had seen on service stayed with them for the rest of their lives. In the 1940s, men were expected 'to be men' and counselling was largely unaffordable or not considered. Many soldiers returned bearing mental as well as physical scars that affected their everyday lives in peacetime, from nightmares and

mood swings to domestic violence. This is now diagnosed as Post-Traumatic Stress Disorder (PTSD).

Some men settled straight back into jobs they had left before the war, others found their vacancy had already been filled. Alternatively, after years of frantic action, some found they were unable to sit for hours behind a desk. This testimony by my partner's grandfather will best explain the experience of servicemen trying to return to 'civvy street'. Corporal Charles Cooper

(1926–2008) served in the Staffordshire Home Guard and later, towards the end of the war, in the British 1st Airborne Division, driving a jeep through Europe, towing a six-pounder anti-tank gun. Charlie told me several poignant and hard-hitting stories about his war service, but when I interviewed him, there was one tale he wanted told the most: '... but enough of the old war stories and all that, tell them how we were treated *after* the war', he snapped, before irritably exemplifying his point.

When we got back, there was very little work for us: certainly no jobs or 'homes for heroes'. As I had served as a driver, I got a job driving a lorry. One trip, I had to drive all the way up from Stoke to Glasgow to deliver some barrels. When I finally arrived after the long journey, (there were no motorways, only A and B roads), as I'm not a very big fella, I asked one of the men in the warehouse if he could give me a hand to unload the barrels. He smirked and just said: 'You squaddies are ten a penny – do it yourself.' I lost it and just punched him flat out, kicked the barrels off the back of the lorry, got in the cab and drove, foot down, all the way back to Stoke.

These feelings of frustration and anticlimax were common to many servicemen on their return to Britain. They had been trained to fight and kill for their country – and they had done so. But they received little help or preparation to readjust back into post-war British society. The nation had moved on – and not all ex-servicemen were helped on the journey.

It is for that reason poet John Maxwell Edmonds' (1875–1958) original 1919 epitaph quoted at the end of the First World War still stood true at the end of the following conflict: 'For your tomorrows, these gave their today' – and it still stands true today.

This slightly faded, red, white and blue 37in by 35in cotton banner welcomed home thirty-five-year-old Sergeant Major Charles Albert Doyle Powell (1910–93) at the war's end. Powell served with the Oxford and Bucks Light Infantry in 1927–49. His grandson recalls Charles served throughout the Second World War and 'he had nine medals'. In peacetime, he continued public service as a prison officer, then a policeman in Watford. This banner was displayed in 1945 and then folded up and put away – now it is permanently displayed in this book.

98: Bomb Damage Mystery, 1945

'Necessity is the mother of invention' and wartime practicality adapted city centre destruction for the war effort. Bombsites became 'victory gardens', growing much-needed food, or unofficial children's playgrounds. Ironically, the debris was also used as a basis to return the destruction to Germany: over a six-month period, 750,000 tons of London rubble was transported on 1,700 trains for the foundation of RAF Bomber Command airfields, while rubble from Birmingham was used to make US air force runways. Some rubble even found its way to the other side of the Atlantic to make new homes: bricks from Bristol bombsites acted as ballast on returning US supply ships, then were used to build an area of New York's Manhattan called the Bristol Basin.

But Britain's housing stock had been severely depleted. By the war's end, around two million British homes had been destroyed in the bombing. Once again, service personnel did not return to 'homes fit for heroes'. The housing shortage was so acute that by summer 1946 around 40,000 people were living as squatters in former army camps and abandoned airfields. They comprised bombed-out families and 'displaced persons', such as Poles, who could not return to their homeland as it was now part of Soviet-controlled Eastern Europe.

As a temporary remedy, back in 1943 the government began the Temporary Housing Programme, earmarking £1 million [£40 million] towards easily erected prefabricated homes. Created on former aircraft factory production lines, by 1948 some 125,000 'prefabs' were built. Despite their stopgap nature, many prefabs soldiered on for many decades and were popular with their residents: indeed, it is a form of housing that, seventy years on, is coming back into production.

While there was no immediate solution to the housing crisis, both local and national government had made long-term plans for the future. In November 1943, Churchill created the Ministry of Reconstruction, moving Lord Woolton from the Ministry of Food as its new chief. The Ministry of Town and Country Planning was also formed. Indeed, as early as 1941, London County Council commissioned Britain's most eminent planner, Professor Patrick Abercrombie (1879–1957), to formulate the capital's reconstruction, creating the 1943 County of London Plan and 1944 Greater London Plan. Other blitzed cities, such as Coventry, also drew up their own plans.

The government also used this opportunity to reduce housing density by building outside existing city limits, creating fourteen new conurbations under the 1946 New Towns Act, eight of them outside London, including Crawley, Bracknell, Hemel Hempstead, Hatfield, Stevenage, Harlow, Basildon and Welwyn Garden City. Today, over two million people live in the new towns.

However, many of these grand quasi-utopian plans for the future were often only partly realised due to cost and changing administrations. Post-war financial constraints also partly explain the poor utilitarian standard of functional urban buildings of the 1950s and beyond. Similarly, such was the huge task facing developers, large bombsite moonscapes remained, even in central London, until the 1960s and '70s, many simply boarded off or used as car parks or playgrounds for post-war children.

As is often pointed out, it's ironic that in many towns and cities more destruction of Britain's irreplaceable built historic heritage was carried out not by the Luftwaffe, but by successive post-war councils and private developers. The destruction continues to this day. One positive that did emerge from all the bombing for which we can thank today is the diversity of surviving heritage. At the height of the Blitz, in November 1940, the Royal Institute of British Architects and the Society for the Protection of Ancient Buildings commissioned 300 architects to photograph and 'list' important buildings. This became the basis of the present listing process, which offers some statutory protection to our built heritage. This means we can still enjoy fine historic buildings that survived Nazi bombs – and will hopefully survive the excesses of overzealous twenty-first-century developers.

In Britain's biggest target, London's built heritage took a battering. It is estimated that a million buildings were destroyed and another 1.7 million damaged. Large and exposed, the capital's historic churches were particularly susceptible to the bombing: 624 of 701 churches were damaged, of which ninety-one were destroyed. In 1991, I picked up this unusual 12in wide by 9in tall wooden object in London's Camden Passage antiques arcade. Clearly, the contemporary 'Blitz London 1941' wording added in gold paint to the front reveals it is bomb damaged. Technically, it is probably the oldest item in my collection – but it's also the most mysterious. It clearly has some age, possibly even medieval, but so far no historian, antique expert or architect has been able to identify exactly what it is from: intricately carved, is it part of a table or chair, perhaps an architectural detail from a grand house, or even a section of reredos altar panel from a London church? Answers on a postcard, please.

One of the prefabricated houses introduced towards the end of the war in an effort to alleviate a looming housing crisis in Britain's towns and cities. This is an example of the 'Aluminum House' pictured in April 1945. Designed by the Aircraft Industries Research Organization on Housing, it was made in four sections, each complete in itself, which are fastened together a few hours after arrival on site. (*Historic Military Press*)

99: School Victory
Souvenir Certificate, 1946

Once the victory celebrations were over, Britons looked forward to a brighter future. They wanted the war to mark a dividing line between the old inequalities and a new way forward. But conditions in Britain would get worse before they got better …

Following VE Day, while the war was still being fought in the Far East, the country's great war leader, Winston Churchill, was defeated at the ballot box on 26 July 1945. Under new Prime Minister Clement Attlee (1883–1967), the Labour party came to power with a massive political landslide. Despite Churchill's popularity during the conflict, voters now saw him as a man of war, not peace. They now wanted to rebuild the country and move on.

However, anyone who thought good times would roll because the war was over were sadly mistaken. Britain was bankrupt. Under the Lend-Lease Act, the country was in massive debt to the US, owing $31.4 billion [£324 billion], which was not finally paid off until 29 December 2006!

Nor did victory bring an end to rationing. Far from it. On 27 May 1945, barely three weeks after VE Day, cuts were made to the basic ration. Bacon went down from 4oz to 3oz, cooking fat from 2oz to 1oz and part of the meagre meat ration had to be taken in corned beef. On

the Continent, agricultural fields had become broken battlefields, creating a worldwide wheat shortage, leading to bread rationing in Britain for two years from July 1946 – something that had never happened even during the darkest days of the war. Home food production was further curtailed by a particularly bad winter of 1946–47.

8th June, 1946

TO-DAY, AS WE CELEBRATE VICTORY, I send this personal message to you and all other boys and girls at school. For you have shared in the hardships and dangers of a total war and you have shared no less in the triumph of the Allied Nations.

I know you will always feel proud to belong to a country which was capable of such supreme effort; proud, too, of parents and elder brothers and sisters who by their courage, endurance and enterprise brought victory. May these qualities be yours as you grow up and join in the common effort to establish among the nations of the world unity and peace.

George R.I.

Similarly, the clothing coupon allowance fell to its lowest immediately the war ended. For eight months, between 1 September 1945 and 30 April 1946, only twenty-four coupons were issued, compared to sixty-six in 1941.

It would require a great national effort to get the country back on its feet. However, with the gradual return of ex-servicemen, labour became available to rebuild the nation and slowly, over time, Britain recovered. From simple luxuries, such as television broadcasts resuming on 7 June 1946, to more important necessities, such as the end of clothes rationing on 15 March 1949 and petrol rationing on 26 May 1950, austerity began to ease.

But due to the post-war anticlimax and voter disappointment, on 25 October 1951, Churchill was voted back into power on a Conservative party manifesto pledge to end rationing. On 5 February 1953, sweets were derationed, sugar following on 26 September and, finally, all food rationing ended on 4 July 1954. Beaming Britons were filmed burning their ration books.

But what of the great social aspirations that were planned during the war? Back at the height of the Blitz in January 1941, *Picture Post* [Object 45] had made a list of future hopes called *A Plan for Britain*, two years before the government's Beveridge Report. Did these aims come to fruition? *Picture Post* wanted a complete overhaul of the schools system: this was actually partly met during the war, with the 1944 Education Act. *Picture Post* wanted to end child poverty with the introduction of targeted subsidies: Child Allowance payments were introduced in 1977. *Picture Post* wanted a minimum wage: this was finally introduced on 1 April 1999. *Picture*

Post wanted full employment: well, that was probably the toughest nut to crack, and with the increased automation of the digital age, may never be achieved.

But perhaps the two greatest testimonies to the efforts of the Second World War generation are our National Health Service, founded on 5 July 1948, ensuring the greatest healthcare Britons have ever had, and the daily freedom we have enjoyed since 1945. For this, we can all give thanks – long may it continue.

One year and one month after the end of the war in Europe, on Saturday, 8 June 1946, national Victory Celebrations were held across Britain, with a large parade through central London featuring troops of all the Allied nations (except Poland, Russia and Yugoslavia, who boycotted the parade for political reasons). Representative services of the nation's wartime CD and Home Guard also marched through the capital. Smaller processions were also held in Britain's cities and towns. Schoolchildren throughout the land were given this 10in by 7in commemorative souvenir certificate from King George VI, bearing a full colour royal crest, with poignant words and meaningful thoughts for the future ahead. On the back is a long list of 'Important War Dates' for future reference. Below it is a space for the recipient to add 'My Family's War Record'. Usually left blank on most surviving certificates, however, this example has been filled in, with the small, ink handwriting of a child: 'Father: The Great War 1914–1918: Royal Army Medical Corps 11th Jan 1915 to Mar 3rd 1918. Last War 1939–1945 Home Guard 55th [Sutton & Cheam] Battalion East Surrey Rgt. Cousin: Last War 1939–1945 War Office'.

100: Railing Stumps Mystery, Today

We end this book with something of an enigma. Our final object from the Home Front is one of the most common, but also, ironically, surrounded by mystery. Whether you live in a British city, town or village, most people probably just pass by without noticing or even realising how they came to be.

Following the successful public response to the request for aluminium salvage in summer 1940, in April 1941, the Ministry of Supply announced the shortage 'of the particular type of scrap metal which may be obtained from railings and which had a special value in the manufacture of ships' cables, chains and other fittings'.

In September 1941, local authorities were ordered to survey unnecessary railings, with tenants having only two weeks to appeal against removal on artistic, historic or safety grounds. This new drive, designed to raise 500,000 tons of scrap, enough for 300 destroyers, coincided with the start of the Warship Weeks savings scheme in October 1941 [see Object 77], with opening publicity given to the removal of some railings outside Buckingham Palace. In December, 3 miles of railings were removed from around Hyde Park, raising 1,000 tons of scrap. By March 1942, London was yielding over 5,000 tons of iron railings and gates from 45,000 properties per week, with more than 40,000 tons already collected.

However, there was an aesthetic cost to this scrap drive. Iron railings became popular in the Georgian eighteenth century and Victorian nineteenth century, with elegant and stylish designs fronting many properties. By the 1940s, this architecture was sometimes seen as bleak and passé, so many householders were glad to get rid of their railings. But, there was a shortage of hacksaws and the correct cutting equipment: oxyacetylene was used to cut through wrought-iron railings but not cast-iron ones, which required too much bottled oxygen, which was in short supply. Instead, sledgehammers were used, often damaging boundary walls, as the chips and scars reveal today.

By the close of this salvage campaign in September 1944, over 1 million tons of railings had been collected – more than was needed or could be processed. What happened to all these railings? There have been various fanciful rumours, such as they were dropped by RAF Bomber Command on Germany, or used as ballast in ships and that 'seaport

buildings in Nigeria still sport rather nice Georgian railings'.

Records suggest that only 26 per cent of the ironwork collected was used for munitions and by the war's end much of it was rusting in depots and railway sidings or overgrown in village dumps. So where did it all disappear to?

In 1984, a letter writer to the *Evening Standard* revealed 'many hundreds of tons of scrap iron and ornamental railings were sent to the bottom in the Thames Estuary, because Britain was unable to process this ironwork into weapons of war. This information came from dockers in Canning Town in 1978, who had worked during the war on 'lighters' that were towed down the Thames to dump vast quantities of scrap metal and decorative ironwork. They claimed so much

was dumped at certain spots in the estuary, such as off Sheerness, ships passing the area needed pilots to guide them, because their compasses were strongly affected by the quantity of iron on the seabed. Similar dumping is said to have occurred in the Solent and Irish Sea.

There has never been any government confirmation of this practice or any explanation as to how hundreds of thousands of tons of railings suddenly disappeared – possibly to avoid official embarrassment. So, this final mystery endures. However, the millions of metal railing stumps that remain to this day for all to see on front garden walls bear testimony to the cost of this nationwide wartime scrap drive on the Home Front.

Railings being salvaged for the war effort in Berkeley Square, Mayfair, London, on 3 March 1941. (*Public Domain*)

Bibliography/Further Reading

Addison, P. (1985): *Now That the War is Over,* BBC/ Jonathan Cape, London.

Auckland, R. G. & Moore, K. B. (1998): *Messages From the Sky Over Britain,* Blatter 24, Psywar Society, Yorkshire.

Barber, M. (2017): *V2: The A4 Rocket from Peenemunde to Redstone,* Crecy, Manchester.

Bourne, S. (2010): *Mother Country: Britain's Black Community on the Home Front 1939–45,* The History Press, Gloucestershire.

Briggs, A. (2000): *Go To It! Working For Victory on the Home Front 1939–1945,* Mitchell Beazley, London.

Brown, M. (1999): *Put That Light Out! Britain's Civil Defence Services at War 1939–1945,* Sutton Publishing, Gloucestershire.

Brown, M. & Harris, C. (2001): *The Wartime House: Home Life in Wartime Britain 1939–1945,* Sutton Publishing, Gloucestershire.

Brown, M. (2004): *Christmas on the Home Front,* Sutton Publishing, Gloucestershire.

Brown, M. (2005): *The Day Peace Broke Out: The VE-Day Experience,* Sutton Publishing, Gloucestershire.

Bungay, S. (2009): *The Most Dangerous Enemy: A History of the Battle of Britain,* Aurum Press, London.

Calder, A. (1992): *The Myth of the Blitz,* Pimlico, London.

Calder, A. (1996): *The People's War: Britain 1939–1945,* Pimlico, London.

Cocroft, W. (2000): *Dangerous Energy: The Archaeology of Gunpowder and Military Explosives Manufacture, English Heritage,* Wiltshire.

Cruickshank, C. (1990): *The German Occupation of the Channel Islands,* Sutton Publishing, Gloucestershire.

Cullen, S. M. (2011): *In Search of the Real Dad's Army: The Home Guard and the Defence of the UK 1940–1944,* Pen & Sword, Yorkshire.

Davies, J. (1993): *The Wartime Kitchen and Garden: The Home Front 1939–45,* BBC Books, London.

de la Haye, A. (2009): *Land Girls: Cinderellas of the Soil,* The Royal pavilion & Museums, Sussex.

Dobinson, C, (2001): *AA Command: Britain's Anti-Aircraft Defences of the Second World War,* Methuen, London.

Doherty, M. A. (2000): *Nazi Wireless Propaganda,* Edinburgh University Press, Edinburgh.

Falconer, J. (1998): *The Bomber Command Handbook 1939–1945,* Sutton Publishing, Gloucestershire.

Fleischer, W. (2004): *German Air-Dropped Weapons to 1945,* Midland Publ., Leicestershire.

Fletcher, L. (1945): *They Never Failed: The Story of the Provincial Press in Wartime,* Newspaper Society, London.

Gardiner, J. (2005): *The Children's War,* Portrait/ IWM, London.

Gardiner, J. (2004): *Wartime Britain 1939–1945,* Headline, London.

Glover, B. (1995): *Brewing For Victory: Brewers, Beer and Pubs in World War II,* Lutterworth Press, Cambridge.

Hall, D. (2002): *The Book of Churchilliana,* New Cavendish, London.

Harrison, T. (1976): *Living Through the Blitz,* Collins, London.

Hickman, T. (1995): *What Did You Do in the War, Auntie? The BBC at War 1939–45,* BBC Books, London.

Hickman, T. (2008): *Called Up, Sent Down: The Bevin Boys' War,* The History Press, Gloucestershire.

Holsken, D. (1994): *V-Missiles of the Third Reich: The V-1 and V-2,* Monogram Aviation Publications, Massachusetts, USA.

Kee, R. (1989): *The Picture Post Album,* Guild Publishing, London.

Knight, K. (2007): *Spuds, Spam and Eating for Victory: Rationing and the Second World War,* Tempus, Gloucestershire.

Kramer, A. (2013): *Conscientious Objectors of the Second World War,* Pen & Sword, Yorkshire.

Kynaston, D. (2007): *Austerity Britain 1945–51,* Bloomsbury, London.

Levine, J. (2015): *The Secret History of the Blitz,* Simon & Schuster UK, London.

Lewis, B. (2017): *Keep Calm and Carry On: The Truth Behind the Poster,* IWM, London.

Longmate, N. (2002): *How We Lived Then: A History of Everyday Life During the Second World War,* Pimlico, London.

Malcolmson, P. and R. (2013): *Women at the Ready: The Remarkable Story of the WVS on the Home Front,* Little, Brown, London.

Maton, M: (2012): *Honour The Civilians: Honours and Awards to Civilians During World War II,* Token Publishing, Devon.

McLaine, I. (1979): *Ministry of Morale: Home Front Morale and the Ministry of Information in World War II,* George Allen & Unwin, London.

McGrory, D. (1997): *Coventry at War: Britain in Old Photographs,* Sutton Publishing, Gloucestershire.

Mills, J. (1993): *A People's Army: Civil Defence Insignia and Uniforms 1939–1945,* Wardens Publ., Kent.

Mills, J. (2001): *In the Space of a Single Day: The Insignia and Uniforms of the LDV and Home Guard 1940–1944 and 1952–1956,* Wardens Publ., Kent .

Mills, J. (2012): *Doing Their Bit: Home Front Lapel Badges 1939–1945,* Sabrestorm Publishing, Kent.

Munoz, G. C. & Gonzalez, S. G. (2013): *Deutsche Luftwaffe: Uniforms and Equipment of the German Air Force 1935–1945,* Andrea Press, Spain.

O'Brien, T. H. (1954): *Civil Defence,* HMSO, London.

Opie, R. (2005): *The Wartime Scrapbook 1939–1945,* PI Global Publishing Ltd, London.

Price, A. (2000): *Blitz on Britain 1939–45,* Sutton Publ., Gloucestershire.

Ramsey, Ed. W. (1987, 1988, 1990): *The Blitz: Then & Now: Vols.1–3,* Battle of Britain Prints International, London.

Ransted, C. (2017): *Bomb Disposal in World War Two,* Pen & Sword, Yorkshire.

Reynolds, D. (1995): *Rich Relations: The American Occupation of Britain 1942–1945,* HarperCollins, London.

Ruddy, A. J. (2004): *British Anti-Invasion Defences 1940–1945,* Historic Military Press, Sussex.

Ruddy, A. J. (2014): *Tested By Bomb and Flame: Leicester Versus the Luftwaffe, 1939–1945,* Halsgrove, Somerset.

Saunders, A. (2015): *Battle of Britain July to October 1940: RAF Operations Manual,* Haynes Publishing, Somerset.

Smith, D. (2011): *The Spade as Mighty as the Sword: The Story of World War Two's Dig for Victory Campaign,* Aurum Press, London.

Summers, J. (2015): *Fashion on the Ration: Style in the Second World War,* Profile Books, London.

Thomas, D. (2003): *An Underworld at War: Spivs, Deserters, Racketeers and Civilians in the Second World War,* John Murray, London.

Titmuss, R. M. (1950): *Problems of Social Policy,* HMSO, London.

Way, C. (1996): *Glenn Miller in Britain Then and Now,* Battle of Britain Prints International, London.

Wood, D. (1992): *Attack Warning Red: The ROC and the Defence of Britain 1925–1992,* Carmichael & Sweet, Hampshire.

Wragg, D. (2006): *Wartime on the Railways,* Sutton Publishing, Gloucestershire.

Index